SPANISH
~ *with a* ~
# MISSION

Worldwide Publishing Group
Your multi-platform publishing partner
7710-T Cherry Park Drive, Suite 224, Houston, Texas 77095
www.WorldwidePublishingGroup.com
(713) 766-4272

The views expressed in this book are the authors and do not necessarily reflect those of the publisher.

Published in the United States of America

Softcover: 978-1-68411-068-1

SPANISH
~ with a ~
MISSION

For Ministry, Witnessing, and Mission Trips

Spanish for Spreading the Gospel

~ *With Coritos and Alabanzas* ~
Spanish Christian songs for all ages

by Mirna Deborah Balyeat

Second Edition

Dedicated to my mother, Rosa Lillyam Arce Montenegro. From a humble family in Nicaragua, her priority was education and the improvement of one's self.

Thank you to my family: David, Alicia, Diego, Cristina, David M., and Lily.
You have supported me extensively through this project. I love you, and I thank God for you.
A special thank you also to Elmin and Betty Howell for your enthusiasm and support.

ACKNOWLEDGEMENTS TO MY *SPANISH WITH A MISSION* TEAM

Alicia Morcillo, Creative Director, Graphic Designer and Photographer
Rosario Welle, Chief Editor
What God provided through these two ladies was far and beyond what I could have asked. They are excellent at what they do and put their whole heart into this project, for which I will always be grateful.

Lucas Nobre, Graphic Designer
Cristina Balyeat, Photographer
The talents and keen eye that they posess have added beauty and an artistic consistency throughout the book.

Many more gave of their time and skills to help with this endeavor:
Ka Riley, David Balyeat, Diego Morcillo, Christina Johnston, Leticia Clark, Lloydene Balyeat, Lily Barnes, Neisy Casanova, Joel Ginsberg, Esther Echaverry, Karen Alexander, Justin Hardin and **Mariel Gonnet.**

¡Gracias!

Preface

"How, then, can they call on the one they have not believed in?
And how can they believe in the one of whom they have not heard?
And how can they hear without someone preaching to them?" Romans 10:14

Spanish with a Mission is written for individual workers and groups of volunteers who go on mission trips or do community outreach to Hispanics. Whether you are volunteering in your community, witnessing to a Hispanic neighbor, or participating on a mission trip, the better you communicate, the more effective your ministry will be.

During my years on the mission field and as a Spanish teacher, it has been my observation that many groups plan for a mission trip or outreach event spending much time and money preparing for what will take place or what will be taught while investing little in learning the language, and often the communication is left to a small bilingual staff. How great and wonderful it would be if the whole ministry staff or group could communicate. As we know, there are always opportunities to share, and if language is a hindrance, there are opportunities that will be missed. *Spanish with a Mission* is a tool that will diminish language barriers.

What makes this textbook different from other Spanish textbooks? This textbook/workbook teaches the basics of Spanish grammar and gives practical thematic vocabulary and exercises to practice and to raise skill levels. In addition, the material is written from a Christian perspective, including religious words and phrases, mission vocabulary, cultural insights, and key Bible verses necessary for Christian outreach and leading someone to Christ.

More over, this book contains many Christian choruses and praise songs that can be sung with children or adults. Included are biographies of Christian artists and composers. These songs are often heard in Hispanic churches and consequently, used in ministry.

So what is the practicality of using this book as a textbook? Though I started my career teaching Spanish as a 22 year old graduate student in a university, I have also had many years experience of teaching on the mission field, in non-credit classes, and in churches. I know that when the situation is outside of academia, there has to be a practical and flexible way to make it fit in schedules. Another objective is to make it easily available to everyone; meaning, you don't have to find a seasoned Spanish teacher to get you through this book.

Spanish with a Mission is written in easy-to-follow lessons, which can be used for individual learning, or can be used in a class taught by a Spanish speaker from the same congregation or community – a Teacher's Guide is available to facilitate this and the book can be covered in less than three months. The information in the book can continue to be used as a resource for review and practice after the lessons are completed.

Moreover, conversation classes can be added for those who want to continue learning and add more fluency to their communication. This book will give enough grammar and thematic vocabulary to launch a conversation class, which can also be taught by a willing Spanish Speaker in your area.

What can you expect in the lessons? The grammar structures in this book are designed to be easy to understand and to teach communication in the present tense, but also include the informal future and simple past so that learners are not limited only to the present tense. (The future is needed to talk about events you're planning, and the past is needed to give your testimony and to tell Bible stories.)

Each lesson takes about 2 hours to complete. Preliminary lessons, A & B, contain information for those who have never taken Spanish. They can be covered in a classroom, or individually since the student can study them at his or her own pace with the audio portion on the author's Web page, www.spanishwithamission.com. In this case, if a group class is organized, instruction may begin with Lesson 1 and be finished in 10 lessons. (The options are laid out in the Teacher's Guide.) The author's suggestion is to cover one lesson per week and to finish the course in 10-12 weeks, perhaps taking two weeks for the Witnessing lesson (lesson 10). It is possible to modify this according to the goal of the individual or group.

Learning the Spanish language and culture is an investment you make in the ministry of reaching more people and spreading the Gospel.

May God bless your ministry.

FOR MORE INFORMATION on how to receive a guide for starting your own *Spanish with a Mission* class in your church or organization, visit *spanishwithamission.com*

Foreword

Deborah Balyeat has scored a spiritual victory for many givers and receivers who will be involved in sharing a Christian witness in a Spanish language and cultural setting. Any size group or individual who wants to really know what to do, how to do it, and how to keep communication priorities in perspective are those who will benefit from her work.
Deborah has written and outlined a wonderful preparation guide that will honor the Lord.

Having been raised in the Spanish culture by a Nicaraguan mother, being married to a son of missionaries from Argentina and presently teaching Spanish at Dallas Baptist University has given Deborah Balyeat a lifetime of training and practical experience that the Lord can identify so the Holy Spirit can work on both ends of the line in a total mission venture.

People who have worked with the Balyeats are very grateful and appreciative of their Christian leadership. They have led mission workgroups to numerous foreign countries for a number of years. They are also active members in their home church, Shiloh Terrace Baptist Church in East Dallas County.

Finally, I would say that the spiritual preparation for any mission-minded group, including each member of the group, is uppermost. You will be reminded of this throughout the manuscript as you learn Spanish.

Respectfully submitted by *Mr. Elmin Howel, Jr.*
Retired Director of the Rio Grande River Ministry
on both sides of the Border of Mexico and Texas. 1968-1996.

ENDORSEMENTS

"I am always receiving requests for different types of ministry resources from my ministry partners. I've had difficulty finding a good resource for people who are trying to learn Spanish. I have found several good resources for people who want to learn and/or teach English. I had not come across a resource for people who want to learn Spanish in preparation for a mission trip or working in a Hispanic community. Recently I was asked to review the book *Spanish with a Mission: Basic Spanish for Spreading the Gospel* by Deborah Balyeat. Not only did I review it but I also asked my wife to review it. She has taught Spanish both in Mexico and the United States. After reviewing the book, both of us came up with the same conclusion, 'This is an excellent book for learning and teaching Spanish.' It is the only book that I have come across that teaches Spanish with a Christian perspective. It not only teaches you the basics of the language but it also gives you the vocabulary you will need to work in different areas of ministry such as: clothes closet, agriculture mission, construction, medical missions, and witnessing. My wife also pointed out to me that the book was written using a very good teaching structure that either a teacher or student would find easy to follow. The book also comes with several resources: teachers guide, web page, Spanish Christian songs. Now when someone asks me for a resource for learning Spanish, I know what to recommend."

E. Daniel Rangel
Director, River Ministry/Mexico Missions
Missions Mobilization Team, BGCT

"You absolutely must learn what is in this book before your next missions trip to Latin America! Here is a very helpful tool for those who want to learn Spanish and use it to serve God. This may be the fastest and easiest way to get some survival skills with key phrases in Spanish. The lessons are simple to learn but give you a lot of understanding about the Spanish language and Latin culture. Since the author is a veteran missionary and an accomplished Spanish teacher, Deborah Balyeat brings the best from both those worlds together for you. ¡Qué Dios le bendiga!"

Dr. Bob Garrett
Piper Chair of Missions
Director, MA in Global Leadership
Dallas Baptist University

"*Spanish with a Mission* is a must-have for every Christian and church wanting to reach Spanish speakers with the Gospel of Jesus Christ. It is an ideal resource for groups going on mission trips or churches located around Spanish speakers. Deborah Balyeat turns conversational Spanish into transformational Spanish as she teaches beginners how to communicate the love of Christ. She specifically targets words and phrases used in the most common types of mission trips including medical missions, construction, Vacation Bible School, and sports evangelism. By translating a variety of Scripture passages used in most Gospel presentations, Balyeat equips Christians to talk about their own faith journey in Spanish and to share key passages used to lead someone to Christ. *Spanish with a Mission* is also a great resource for teaching popular worship songs. Now, church groups can be prepared to lead worship for children and adults—not through the rote memorization of words—but by praising God in Spanish from the heart. *Spanish with a Mission* is the most practical, Gospel-oriented resource on the market today. If you want your mission trip to have the greatest, Kingdom impact possible, you must ask every traveler to read *Spanish with a Mission*. This book will change the future of Spanish missions forever."

Craig C. Christina, Ph.D.
Senior Pastor, Shiloh Terrace Baptist Church

"*Spanish with a Mission* is a wonderful resource to prepare you or your group for a mission opportunity to a Spanish speaking country. Deborah Balyeat has done a wonderful job of making this book relevant to missions and ministry needs, and very easy to use as a training tool for your team to prepare for their experience. I am grateful for the work and thought she put into this guide to help spread the Gospel of Jesus Christ. I hope you will consider this book for learning the language and the culture for your next mission endeavor to a Spanish speaking people group."

Rene Maciel
President of Baptist University of the Americas

"Short practical lessons mixed with cultural tidbits makes *Spanish with a Mission* the perfect language tool for Christians with a cross-cultural mission for learning Spanish. The need for conversational Spanish both in the U.S. and abroad is essential for building relationships and communicating the Gospel. Anyone with a desire to serve Hispanic people will find it easy to build vocabulary, learn verb tenses, and use idiomatic expressions in less than three months. Learning Spanish songs and being able to share a faith story in Spanish equips believers for 'ministry, witnessing, and mission trips.'"

Jim and Viola Palmer
Career Missionaries, Latin America

Table of Contents

Introduction for the language learner:

Congratulations on taking a step toward learning or improving your Spanish! Another language opens up another world of opportunities. God has a plan! Whatever your motivation is for learning Spanish, make sure you remember that motivation to help you spend the time you need for learning Spanish and dedicating your time to it.

Motivation + time = success. Make a commitment to take time to study consistently because this is the combination that will help you succeed. Everyone has different aptitudes for learning a foreign language, whether you learn quickly or not, the biggest personal factor is motivation. God has given you a desire and reason to learn Spanish; make sure you are committed to give it your time. The more time you spend and immerse yourself within Spanish, the more you will advance and be able to communicate.

As you start this book, you will find that the first lessons are preliminary lessons A & B. These lessons can be covered in a classroom or on your own by going online to the website www.spanishwithamission.com. Both preliminary lessons are covered here. Follow along with your book and listen as many times as you need to hear and to repeat the sounds; it is like having your own personal teacher.

Feel free to go at your own pace, but it is important when you are studying a language not to let too much time go by without studying. As mentioned before, be consistent. Ideally, exposure every day gives the best result, even if it is only 15 minutes. Repetition is extremely important in language learning.

My goal for this book was to keep it simple, but complete enough to give you the tools you need to start communicating. This book offers work to do at home after every lesson. Spend time on this section, and finish the work. The answers are in the back of the book for you to check and to correct the work you do on your own. Learn the Bible verses that are at the beginning of each lesson, and become familiar with a Spanish or bilingual Bible. There are also songs at the end of each lesson. Look up these songs online, and sing along. Music is a great way to learn a language and gives the opportunity to repeat in a fun way. It is also practical to learn these songs because you may have the opportunity to share them on a mission trip or outreach.

My prayer is that you take what you learn in this book and then practice Spanish in real situations; this will be the key to acquisition. Make learning Spanish an incessant task and the true fruit of your labor will come. Use every opportunity God gives you!

M. D. Balyeat

Preliminary Lesson A
Beginnings

Pronunciation I / Basic Greetings and Other Information / Alphabet /
1-30 / Names / Hispanic Countries / Making Plurals / Gender of Nouns /
Definite Articles / Pronunciation II / Subject Pronouns / Verb Introduction

Lección Preliminar A

A.1 PRONUNCIACIÓN I | *PRONUNCIATION I*

VOWELS

Each vowel in Spanish has only one sound. The sound should be steady, meaning, do not move your tongue or "glide" the vowels as in English.

Listen and repeat. (*Escuchen y repitan.*) You can listen at www.spanishwithamission.com.

a ah like in **A**mish

e eh, like in m**e**ts

i ee, like in s**ee**

o oh, like in s**o**ldier

u u, like in S**u**e

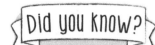

Did you know?

Spanish is the third most spoken language in the world.

Listen and repeat these words.

a *la, mamá, papá, mapa, Ana, ama*

e *el, es, ese, fe, me, leche*

i *mi, sí, Lima, Chile, chica, Iris*

o *lo, no, mono, nosotros, Lola, Rodolfo*

u *tú, luz, muy, su, Jesús*

Practice saying the vowels with a consonant preceding.

ma, me, mi, mo, mu   la, le, li, lo, lu   sa, se, si, so, su   ta, te, ti, to, tu   fa, fe, fi, fo, fu

CONSONANTS PART I

h	is silent	*hola, hasta, hora, ahora, hospital*
ll	English "y" sound, like in "yes"	*llama, silla, llamo, pollo*
r	single trill of the tongue, like the "dd" in "ladder"	*libro, profesor, escritorio, nombre*
rr	multiple trill of the tongue (also when "r" begins a word)	*perro, barra, Rosa*
z	makes an English "s" sound	*lápiz, La Paz, luz, cruz*
ñ	makes the "ny" sound like in "canyon"	*niño, baño, Señor*
j	makes the English "h" sound, like in "hello"	*Juanita, Jesús, José, Jamaica*
t/d/p	are like the English equivalent, but a little softer	*Tomás, Dora, tú, todo, peso, pila*
b/v	there is no true distinction, both sound like English "b"	*vaca, burro, vaso, bueno*

ACCENT MARKS PART I

When you see an accent mark, stress the syllable or vowel that carries it.

Listen and repeat: *Raúl, papá, lápiz, dieciséis, Jesús, corazón*

Question words have accent marks. The accent mark goes over the vowel heard strongest.

Listen and repeat: *¿Qué? ¿Dónde? ¿Cómo? ¿Cuántos?*

A.2 LOS SALUDOS | *BASIC GREETINGS* (AND OTHER INFORMATION)

Spanish	English	Spanish	English
Hola.	*Hello.*	nombre	*name*
¿Qué tal?	*How's it going?*	apellido	*last name*
¿Cómo se llama?	*What is your name?*	número de teléfono	*telephone #*
(Yo) me llamo ____.	*My name is ____.*	la dirección, el domicilio	*address*
(Yo) soy de ____.	*I'm from ____.*	la calle	*the street*
¿Cómo se escribe?	*How do you spell it?*	(Yo) vivo en ____.	*I live in ____.*
¿Cuántos hijos tiene?	*How many children do you have?*	Gracias.	*Thank you.*
Más despacio, por favor.	*(Speak) slowly please.*	Más lento, por favor.	*Slowly please.*

1. Introduce yourself by saying, "Hola, me llamo_____."   *2.* "(Yo) soy de_____."

A.3 EL ALFABETO | *THE ALPHABET*

a	a	**h**	hache	**ñ**	eñe	**u**	u
b	be	**i**	i	**o**	o	**v**	ve *or* uve
c	ce	**j**	jota	**p**	pe	**w**	doble ve *or* doble uve
d	de	**k**	ka	**q**	cu	**x**	equis
e	e	**l**	ele	**r**	ere	**y**	i griega *or* ye
f	efe	**m**	eme	**s**	ese	**z**	zeta *or* ceta
g	ge	**n**	ene	**t**	te		

1. Spell your first and last name.

2. Spell a friend's name while you write it down. If in a class, someone else can write it down as you say it.

3. Listen to the names spelled out, write them down as you hear them.

_____   _____   _____

A.4 LOS NÚMEROS (1-30) | *NUMBERS*

0	**cero**	8	**ocho**	16	**dieciséis**	24	**veinticuatro**
1	**uno**	9	**nueve**	17	**diecisiete**	25	**veinticinco**
2	**dos**	10	**diez**	18	**dieciocho**	26	**veintiséis**
3	**tres**	11	**once**	19	**diecinueve**	27	**veintisiete**
4	**cuatro**	12	**doce**	20	**veinte**	28	**veintiocho**
5	**cinco**	13	**trece**	21	**veintiuno**	29	**veintinueve**
6	**seis**	14	**catorce**	22	**veintidós**	30	**treinta**
7	**siete**	15	**quince**	23	**veintitrés**	31	**treinta y uno**

Note: after 30, the "y" is used in between the ten's and the one's.

Ask a partner for information, write it down and check it:

1. Say your phone or work number in Spanish.

2. Say your address in Spanish, spelling out the name of street and city.

3. Count how many students, chairs, books, pens, etc., are in the room.

A.5 NOMBRES | *NAMES*

FIRST NAMES
Most Hispanics have two first names, like *Ana María* or *José Alberto*.
Often they are named after the Saint that represents their birthdate.

Find out what your first name is in Spanish.
Sometime the name translates easily, (John → *Juan*) or (Monique → *Mónica*).
Other times it may not have an easy translation but you can say the name with a Spanish accent or change it a little to make it easier to say. Example: *Courtney* is a name that is hard for Hispanics to say, but you could change it to *Cora* to make it more "Spanish friendly".

LAST NAMES
Hispanics have two last names, a primary and a secondary.
The primary is their father's last name. The secondary is their mother's last name.
In the name, *María Elena Romero Losa*, her father's last name is *Romero* and her mother's maiden name is *Losa*.

When a woman marries, she does not lose her primary last name. She usually drops her secondary last name and replaces it with *de* followed by the husband's primary last name.
Example:
> If, *María Elena Romero Losa* marries *Juan Francisco Gutiérrez Arce,*
> She will become: *María Elena Romero de Gutiérrez.*

What would your full name be if you were born in a Hispanic country? Write it below.

_____

REPÚBLICA DE PERÚ
SERVICIO DE REGISTRO CIVIL E IDENTIFICACIÓN
CÉDULA DE IDENTIDAD

APELLIDOS
MARTINEZ
HERRERA
NOMBRES
ELSA LORENA
SEXO   PAÍS DE NACIONALIDAD
F   PERÚ
FECHA DE NACIMIENTO
21 ENERO 1983
FECHA DE EMISIÓN
15 NOV 2011
FECHA DE VENCIMIENTO
15 NOV 2021

FIRMA DEL TITULAR

FE 298.74.9837-54

(ID shown is not valid)

Listen, and repeat the countries and their capitals in Spanish.

Europa, México, Centroamérica, el Caribe
Madrid, España
México D.F. , México
Ciudad de Guatemala, Guatemala
San Salvador, El Salvador
Managua, Nicaragua
San José, Costa Rica
Tegucigalpa, Honduras
Ciudad de Panamá, Panamá
La Habana, Cuba
San Juan, Puerto Rico
Santo Domingo, República Dominicana

Sudamérica
Caracas, Venezuela
Quito, Ecuador
Bogotá, Colombia
La Paz, Bolivia
Lima, Perú
Santiago, Chile
Buenos Aires, Argentina
Asunción, Paraguay
Montevideo, Uruguay

Los Estados Unidos (*The United States*)
Canadá

*Hola, me llamo
Guillermina.
Soy de
Argentina.*

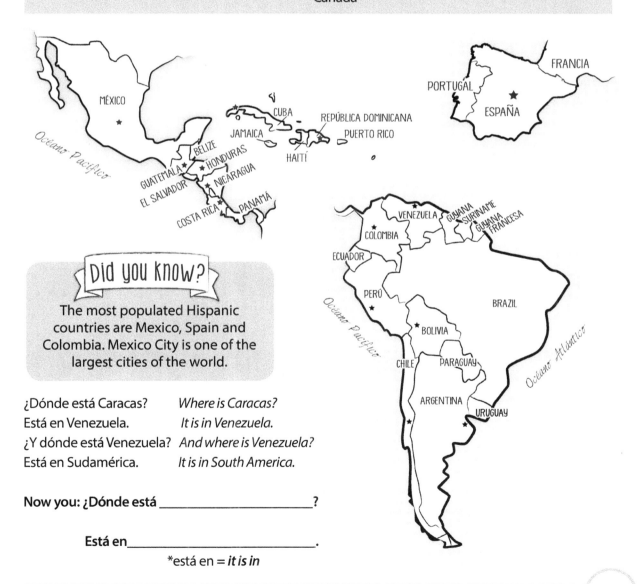

Did you know?

The most populated Hispanic
countries are Mexico, Spain and
Colombia. Mexico City is one of the
largest cities of the world.

¿Dónde está Caracas?   *Where is Caracas?*
Está en Venezuela.   *It is in Venezuela.*
¿Y dónde está Venezuela? *And where is Venezuela?*
Está en Sudamérica.   *It is in South America.*

Now you: **¿Dónde está** _____?

Está en_____.

*está en = **it is in***

A.7 MAKING PLURALS

The plural of a word is made by adding an –*s* or –*es*.

In general, if the word ends in a vowel, add -*s*.

chico—chicos   silla—sillas

If the word ends in a consonant, add -*es*.

papel—papeles   borrador—borradores

If the word ends in -*z*, change it to -*c* and add -*es*.

luz—luces   lápiz—lápices

A.8 GENDER OF NOUNS

Since Spanish derives from Latin, all nouns are either masculine or feminine. This is easy when we are talking about people but for nouns that refer to things, there is no reason why something is masculine or feminine. Usually it is because that is what it was in Latin.

Many times you can know if it is masculine or feminine by the ending of the word.

1. Most nouns that end with -*o* are masculine, and with -*a* are feminine. There are, though, exceptions.
2. Nouns that end in -*ción* or -*dad* are feminine.
3. Nouns that end in consonants or -*e* can go either way, though most will be masculine.
4. Nouns referring to people will be the gender of the person.
5. Nouns that end with -*nte* or -*ista* will refer to people and will be the gender of the person.

Masculine	Feminine
chico	chica
libro	Biblia
lápiz	luz
papel	universidad
tomate	canción
padre	madre
estudiante	estudiante
artista	artista

niño

niña

A.9 DEFINITE ARTICLES

There are 4 definite articles in Spanish that are the equivalent to the article "the."
The masculine article is **el**, the feminine article is **la**. These accompany a singular noun.

el libro   el chico   el escritorio

la profesora   la señora   la Biblia

If the noun is plural, you must use a plural article.
Los is for a masculine plural noun. **Las** is for a feminine plural noun.

los libros   los chicos   los escritorios

las profesoras   las señoras   las sillas

Here are all 4 definite articles.

definite articles	masculine	feminine
singular	**el**	**la**
plural	**los**	**las**

LEARNING THE GENDER OF VOCABULARY WORDS

When you learn vocabulary words, they will be introduced with the article so you can know if the word is masculine or feminine. Since the ending of the word does not always let you know, learn the word with the article so you can learn the gender.

Under each picture, state if it's masculine or feminine. Then if singular, make plural and vice versa.

1. la casa

F

las casas

2. el carro, el auto

_____

_____

3. la cruz

_____

_____

4. el corazón *

_____

*Will not need an accent mark in plural.

5. la playa

_____

_____

6. los perros

_____

_____

7. el supermercado

_____

_____

8. la iglesia

_____

_____

9. los niños

_____

_____

Note: Use the definite article with titles when talking about the person, but not when addressing them directly.

—Sr. López, ¿Cómo están **la** Sra. López y **el** Dr. Ortega?   *Mr. López, how are Mrs. López and Dr. Ortega?*

In referring to families, last names are never made plural, just the article. Ex.: The Smiths = *Los Smith*.

VOWELS | DIPTHONGS PART I - <u>For a deeper explanation of these rules go to Appendix IV.</u>

The vowels **u** and **i** are weak vowels. The other vowels (**a, e, o**) are strong. When you have two vowels together in which one is an **i** or **u** (or both), it forms what is called a **dipthong**. Dipthongs combine the vowels to make a joining sound to make one syllable.

Listen and repeat these words. *Escuchen y repitan.* You can listen at www.spanishwithamission.com.

ai, ia	*bailar, Colombia, California, iglesia, Biblia*
au, ua	*Guatemala, Uruguay, Paraguay, cuando, Ecuador*
ei, ie	*seis, siete, bien, diez*
eu, ue	*Venezuela, bueno, Buenos Aires, Puerto Rico, nueve*
oi, io	*pronunciación, canción, soy, Mario*
ui, iu	*ciudad, muy*

If the vowels are not supposed to combine and make a dipthong, an accent mark must be put over the weak vowel to separate them.

Mario   the *-io* combine into a dipthong and one syllable.

María   an accent is placed over the *-i* because the pronunciation requires the *-i* to be separate from the *-a* and not combine into a dipthong.

CONSONANTS PART II

c   makes an English **k** sound as in the word *"cat,"* <u>unless</u> it has an *-e* or *-i* that follows it, in which case it makes an **s** sound like in "Sam." Listen and repeat.

Costa Rica, Colombia, Ecuador, casado, castaño, California, Cristo, clase, cuatro

ce	*cero, once, doce, centavo*
ci	*cinco, dieciséis, ciudad, Florencia*

The way Spanish makes the **k** sound with *-e* and *-i*, is to write it like this:

que	*que, porque, queso*
qui	*quien, Quito, quince*

g   makes a hard **g** sound as in the word *"go,"* <u>unless</u> it has an *-e* or *-i* that follows it, in which case it makes an **h** sound like in *"hello."* Listen and repeat.

gato, gozo, grande, gracias, gusto, pregunta

ge	*generoso, general, gente, Argentina*
gi	*página, Gilberto, gigante*

The way Spanish makes the hard **g** sound with *-e* and *-i*, is to write it like this, (the *-u* is silent):

gue	*guerra, guerrilla, pague*
gui	*Guillermo, Guido, guitarra*

Note: The exception is if the "u" has a "diéresis" over it: *ü*. The *-u* will not be silent: *lingüista, vergüenza*

A.11 SUBJECT PRONOUNS

yo	I
tú	you (informal)
usted	you (formal) - *abbreviated as* **Ud.**
él	he
ella	she
nosotros, nosotras	we (masculine/feminine)
ellos, ellas	they (masculine, feminine, mixed)
ustedes	you plural (formal and informal) - *abbreviated as* **Uds.**
*vos	used in many countries instead of *tú* (most of Central America, many parts of South America, especially Argentina).
*vosotros, vosotras	used only in Spain instead of *ustedes*.

Pronouns	Singular	Plural
1st person	**yo**	**nosotros, nosotras**
2nd person	**tú**	
	usted (Ud.)	**ustedes (Uds.)**
	*vos	***vosotros, vosotras**
3rd person	**él, ella**	**ellos, ellas**

*****Vos** *and* **vosotros/as** *conjugations will not be covered in this text because they are not as commonly used. For a comprehensive look at the* **vos** *and* **vosotros** *conjugations, consult Appendix V in the back of the book.*

When there is a group of mixed (masculine and feminine), the masculine form is used.

Example: *María, Susana y José* = **ellos** (If José were not there, it would be *ellas*.)

Third person singular and plural is also used for things. There is not an "it" subject pronoun like in English.

IMPORTANT NOTE:

There are 3 ways to say "you" in the singular form. Different countries have their own rules as to which ones to use for whom. The most respectful "you" is **usted**. In most countries this is the form you use with people older than yourself or with someone you have just met. **Tú** is most widely used, since it is the one that is used with friends, children, family, and peers. This is the rule used in Mexico, the Caribbean, Spain and most of the other Hispanic countries. Many countries use **vos** instead of *tú*, but will understand **tú** if used. Since you cannot go wrong using **usted** in any country, many of the examples in this book will use **usted** in the questions. **Vos** has a different conjugation that is not difficult and can be learned in the country if needed. (Look at Appendix V.)

If you are going on a mission trip, before leaving, try to find out which rule is used. This will ensure that you speak to the people there in the way in which they are accustomed, and this also gives you a chance to practice it before the trip.

If you are working with Hispanics in the United States, using **tú** will be the norm, though I suggest addressing older adults with **usted** to show respect.

Decide which pronoun you would use for:

1. talking to your good friend   *tú*

2. talking to your teacher   _____

3. talking to a person you don't know or just met   _____

4. talking to a child   _____

5. talking about a man   _____

6. talking about a woman   _____

7. talking about a group of men and women   _____

8. talking to an officer   _____

9. a large group of people you are speaking to   _____

10. talking about yourself and your friends   _____

11. In Argentina, talking to a good friend   _____

12. In Spain, talking to a group of people   _____

A.12 VERBS | AN INTRODUCTION

The **infinitive form** is the most basic form of a verb, it is the non-conjugated form. This is equivalent to the English form of **TO BE** or **TO SEE**. This form is not conjugated for any subject. This is the form that you would find in the dictionary when you look it up. For example: **Soy** is the conjugated form of *SER*. It means "I am." If you look up **soy**, you will not find it in the dictionary, it is a conjugated form of the verb **SER** which means "to be." **SER** is what you would find in the dictionary because it is the **infinitive form**.

There are 3 forms of infinitives. *-ar, -er, -ir.*
> *hablar* - to speak | *comer* - to eat | *vivir* - to live

The infinitives are made up of **the root** (or **stem**), and the **ending**.
> *hablar* | *habl-* stem | *-ar* ending

Verbs come under the category of **regular** or **irregular** conjugations. If they follow the regular pattern, they are regular. If they change in either the ending or the root, then they are considered irregular.

Verb conjugations are important to learn since there is much more inflection or change of endings than in English. Repetition is the best way to learn them.
The pronouns are not always needed, as in English. For example, **soy** means "I am." You can say "*Yo soy*" but the **yo** is not needed since **soy** only means "I am." Many times the verbs can be used without the pronouns and be understood.

Cultural Note

At the end of each lesson, you will be introduced to some **CORITOS**. These are choruses/songs sung in Hispanic churches. There are many *coritos* so there can be different variations of the same *corito* that has changed from country to country. Many times they are sung with only clapping or a guitar. If you go to a Hispanic church, even one in the U.S., you will most likely hear the *coritos*/songs. They are great to know for mission trips. Many of the *coritos* here in the lessons are songs you can sing with children. It also makes a fun way to learn Spanish. You can find the *coritos* and Praise and Worship songs in the back pages of this book and you can listen on the web page, www.spanishwithamission.com.

Coritos

GLORIA A DIOS (*Praise Ye the Lord*)

  A. - Alelu, alelu, alelu, aleluya.

  B. - gloria a Dios *2 x*   *Glory to God*

  B. - gloria a Dios

  A. - aleluya *3 x*

  A. & B. ¡GLORIA A DIOS!

- Anonymous translation.

GRANDE ES (*Deep and Wide*)

Grande es, grande es,   *big/great is the love of Christ my Lord*
El amor de Cristo mi Señor
Grande es, grande es,
El amor de Cristo mi Señor

- Anonymous translation.

Written Work (Answers found in appendix VII)

Write the Spanish Bible verse for this lesson. Repeat it several times, and learn it.

A. Write the names of some relatives, spell out their names in Spanish as you write them.

A.3 (This is the section that corresponds to the exercise, if you need to review.)

1._____   3._____

2._____   4._____

B. Say and write the number after the typed number. **A.4**

0 - _____   7 - _____   14 - _____

1 - _____   8 - _____   15 - _____

2 - _____   9 - _____   16 - _____

3 - _____   10 - _____   20 - _____

4 - _____   11 - _____   21 - _____

5 - _____   12 - _____   30 - _____

6 - _____   13 - _____   35 - _____

C. Taking into consideration that most nouns that end with -o are masculine and that end in -a, -dad and -ción are feminine. Write the correct article before. (el, la, los, las). **A.8**

1.____*la*____ silla   4._____chico   7._____Biblia

2._____tortillas   5._____amigos   8._____universidad

3._____tacos   6._____ iglesias   9._____dirección

D. Make these nouns plural, then translate: *el teléfono -* **los teléfonos;** *el pupitre -* **los pupitres;** *la universidad -* **las universidades. A.2 and A.7**

1. el hospital ____*los hospitales*____ (*the hospitals*)_____

2. el profesor_____

3. la chica _____

4. la cruz _____

5. la calle _____

6. el nombre _____

7. la estudiante _____

8. la universidad _____

9. el apellido _____

10. la luz (*light*) _____

E. *Sopa de Letras* - Word Search

Learn some words while you find and circle them. How many do you already know?

```
E  V  I  D  A  D  R  P  E  R  D  O  N  D  A
B  A  U  T  I  Z  O  F  Y  O  C  L  D  U  M
M  I  S  E  R  I  C  O  R  D  I  A  T  S  A
S  C  H  A  M  O  R  I  T  A  J  I  H  Z  L
L  A  G  B  T  N  H  B  O  G  R  A  C  I  A
U  I  L  S  A  N  T  O  Z  I  S  J  A  R  B
V  G  D  V  T  S  I  U  P  Z  O  A  L  M  A
E  L  E  B  A  A  D  S  O  R  A  C  I  O  N
R  E  N  I  R  C  E  G  D  A  C  A  U  T  Z
S  S  E  B  O  Q  I  N  E  J  B  H  L  M  A
I  I  F  E  I  U  P  O  R  V  E  R  D  A  D
C  A  V  J  S  B  V  A  N  F  N  S  O  G  I
U  I  S  R  A  E  L  F  S  I  O  P  U  V  O
L  R  E  D  E  N  C  I  O  N  P  Q  A  S  S
O  P  A  Z  G  I  U  V  A  C  R  I  S  T  O
```

AMOR	GRACIA	PODER
ALABANZA	IGLESIA	REDENCIÓN
ALMA	ISRAEL	SALVACIÓN
BIBLIA	JESÚS	SANTO
BAUTIZO	MISERICORDIA	VERDAD
CRISTO	ORACIÓN	VERSÍCULO
DIOS	PAZ	VIDA
ESPÍRITU	PERDÓN	

Translation: (Traducción)

LOVE, PRAISE, SOUL, BIBLE, BAPTISM, CHRIST, GOD, SPIRIT, GRACE, CHURCH, ISRAEL, JESUS, MERCY, PRAYER, PEACE, FORGIVENESS, POWER, REDEMPTION, SALVATION, HOLY, TRUTH, VERSE, LIFE

Preliminary Lesson B
Meeting People / The Classroom

Greetings and Titles Vocabulary / *SER* / Making Questions
and Answering Yes and No Questions / Dialogues / Classroom
Vocabulary / 10-100 / Indefinite Articles / *¿Dónde está?* / Hay /
¿Cuántos? / Negative Statements / Written Accent Rules

Lección Preliminar B

Soy el Alfa y la Omega, el principio y el fin. Apocalipsis 22:13

I am the Alpha and the Omega, the beginning and the end. Revelation 22:13

B.1 LOS SALUDOS | *GREETINGS AND TITLES*

Hola, buenos días/buenas tardes.	*Hello, good morning/good afternoon.*
Buenas noches/¿Qué tal?	*Good evening/How's it going?*
¿Cómo está usted?	*How are you?*
Bien, gracias.	*Fine, thank you?*
Muy bien,¿y usted?	*Very well, and you?*
¿Cómo se llama usted?	*What is your name?*
(Yo) me llamo…	*My name is… (I call myself…)*
(Él / Ella) se llama…	*His/her name is (He/she calls himself/herself)*
¿De dónde es usted?	*Where are you from?*
¿Y usted?	*And you?*
(Yo) soy de…	*I'm from…*
Mucho gusto.	*Nice to meet you.*
El gusto es mío.	*The pleasure is mine.*
Por favor/gracias/de nada	*Please/thank you/you're welcome*
Lo siento (mucho).	*I'm (very) sorry.*

junction words:	y - and o - or

Adiós.	*Goodbye.*		
Hasta luego.	*Until later.*	(Que) Dios le bendiga.	*(May) God bless you. (formal)*
Hasta mañana.	*Until tomorrow.*	(Que) Dios te bendiga.	*(May) God bless you. (informal)*
Nos vemos.	*See you later.*	Gloria a Dios.	*Praise the Lord.*
Chau.	*Bye.*		

Titles: Señor (Sr.)   *Mr.*   Señora (Sra.)   *Mrs.*   Señorita (Srta.)   *Miss*
Don and *Doña* are titles of respect used with the first name.   Example: **Don Pablo**
Hermano and *Hermana* (brother/sister) are also used with first names in Christian circles.

*Hola, me llamo Claudia.
Soy de Costa Rica.
Mucho gusto.*

In Hispanic countries, a kiss on the cheek is the most common greeting among women.
Greetings with men can be a kiss or a hand shake, depending on the country.

If you are in a class

Get in a group of 3-4 classmates, and greet each other, ask their name and where they are from.
"¿Cómo se llama?" game. Can you remember everyone's name? Get in a circle and start with one person who says, "Me llamo _____." The next person says their own name, "Me llamo _____." Then says the last person's name, "Se llama _____."
As you add people, you add the names each person has to remember.

The verb *SER* (to be) is the most common verb in Spanish. It is conjugated in the ***present tense*** like this:

Verb conjugation for *SER* (to be)	
yo soy	(I am)
tú eres	(you are - informal)
él es	(he is)
ella es	(she is)
usted es	(you are - formal)
nosotros somos	(we are)
ellos son	(they are)
ellas son	(they are - feminine)
ustedes son	(you are - plural)

As you can see, **soy** only goes with *yo*, **eres** only goes with *tú*, and **somos** only goes with *nosotros*. The pronoun can be eliminated, and the subject will still be understood.

Examples: *Yo soy* de Texas.   *Soy* de Texas.   Both mean "I'm from Texas."

Tú eres de Texas.   *Eres* de Texas.   Both mean "You (informal) are from Texas."

Nosotros somos de Texas.   *Somos* de Texas.   Both mean "We are from Texas."

Es and **son** on the other hand, can be used with different pronouns.

Es can go with either *él, élla, or usted*.   **Son** can go with either *ellos, ellas, or ustedes*.
You will need to specify if the pronoun is not clear.

¿De dónde **es** Juan?   *Where is Juan from?*
Es de México.   *He is from Mexico.*

¿De dónde **son** ellos?   *Where are they from?*
Son de México.   *They are from Mexico.*

When referring to things: **Es** can also mean "it is."   Example: **Es** la una.   *It is one o'clock.*

Son can also mean "they are".   Example: **Son** clínicas.   *They are clinics.*

Fill in with correct form of the verb *SER*:

1. Usted ___*es*___ pastor.   Yo _____ estudiante.

2. Él _____ un excelente profesor.   Nosotros _____ artistas.

3. Tú _____ de Honduras.   Ustedes _____ cubanos.

4. María _____ católica. Yo _____ bautista. Ellos _____ misioneros.

Note: Nationalities, languages and religious affiliations are not capitalized in Spanish.

To change a statement in Spanish into a question is not hard but there are different ways to do it. An inverted question mark is always placed at the beginning of a question.

1. Simply add question marks to the statement, but you must raise your voice at the end so the inflection is heard and can be understood to be a question.

> Statement: Mario es hondureño.   *Mario is Honduran.*
> Question: ¿Mario es hondureño?   *Is Mario Honduran?*

Important: You must be sure to raise your voice at the end for the question. Listen and repeat.

2. Add a question word tagged on at the end of the statement.

> Mario es hondureño, ¿no?   *-Or-* Mario es hondureño, ¿verdad?[true?]

3. Invert the subject with the verb.

> ¿Es Mario hondureño?

4. Start with the verb, and put the subject at the end.

> ¿Es hondureño Mario?

A. Using rules 1, 3 and 4, make the statement into questions. There are 3 possible ways. Follow the model.
Example: Josefina es mexicana.

> *¿Josefina es mexicana?*
> *¿Es Josefina mexicana?*
> *¿Es mexicana Josefina?*

Jorge y Susana son colombianos.

_____

_____

_____

HOW TO ANSWER YES OR NO QUESTIONS

¿Es Lidia mexicana? *Is Lidia Mexican?*

—**Sí**, Lidia es mexicana. *Yes ,she is Mexican.* - OR - —**No**, Lidia **no** es mexicana. *No, she's not Mexican.*

Notice: The verb "do/does" used in English for questions and negative, does not exist in Spanish.

> Example: ¿Vive Rosa en Dallas?   ***Does** Rosa live in Dallas?*
> —No, no vive en Dallas.   *No, she **does** not live in Dallas.*

B. Answer affirmatively and then negatively:

¿Es David chileno? Sí, _____

No, _____

Diálogo 1. Listen, then practice with a partner or read them aloud.

Alan:	Buenas tardes.
Esteban:	Buenas tardes. ¿Cómo está usted?
Alan:	Estoy muy bien, gracias. ¿Y usted?
Esteban:	Bien, gracias.
Alan:	Yo me llamo Alan. ¿Cómo se llama usted?
Esteban:	Me llamo Esteban. Mucho gusto.
Alan:	El gusto es mío.
Esteban:	¿De dónde es usted?
Alan:	Soy de Texas. Soy pastor de mi iglesia en Texas. ¿Y usted?
Esteban:	Soy estudiante. Tengo que ir a clase. *(I have to go to class)*
Alan:	Bueno, hasta luego. Que Dios le bendiga.*
Esteban:	Muchas gracias, hasta luego.

*This is the formal way (usted) to say "God bless you." "Que Dios te bendiga" is the informal way (tú).

Diálogo 2.

Sra. López:	Hola, Marisol. ¿Cómo estás tú?
Marisol:	Bien, profesora. ¿Y usted?
Sra. López:	Yo estoy bien, gracias.
Marisol:	Me gusta la clase. *(I like the class.)*
Sra. López:	Gracias. ¿Nos vemos mañana en la clase?
Marisol:	Sí, hasta mañana. Gracias y adiós.
Sra. López:	Adiós, ¡que Dios te bendiga!

> **Did you know?**
>
> Puerto Rico is a territory of the U.S. and Puerto Ricans are U.S. citizens. English is a required school subject.

Answer these questions about the dialogues:

1. ¿Cómo se llama el pastor de Texas? _____

2. ¿Cómo se llama <u>el</u> estudiante? _____ ¿Y <u>la</u> estudiante? _____

3. ¿Cómo se llama la profesora? _____

4. Which pronouns do the people use to talk to each other in the dialogues? *¿Tú or usted?*

Dialogue #1 _____ Dialogue #2 _____

Why do you think they do that? _____

el libro	book	la tarea	homework / task
el lápiz	pencil	la computadora	computer
la pluma	pen	el teléfono (celular)	(cell) phone
el papel	paper	el/la estudiante	student
el escritorio	desk	el/la alumno/a	student
la silla	chair	el/la maestro/a	teacher
la luz	light	el/la profesor/a	professor
las luces	lights	el niño	little boy
la ventana	window	la niña	little girl
la puerta	door	el chico	guy (boy)
el mapa, el plano	map	la chica	young lady (girl)
el cuaderno	notebook	el hombre	man
la mochila	backpack	la mujer	woman
la pizarra	blackboard	la pregunta	question
el reloj	clock	la respuesta	answer
la mesa	table	la escuela	school
la página	page	el colegio	school (not college)
el baño	bathroom	la iglesia	church
la escuela dominical	Sunday School	la universidad	university
la clase bíblica	Bible class	la biblioteca	library

¿Dónde está(n) ...?	Where is (are) ...?	No sé.	I don't know.
Está(n) aquí.	It is (They are) here.	Está(n) allí.	It is (They are) there.
¿Cuántos?/¿Cuántas?	How many?	hay	there is, there are

B.6 LOS NÚMEROS DE 10 A 100 | *NUMBERS 10–100*

10	diez	19	diecinueve	100	cien
11	once	20	veinte	101	ciento uno
12	doce	30	treinta	102	ciento dos
13	trece	40	cuarenta	115	ciento quince
14	catorce	50	cincuenta	121	ciento veintiuno
15	quince	60	sesenta	132	ciento treinta y dos
16	dieciséis	70	setenta	143	ciento cuarenta y tres
17	diecisiete	80	ochenta	167	ciento sesenta y siete
18	dieciocho	90	noventa	198	ciento noventa y ocho

Remember that "y" is used in numbers 31 - 99. Don't use "y" with numbers greater than 100.
Cien is 100 even. After that it changes to *ciento*. (not "*cien y...*")

1. Listen, and write the number you hear.

_____ _____ _____ _____ _____ _____ _____ _____ _____

2. Count to one hundred by ten's without looking. Then count by five's to one hundred.

3. Say phone numbers, separating them like this to practice: 21-42-52-16-48 *(214-252-1648)*
(Many times the phone numbers are separated this way, by groups of two, in Europe and Latin America.)

B.7 INDEFINITE ARTICLES

The indefinite articles in English are "a" and "some." The word for "one" (*uno*) is used as an **indefinite article** in Spanish.   It must change to agree with the noun.
(The -*o* is dropped before a masculine singular noun, the -*o* is changed to an -*a* for feminine, -*s* is added for plural)

un libro	*a book (one book)*	**una** mesa	*a table*
unos libros	*some books*	**unas** mesas	*some tables*

indefinite articles	masculine	feminine
singular	**un**	**una**
plural	**unos**	**unas**

Write the correct indefinite article for the noun:

1. ___*un*___ papel

2. _____ profesora

3. _____ escritorios

4. _____ plumas

5. _____ papeles

6. _____ luz

7. _____ teléfono celular

8. _____ sillas

Note: With numbers that end with "one", change *uno* to **un** before masculine nouns, and change to *una* before feminine nouns.
Example: veintiún libros *twenty-one books*   treinta y una mochilas *thirty-one backpacks*

B.8 ¿DÓNDE ESTÁ(N)? | *WHERE IS IT? WHERE ARE THEY?*

Dónde means "where"; *está* and *están* are verbs used for location.
Use **está** when asking about one thing (singular).
Use **están** when asking about more than one thing (plural).

¿Dónde está la puerta?	*Where is the door?*
¿Dónde están las ventanas?	*Where are the windows?*
¿Dónde está el baño?	*Where is the bathroom?*

Write in **está** or **están**:

1. ¿Dónde_____*está*_____la profesora?

2. ¿Dónde_____el pastor?

3. ¿Dónde_____los estudiantes?

4. ¿Dónde_____las luces?

5. ¿Dónde_____la mochila?

Did you know?

Costa Rica has no army. Per the Rio treaty, if they were attacked, they would be defended by the U.S. and American Continent nations.

They choose to put more money into education and have a 95% literacy rate, one of the highest in Latin America. The lowest literacy rates are in Nicaragua and Guatemala.

Answer these questions about the classroom or room you're in now.

1. ¿Dónde está la puerta?
2. ¿Dónde están las ventanas?
3. ¿Dónde está el libro de español?
4. ¿Dónde están las plumas?
5. ¿Dónde está la silla?
6. ¿Dónde está el baño?

aquí:	*here*
allí:	*there*

The verb **hay** means "t*here is*" or "*there are.*" It doesn't make a difference if it is a singular, plural, masculine or feminine noun.

Examples: Hay un reloj.   *There is a clock.*
             Hay una mesa.   *There is one table.*
             Hay cuatro sillas.   *There are four chairs.*
             Hay veintiún alumnos.   *There are twenty-one students.*

Note: If the number ends in "*uno*", the -*o* will be dropped before a masculine noun and -*a* added for a feminine noun.

In your classroom, or room, write how many there are of the indicated nouns.
Examples: **sillas:** Hay catorce sillas.   *There are 14 chairs.*
             mapas: No hay mapas.   *There are no maps.*

1. ventanas: *Hay una ventana.* _____

2. sillas: _____

3. plumas: _____

4. puertas: _____

5. luces: _____

¿Cuánto(s)? is the interrogative word for "*how much?*" or "*how many?*" It must agree with the noun it modifies.

¿Cuántos libros hay?   *How many books are there?*
¿Cuántas mesas hay?   *How many tables are there?*
¿Cuánto dinero hay?   *How much money is there?*

> ### Did you know?
>
> In Hispanic countries, there is primary (elementary) school and secondary (high) school, but no middle school buildings.

A. Write ***Cuántos*** or ***Cuántas*** in the blank:

1. ¿ _____ relojes hay?

2. ¿ _____ sillas hay?

3. ¿ _____ teléfonos celulares hay?

B. Answer:

1. ¿Cuántos estudiantes hay en el salón de clase? _____

2. ¿Cuántos niños hay en tu iglesia? _____

3. ¿Cuántas páginas hay en el libro de español? _____

4. ¿Cuántas personas hay en tu casa? _____

5. ¿Cuántos/as_____ hay en el salón de clase?
             (Use B.5 vocabulary words.)

B.11 NEGATIVE STATEMENTS

To make a statement negative in Spanish, place **_no_** before the verb or verb phrase to negate it.

No hay un reloj en el salón de clase.   *There isn't a clock in the classroom.*
No soy de California.   *I am not from California.*
No me llamo María.   *My name is not María. (I **don't call myself** María.)*

Make the following senteces negative:

1. Hay tres sillas. _____

2. Soy de Texas. _____

3. Federico es de Guatemala. _____

4. En la clase hay una profesora. _____

5. Tú eres estudiante. _____

6. (Using the vocabulary B.5, state what is not in the room.) "No hay _____."

B.12 WRITTEN ACCENT RULES

Where you stress the word is important in Spanish. If you stress the wrong syllable, you could change the word. Look at these 2 words. The stressed syllable is underlined:

       <u>pa</u>pa *potato*   **pa<u>pá</u>** *father*

The rule is:
#1. If the word ends with a vowel, *-n,* or *-s,* stress the <u>next to the last syllable.</u>
#2. If not (not ending in a vowel, *-n,* or *–s*), stress the <u>last syllable</u>.
#3. If the word does not follow these rules, (meaning it is pronounced with a different stressed syllable), there will be a written accent mark to stress the correct syllable.
Here are examples of each rule:

#1. a<u>mi</u>go, <u>can</u>tan, tor<u>ti</u>llas   **#2. co<u>mer</u>, a<u>zul</u>, universi<u>dad</u>**   **#3. te<u>lé</u>fono, <u>fá</u>cil, na<u>ción</u>**

ONE-SYLLABLE WORDS THAT HAVE WRITTEN ACCENT MARKS (FOR REASON OF DEFINITION)
Some words are said exactly the same, but one will have an accent mark, the other won't so as to distinguish the meaning.

tu (your)	tú (you)	si (if)	sí (yes)	te (pronoun)	té (tea)
el (the)	él (he)	mi (my)	mí (me)	se (pronoun)	sé (I know)
mas (but)	más (more)	de (of, from)	dé (give)		

* For more information on the rules for written accents, look in Appendix IV.

Coritos

HAY VIDA EN JESÚS (*There is life in Jesus*)

Hay vida, hay vida, hay vida en Jesús.	*There is life in Jesus*
Hay vida, hay vida, hay vida en Jesús.	
Yo voy a morar en la Patria Celestial,	*I'm going to live in heaven*
Porque hay vida, hay vida en Jesús.	*because there is life in Jesus*
- Gozo	*joy*
- Canto	*song*

Traditional song from Cancionero Latinoamericano.

SALMO 23:1. JEHOVÁ ES MI PASTOR (Psalm 23:1. *The Lord is my shepherd*)

Jehová es mi pastor,	*The Lord is my shepherd (3X)*
Jehová es mi pastor,	
Jehová es mi pastor,	
Y nada me faltará.	*And I shall not want*

Traditional song from Cancionero Latinoamericano.
The complete song is in the Praise and Worship section.

Written Work

Write the Spanish Bible verse for this lesson. Repeat it several times, and learn it.
Notice there is no "ph" in Spanish, it will always be an "f."

_____

_____

A. Pretend you just met someone and you want to introduce yourself. Fill in the blanks: **B.1**

1. Hola. _____Buenos_____ días. ¿ _____ está usted?

2. Muy _____, gracias. ¿ _____ usted?

3. _____ llamo _____.

4. _____ soy de _____.

5. Mucho _____.

6. El gusto _____ mío.

B. Match the subject pronoun with the correct form of the verb *SER*. **B.2**

yo	es
tú	son
él	soy
ella	son
usted	eres
nosotros	son
ellos	es
ellas	somos
ustedes	es

Draw lines to match the subject w/ conjugation.

C. Answer each question first affirmatively then negatively. **B.3**

1. ¿Eres tú estudiante? *Sí, yo soy estudiante. No, yo no soy estudiante.*

2. ¿Eres tú mexicano? _____

3. ¿Uds. son de los Estados Unidos? (Answer with nosotros.) _____

_____

D. Answer the question by stating how many objects there are. **B.6 + B.10**

1. ¿Cuántas plumas hay? (34) *Hay treinta y cuatro plumas.*

2. ¿Cuántos estudiantes hay? (25) _____

3. ¿Cuántos escritorios hay? (7) _____

4. ¿Cuántas mochilas hay? (18) _____

5. ¿Cuántos libros hay? (59) _____

ACROSS

1   homework
4   what you sit in
5   what you write with
6   a quiet place to study
7   adulta (feminina)
8   use it to talk to people far away
11 school (not "escuela")
13 casa de Dios
14 tells you the time
15 student

DOWN

2   answer
3   where you sit down to write
5   you open this to go into a room
9   adulto (masculino)
10 you keep your things in it
11 a young boy or guy
12 table

Made at puzzle-maker.com

F. Change the definite article to the indefinite article (*un, una, unos, unas*). Then translate. **B.5** and **B.7**

1. el papel   _un_ papel   _a paper_

2. el lápiz   _____ lápiz   _____

3. la luz   _____ luz   _____

4. los cuadernos   _____ cuadernos   _____

5. las puertas   _____ puertas   _____

6. el mapa   _____ mapa   _____

7. los niños   _____ niños   _____

8. la pregunta   _____ pregunta   _____

9. las escuelas   _____ escuelas   _____

10. el hombre   _____ hombre   _____

G. Write the correct form of *está* or *están*. **B.8**

1. ¿Dónde _están_ los relojes?

2. ¿Dónde _____ la tarea?

3. ¿Dónde _____ las mesas?

4. ¿Dónde _____ el teléfono?

5. ¿Dónde _____ la biblioteca?

H. Make the sentence negative, then translate. **B.11**

1. La profesora es de California. _____

_____

2. Los niños son estudiantes. _____

_____

3. Yo soy profesora. _____

_____

4. Los libros están allí. _____

_____

5. Ellos son argentinos. _____

_____

I. Write a paragraph describing what is in your classroom/meeting room. **B.5** and **B.9**

Practice writing the vocabulary words. Start with, *"En mi salón (de clase) hay . . ."* _____

_____

_____

_____

_____

_____

_____

_____

_____

J. *DIOS ES*: **Who** and **what** is God? Find and write the English equivalent.

Padre _____

Hijo _____

Espíritu Santo _____

Rey _____

Amor _____

Paz _____

Consuelo _____

Vida Eterna _____

Bueno _____

Fiel _____

Lección 1
Describe Yourself

Professions / Review of *SER* / Descriptions of People / Adjective Gender-Number Agreement / Giving Compliments / Comparisons With *Más/ESTAR* / Feelings and Conditions / *SER* vs. *ESTAR*

Lección 1

1.1 PROFESIONES | PROFESSIONS (English alphabetical order)

contador/a	accountant	**misionero/a**	missionary
actor, actriz	actor, actress	**gerente**	manager
arquitecto/a	architect	**músico/a**	musician
artista	artist	**enfermero/a**	nurse
autor/a	author	**pintor/a**	painter
jefe/a	boss	**pastor**	pastor
hombre de negocios	business man	**cura, padre**	priest
mujer de negocios	business woman	**farmacéutico/a**	pharmacist
cocinero/a	cook	**fotógrafo/a**	photographer
consejero/a	counselor, adviser	**plomero**	plumber
dentista	dentist	**policía**	police
director/a	director	**político**	politician
médico/a	doctor	**profesional**	professional
doctor/a	doctor	**profesor/a**	professor
conductor/a, chofer	driver	**jubilado/a, retirado/a**	retired
empleado/a	employee	**vendedor/a**	salesperson
ingeniero/a	engineer	**secretario/a**	secretary
jardinero/a	gardener	**cantante**	singer
ama de casa	housewife	**soldado**	soldier
periodista	journalist	**estudiante**	student
juez/a	judge	**maestro/a**	teacher
abogado/a	lawyer	**mesero/a**	waiter, waitress
bibliotecario/a	librarian	**trabajador/a**	worker, laborer

*-o endings are for men, -a endings are for women. -ista and -e endings are male and female.

A. ¿Cuál es su profesión? What profession are you?

Yo soy _____. ¿Y Ud.?

B. What professions are other people in class?
What professions are the members of your family?

REVIEW OF THE VERB *SER*
Remember, the verb "ser" means "to be" and is irregular.

> **Did you know?**
> The word "pastor" in Spanish also means "shepherd."

singular		plural	
yo	**soy**	nosotros/as	**somos**
tú	**eres**		
él, ella, Ud.	**es**	ellos, ellas, Uds.	**son**

Yo **soy** estudiante.	*I am a student.*
Ustedes **son** meseras.	*You (plural) are waitresses.*
Tú **eres** artista.	*You (inform, sing.) are an artist.*
Ellos **son** alumnos.	*They (masc.) are students.*
Ella **es** profesora.	*She is a professor.*
Ellas **son** alumnas.	*They (fem.) are students.*
Nosotros **somos** doctores.	*We are doctors.*

Remember that when the subject is a thing or things, the 3rd person conjugation is used.
Example: Mi mochila es vieja.   *My backpack is old.*
            Las Biblias son hermosas.   *The Bibles are beautiful.*

C. Fill in the correct form of *SER*.

1.   Tú_____*eres*_____mi amiga.
2.   Pedro_____de Nicaragua.
3.   Nosotras_____estudiantes.
4.   Los libros _____de Colombia.
5.   Ellos_____de Costa Rica
6.   Yo no_____ secretaria.
7.   Ustedes no_____artistas.
8.   Usted_____pastor.

Ellas son amigas.

1.2 DESCRIPCIONES DE PERSONAS | *DESCRIPTIONS OF PEOPLE* (WITH SER)

muy	*very*	**joven**	*young*	**amable**	*nice, friendly*
alto/a	*tall*	**viejo/a**	*old*	**tímido/a**	*shy*
bajo/a	*short*	**simpático/a**	*pleasant, nice*	**paciente**	*patient*
bonito/a	*pretty*	**inteligente**	*intelligent*	**casado/a**	*married*
feo/a	*ugly*	**generoso/a**	*generous*	**soltero/a**	*single*
hermoso/a	*beautiful*	**trabajador/a**	*hard working*	**cristiano/a**	*Christian*
guapo/a	*handsome*	**organizado/a**	*organized*	**creyente**	*believer*
gordo/a	*fat*	**activo/a**	*active*	**metodista**	*Methodist*
delgado/a	*thin*	**chistoso/a**	*funny*	**católico/a**	*Catholic*
rubio/a	*blond(e)*	**divertido/a**	*fun*	**presbiteriano/a**	*Presbyterian*
moreno/a	*dark skinned*	**puntual**	*punctual*	**bautista**	*Baptist*
rico/a	*rich*	**optimista**	*optimist*	**evangélico/a**	*evangelical*
pobre	*poor*	**lindo/a**	*cute*	**pentecostal**	*Pentecostal*

*If the adjective ends with *-o/a*, end it with an *-o* for a male, and an *-a* for a female.

1.   Mi mamá es muy_*activa*_. (*active*)
2.   El Sr. Martínez es muy _____ . (*friendly*)
3.   Sofía es _____. (*shy*)
4.   El fotógrafo es _____ . (*tall*)

Describe yourself. Yo soy _____ y _____ y _____ .

Now describe others.   Examples: Miriam es_*rubia*_.   Mi amigo es _____.

Did you know?

"*Gringo*" is a Latin American expression for "American." "*Güero/a*" is a Mexican expression for a light-skinned and lighter brown or blond hair person. "*Güey*" (said like English word 'way') is an expression for "dude" among younger Mexicans, but can be taken offensively by the older generations.

Remember that all nouns in Spanish are either male or female. The gender for the noun is set and any adjective that describes that noun must agree in gender and number.

In Spanish, the noun comes first, then the adjective. You first say what it is, then you describe it.

El chico alto.   *The tall boy.*   La mujer simpática.   *The nice lady.*

Every adjective has a "main form" that is used to describe a singular, male noun. (Example: alto) If that adjective ends in -o, it will change to -a when describing a female noun. If the noun is plural, you must add an -s to make the adjective plural. Look at the Spanish word for TALL, there are four forms.

	masculine	feminine
singular	**alto**	**alta**
plural	**altos**	**altas**

The noun is what determines which form of the adjective to use.
It must be the form that agrees with the noun in number and in gender. Change the -o to -a for feminine.
Look at these examples and see how the article and the adjectives must agree with the noun it's modifying.

el chico <u>alto</u>   *the tall boy*   la chica <u>alta</u>   *the tall girl*
los chicos <u>altos</u>   *the tall boys*   las chicas <u>altas</u>   *the tall girls*

If the adjective's main form does not end with -o, then that form can be used for masculine or feminine nouns, and you do not have to change it unless you have to make it plural.*
These adjectives may end in -e, -ista, -r, -l or -n.
Take a look at the Spanish word for INTELLIGENT, there are only 2 forms.

	masculine	feminine
singular	**inteligente**	**inteligente**
plural	**inteligentes**	**inteligentes**

El médico es <u>inteligente.</u>   El profesor <u>amable.</u>
La enfermera es <u>inteligente.</u>   La profesora <u>amable.</u>
Los niños son <u>inteligentes.</u>   Los profesores <u>amables.</u>
Las niñas son <u>inteligentes.</u>   Las profesoras <u>amables.</u>

*There are exceptions, especially with nationalities as in *español/a* and adjectives that end in -dor, as in *trabajador/a.*

Write the adjective given in the main form and change it according to the noun it is modifying. Make sure you pay attention to the definite article to know if it is masculine or feminine.

1. BAJO

La maestra es ___*baja*___

El arquitecto es ___*bajo*___

Los meseros son ___*bajos*___

Las misioneras son ___*bajas*___

2. GENEROSO

El músico es _____

La escritora es _____

Los pastores son _____

Las estudiantes son _____

3. AMABLE

El pastor es _____

Mi jefe^{boss} es _____

Las secretarias son _____

Los dentistas son _____

4. PUNTUAL

La profesora es _____

Los doctores son _____

El chofer es _____

Las maestras son _____

5. CRISTIANO

El arquitecto es _____

La cocinera es _____

Las vendedoras son _____

Los pintores son _____

6. SIMPÁTICO

El abogado es _____

Los plomeros son _____

La enfermera es _____

Las directoras son _____

Remember: *amable* and *puntual* are forms for both masculine and feminine nouns.

1.4 HOW TO GIVE A COMPLIMENT

A compliment can be a great way to begin a conversation.

There are 2 simple ways to give compliments.

1. **Él es muy inteligente.** *He is very intelligent.*   **Ella es muy bonita.** *She is very pretty.*

2. "Qué + adjective":   **¡Qué bonita!** *How pretty!*   **¡Qué alto!** *How tall!*

¡Qué interesante! *How interesting!*   **¡Qué increíble!** *How incredible!*   **¡Qué divertido!** *How fun!*

1.5 COMPARISONS | USING "MÁS"

A. *Más* is the word that means "more."

"No **más**."	No **more**.
"Hay **más** libros."	There are **more** books.
"Yo necesito **más** tiempo."	I need **more** time.

B. It can be used with adjectives to make comparisons. *Más* + adjective

Mi casa es grande.	My house is big.
Tú casa es **más** <u>grande</u>.	Your house is <u>bigger.</u>

If the adjective is gender specific, you must make it agree with the noun.

Él es más <u>bajo</u>.	He is shorter.
Ella es más <u>baja</u>.	She is shorter.
Tú eres más <u>alto</u>	You are taller.

Él es más alto que ella.

C. Comparisons using "more…than" is expressed with "*más…que*" in Spanish.

Rodrigo es **más** inteligente **que** José.   Rodrigo is **more** intelligent **than** José.

Más + alto + que = *taller than*.

Él es **más** alto **que** ella.	He is taller than her.
Manuel es **más** bajo **que** tú.	Manuel is shorter than you.
Diana es **más** inteligente **que** yo.	Diana is smarter than I.

> **Did you know?**
>
> The most southern city on the globe is Ushuaia, Argentina.

D. Fill in the blank with vocabulary from 1.2:

1. Jorge es más _____ que tú . (*active*)

2. Roberto es más _____ que Jay. (*shy*)

3. Mariana es más _____ que Roberto. (*funny*)

4. Mi amigo es más _____ que yo. (pick from 1.2)

5. Yo soy más _____ que mi amigo. (or compare yourself to other students)

E. There are special adjectives used for comparison:

mejor	*better*	**mayor**	*older*
peor	*worse*	**menor**	*younger*

For example, you do not say "*más bueno,*" you say "*mejor.*"

1. Yo soy _____ *menor* _____ que mi padre.

2. Yo soy _____ que mi hermano/a.^brother/sister (*younger* or *older*)

3. La computadora es _____ que el papel y lápiz. (*better* or *worse*)

4. Un libro es _____ que la televisión. (*better* or *worse*)

1.6 THE VERB *ESTAR*

ESTAR is another verb that means "to be."

This is how you conjugate the verb *ESTAR*. It is an irregular verb and you must learn the conjugation by repeating, and memorizing it. Here is the Present tense conjugation.

singular		plural	
yo	**estoy**	nosotros/as	**estamos**
tú	**estás**	Uds.	**están**
él, ella, Ud.	**está**	ellos, ellas	**están**

If you remember from Lesson 1, the verb *ESTAR* is used when you want to talk about the location of something. ¿Dónde <u>está</u>? *Where is it?*

¿Dónde <u>está</u> el baño?   *Where is the bathroom?*

¿Dónde <u>están</u> los niños?   *Where are the children?*

1.7 FEELINGS AND CONDITIONS USED WITH *ESTAR*

bien	well, fine	**cansado/a**	tired	**nervioso/a**	nervous
mal	bad off	**aburrido/a**	bored	**enfermo/a**	sick
feliz, alegre	happy	**enojado/a**	mad, angry	**ocupado/a**	busy
contento/a	content, happy	**triste**	sad	**preocupado/a**	worried

ESTAR is also used for saying how one "feels." Remember the greeting:

¿Cómo <u>está</u> Ud.?   *How are you?*   —<u>Estoy</u> bien, gracias.   *I'm fine, thank you.*

You can also answer: —Estoy feliz. *I'm happy.*   or   —Estoy cansado/a. *I'm tired.*

ESTAR is used with <u>feelings</u> and <u>conditions</u>.

A. Answer: **¿Cómo está usted?** Pick an adjective to fill in the blank. Make sure you agree with gender.

Estoy _____   No estoy _____

B. Ask a partner (using the *tú* form) how he/she feels in each place:

1. ¿Cómo estás tú ahora^now? _____*feliz*_____   *2.* ¿Cómo estás tú en la iglesia? _____

3. ¿Cómo estás tú en el hospital? _____   *4.* ¿En el trabajo? _____

5. ¿En un funeral? _____   *6.* ¿En la escuela? _____

C. Fill in the blank with the correct form of *ESTAR*, then translate.

1. El pastor _____ ocupado. _____

2. Alejandra y Mario _____ aburridos. _____

3. Nosotros _____ alegres. _____

In English, there is only one verb that means "to be." In Spanish there are 2 verbs, **ser** and **estar**, that can be translated to mean "to be," but are used differently.

SER is used for more "permanent" or inherent characteristics.
Such as <u>profession, origin or physical</u> / <u>personality characteristics</u>. (1.2)

   1. Yo soy **estudiante**.   Tú eres **artista**.   (profession)

   2. Marcelo es **de**^{from} **México**.   Ustedes son **de California**. (origin)

   3. Nosotros somos **altos**.   Ellos son **simpáticos**.   (physical/personality characteristics)

ESTAR is used for <u>location</u> and "temporary" situations, such as <u>feelings</u> and <u>conditions</u>. (1.7)

   1. Yo estoy **en**ⁱⁿ **casa**.   La iglesia está **en Dallas**. (location)

   2. Tú estás **alegre**.   Nosotros estamos **tristes**. (feelings)

   3. Ellos están **enfermos**.   Ella está **cansada**. (conditions)

El bebé está feliz.

A. SER or ESTAR? Fill in the blank with the correct verb.
Make sure you conjugate it correctly. Use charts 1.2 and 1.7

1. El Señor Martínez _____ *es* _____ muy puntual. (ser)

2. Tú _____ abogado^{lawyer}.

3. El Pastor _____ de Texas, pero _____ en Argentina.

4. Yo _____ preocupada^{worried}.

5. Los niños _____ inteligentes, pero _____ aburridos^{bored}.

6. Mario y yo _____ amables y divertidos^{fun}.

7. Ustedes _____ en la iglesia.

8. Rosario _____ morena^{dark skinned} y muy bonita^{pretty}.

A. 2. eres 3. es, está 4. estoy 5. son, están 6. somos 7. están 8. es

B. Write about each person(s). Choose *SER* or *ESTAR* according to the correct expression:

Mi amigo: _____ *Mi amigo está cansado.* _____(is tired)

El/la profesor/a: _____(is patient)

El/La estudiante: _____(is punctual)

Mi jefe^{boss}: _____(is angry)

Cultural Note
MARCOS WITT

Marcos Witt is an Internationally known Christian Singer/ Composer. Marcos grew up in Mexico as the son of missionaries. The multi-GRAMMY® Award winner has written many songs that are used in Praise and Worship throughout Latin America. He also founded an Institute dedicated to preparing worship leaders and music ministers. Marcos lives in Houston, Texas and was the Hispanic Pastor for the Lakewood Church from 2002-2012. One of his best known songs is about God's faithfulness.

TU FIDELIDAD *(Your faithfulness)*

Tu fidelidad es grande.	*You faithfulness is great.*
Tu fidelidad, incomparable es.	*Your faithfulness is incomparable.*
Nadie como Tú, bendito Dios,	*No one like you, blessed God,*
Grande es tu fidelidad.	*Great is your faithfulness.*

Words and music by Miguel Cassina
©1993 Miguel Cassina. Admin by CanZion Editora. All Rights Reserved. Used by permission.

Coritos

YO TENGO GOZO, GOZO EN MI CORAZÓN   *(I have the joy, joy, joy, joy down in my heart)*

Yo tengo gozo, gozo en mi corazón,
¿Dónde?
En mi corazón.
¿Dónde?
En mi corazón.

Yo tengo gozo, gozo en mi corazón,	
¿Por qué? Porque Cristo me salvó.	*I have joy in my heart*
	because Christ saved me
Y estoy alegre, sí muy alegre.	*and I'm happy, yes, very happy*
Yo tengo el amor de Cristo en mi corazón	*I have the love of Christ in my heart*
Y estoy alegre, sí muy alegre,	
Porque Cristo me salvó.	

Anonymous translation.

Written Work

Write the Spanish Bible verse for this lesson. Repeat it several times, and learn it.

_____

_____

A. What professionals would you see at these places.? **1.1**

1. El hospital: _un médico, ..._____

2. El restaurante:_____

3. En la corte (*court*):_____

4. En la escuela o la universidad:_____

5. En un teatro (*theater*):_____

6. En una iglesia: _____

B. Write the correct pronoun(s) with *SER. - yo, tú, él, ella, nosotros, ellos, ellas.* **B.2**

1. _____ soy.   *2.* _____ eres.   *3.* _____ es.

4. _____ somos.   *5.* _____ son.

C. Write the correct pronoun(s) with *ESTAR. - yo, tú, él, ella, nosotros, ellos, ellas.***1.6**

1. _____ estoy.   *2.* _____ estás.   *3.* _____ está.

4. _____ estamos.   *5.* _____ están.

D. Write the correct form of the <u>descriptive adjectives (that use *SER*).</u>

Make sure to match the gender/number of the noun. **1.2 and 1.3**

1. Roberto es _____ y _____. (*tall/handsome*)

2. La casa es _____ y _____. (*old / ugly*)

3. Alberto y yo somos _____. (*friendly*)

4. Estela es _____ y _____. (*pretty / nice*)

5. El pastor es _____ . (*very generous*)

6. Ellos son _____ y _____. (*short / fat*)

7. Las secretarias son _____. (*organized*)

8. Ellas son _____ y _____.(*blonde / thin*)

E. Write the correct form of the adjectives of <u>feelings or conditions (that use *ESTAR*)</u> to match the gender/number of the noun. **1.7**

1. Ricardo está _____ y _____ . *(tired / sick)*

2. Rosita está _____ y _____ . *(worried / nervous)*

3. Alberto y yo estamos _____ . *(tired)*

4. Estela está _____ y _____ . *(happy / content)*

5. El pastor está _____ . *(very busy)*

6. Ellos están _____ y _____ . *(bored / sad)*

7. Las mujeres están _____ . *(mad, angry)*

F. Write the correct form of either *SER* or *ESTAR*. **1.2 and 1.7**

1. Mi profesora _____*está*_____ feliz.

2. El arquitecto _____*es*_____ inteligente.

3. El dentista _____ enfermo.

4. Los abogados _____ preocupados.

5. El pastor _____ alto.

6. La mesera _____ amable.

7. El estudiante _____ aburrido.

G. Finish the sentence correctly after either *SER* or *ESTAR*. **1.2 and 1.7**

1. Yo **soy** _____*estudiante*_____

2. En este momento yo **estoy** _____

3. Mi profesor/a **es** _____

4. Mis primos **están** _____

5. Mis amigos **son** _____

H. Translate. 1.1 and 1.2

1. The missionary is generous. _____

2. The cook is punctual. _____

3. The soldier is intelligent. _____

4. The salesman is busy. _____

5. The judge is a believer. _____

I. Write about yourself. Start by introducing yourself and saying where you are from. Then tell your profession and finish by saying what kind of a person you are (1.2) and how you feel (1.7).

Then write about another person in your life. (One of opposite sex.)

Example: mi esposo/a (*husband/wife),* mi mamá , mi papá, or mi amigo/a.

Use as many vocabulary words as you can.

Make sure you make the adjectives agree and your verbs are conjugated correctly.

_____

_____

_____

_____

_____

_____

_____

_____

_____

_____

_____

_____

_____

_____

_____

_____

_____

Lesson 2
The Family & Descriptions

Family Vocabulary / What are you like? / *TENER* - Expressing
Possession and Age / Possessive Adjectives and Pronouns /
Interrogative Words / Positive and Negative Words

Lección 2

Padre nuestro que estás en el cielo, santificado sea tu nombre. Mateo 6 : 9
Our Father who is in heaven, hallowed be your name. Matthew 6:9

2.1 LA FAMILIA | *FAMILY*

el padre, papá	*father*	**el hijo**	*son*
la madre, mamá	*mother*	**la hija**	*daughter*
los padres	*parents*	**los hijos**	*children*
el hermano	*brother*	**el nieto**	*grandson*
la hermana	*sister*	**la nieta**	*grandaughter*
los hermanos	*siblings*	**los nietos**	*granchildren*
el abuelo	*grandfather*	**el primo**	*male cousin*
la abuela	*grandmother*	**la prima**	*female cousin*
los abuelos	*grandparents*	**los primos**	*cousins*
		el sobrino	*nephew*
el tío	*uncle*	**la sobrina**	*niece*
la tía	*aunt*		
los tíos	*aunts and uncles*	**el cuñado**	*brother-in-law*
		la cuñada	*sister-in-law*
el suegro	*father-in-law*		
la suegra	*mother-in-law*	**el yerno**	*son-in-law*
los suegros	*parents-in-law*	**la nuera**	*daughter-in-law*
el esposo	*husband*	**el novio**	*boyfriend (also groom)*
la esposa	*wife*	**la novia**	*girlfriend (also bride)*

mi(s)	*my*	**la mamá de mi mamá**	*my mom's mom*
tu(s)	*your (informal)*	**¿Cómo se llama?**	*What is his/her name?*
su(s)	*your (formal)*	**mayor/menor**	*older/younger*
de	*of, belongs to*	**¿Cómo es?**	*What is he/she like?*
tengo	*I have*	**no tengo**	*I don't have*

1. La mamá de mi mamá es mi _____

2. El hermano de mi papá es mi _____

3. La madre de mi esposo/a es mi _____

4. La hija de mi hijo es mi _____

5. Ask about different family members: ¿Cómo se llama tu _____? — Se llama _____.

<u>Write the number. Spell it out.</u>

6. Yo tengo _____ hermanos.

7. Yo tengo _____ primos.

8. Yo tengo _____ hijos.

9. Circle one: <u>Tengo</u> / <u>No tengo</u> esposo/a.

2.2 ¿CÓMO ES? | *WHAT IS HE/SHE LIKE?*

¿Cómo eres? asks the question, *what are you like?*
(NOT "¿Cómo estás?" which means, "*how are you doing/feeling?*")
By using the verb *SER*, you are asking, how are you as a person? in other words, "*What are you like?*"
Here are some sample questions with answers. To answer use *SER*. (B.2)

¿Cómo eres tú?	*What are you (informal) like?*	—Soy alto.
¿Cómo es María?	*What is María like?*	—Ella es alta.
¿Cómo es usted?	*What are you (formal) like?*	—Soy amable.
¿Cómo son ellas?	*What are they like?*	—Ellas son bonitas.
¿Cómo son tus padres?	*What are your parents like?*	—Son generosos.

With a partner, take turns telling about your family members.
Using the adjectives in chart 1.2, describe your family members.

Example: Ask: ¿Cómo es tu **tía**? (The answer can be as follows:)
Answer: Mi **tía** se llama Isabel. Ella es **chistosa**. *My **aunt** is called Isabel. She is **funny**.*
(Don't forget to change -o to an -a for females)

Mi _____ se llama _____. Él/Ella es _____.
  (*relative*)   (*name*)   (*adjective*)

You can also add where he/she lives: Él/Ella vive en _____.
                                                                (*city*)

*If you have pictures you could show them to a partner as you talk about them.

2.3 THE VERB *TENER* | EXPRESSING POSSESSION AND AGE

The verb *tener* means "to have." Like most common verbs, it is irregular. Here is the present tense conjugation. The best way to learn irregular verbs is to repeat several times, and memorize.

singular		plural	
yo	**tengo**	nosotros/as	**tenemos**
tú	**tienes**	Uds.	**tienen**
él, ella, Ud.	**tiene**	ellos/ellas	**tienen**

María **tiene** dos hijas. *María **has** two daughters.*
Yo **tengo** una prima. *I **have** a (girl) cousin.*
Ellos **tienen** tres hijos. *They **have** three children.*

A. Ask someone:

1. ¿Cuántos **hermanos** tienes?
2. ¿Cuántas **tías** tienes?
3. ¿Cuántos _____ tienes? (Choose from 2.1)

> ♦ Did you know? ♦
>
> Nursing homes are not as common in Latin America as in the U.S. Most elderly live with their son/daughter and grandchildren.

TENER is the verb also used to express age.

In Spanish you must say you HAVE an amount of years in age.   *TENER* + years.

¿Cuántos años tienes?   *How old are you? (How many years do you have?)*
Yo tengo veinte años (de edad).   *I have 20 years (of age).*

Example: ¿Cuántos años **tiene** tu hermano? —Mi hermano **tiene** 15 años.

B. Write the correct conjugated form of *TENER*: (2.3)

1. Yo _____ 25 años.

2. Los niños _____ 9 años.

3. Ella _____ 40 años.

4. Tú _____ 36 años.

5. Nosotros _____ 50 años.

El niño tiene un año.

C. Ask someone how old his/her family members are or answer for your family.

Example: ¿Cuántos años tiene <u>tu hija</u>?   —<u>Mi hija</u> tiene <u>veinte</u> años.

1. primo/a   *3.* esposo/a   *5.* hijo/a

2. papá   *4.* tío/a   *6.* abuelo/nieto

2.4 POSSESSIVE ADJECTIVES

Possessive adjectives must agree with the noun. ***Mi***, which means "my" is a possessive adjective.

All possessive adjectives must agree in <u>number</u> with the noun they modify.

The only possessive adjective that must agree with gender as well as number is "nuestro/a" - our.

my	**mi(s)**
your (informal)	**tu(s)**
his/her/your (formal)	**su(s)**
our	**nuestro/a(s)**
their/your (plural)	**su(s)**

mi libro   *my book*   **mis** libros   *my books*
tu hermana   *your* (informal) *sister*   **tus** hermanas   *your sisters*
su pluma   *his/her/your* (formal) *pen* **sus** plumas   *his/her/your* (formal) *pens*
su carro   *their/your* (plural) *car*   **sus** carros   *their/your* (plural) *cars*

nuestro auto   *our car*   **nuestra** computadora   *our computer*
nuestros amigos *our friends*   **nuestras** bicicletas   *our bikes*

Note: Possessive adjectives agree with the noun, not the possessor.

"Their dog." is **"Su** perro." NOT "Sus perro." The only time it would be "sus" is if the noun is plural.

Example: Su gato es tímido, pero sus perros son activos.   *His cat is shy, but his dogs are active.*

"Su perro" has various meanings. If the meaning of "su perro" is not clear, this is how you would clarify it.

su perro →
El perro <u>de usted</u>.
El perro <u>de él</u>.
El perro <u>de ella</u>.
El perro <u>de ustedes</u>.
El perro <u>de ellos</u>.
El perro <u>de ellas</u>.

Es su perrito. / Es el perrito de ella.

Fill in the blank with the correct possessive adjective. 2.4

1. _____*Su*_____ hermano es alto. (his)

2. _____ hijos son muy inteligentes. (my)

3. _____ madre se llama Rosa. (our)

4. _____ mesa es muy bonita. (your, informal)

5. _____ esposa no está aquí. (your, formal)

6. _____ pluma es roja. (her)

2.5 POSSESSIVE PRONOUNS   (OPTIONAL)

If the noun is omitted to avoid repetition, instead of the possessive adjective, the possessive **pronoun** will be used. It is a longer form of the possesive adjective. Examples: (The verb *SER* is used with possession.)

Es **mi** libro. → *It is **my** book.*   Es **mío**. → *It is **mine***

Son **tus** plumas. → *They are **your** pens.*   Son **tuyas**. → *They are **yours**.*

All possessive pronouns must agree in gender and number with the noun it modifies, **not** the person who owns it.

Possessive Adjectives		Possessive Pronouns	
my	**mi(s)**	mine	**mío/a(s)**
your (informal)	**tu(s)**	yours (informal)	**tuyo/a(s)**
his, her, your (formal)	**su(s)**	his, hers, yours	**suyo/a(s)**
our	**nuestro/a(s)**	ours (does not change)	**nuestro/a(s)**
their / your (plural)	**su(s)**	theirs, yours	**suyo/a(s)**

A. Fill in the blank with the correct possessive pronoun:

1. Son mis libros. Son ___*míos*___. (mine)

2. Es tu mochila. Es _____. (yours-informal)

3. Es su teléfono. Es ___*suyo*___. (hers)

4. Son nuestros perros. Son ___*nuestros*___. (ours)

5. Es mi pluma. Es _____. (mine)

6. Es su hermana. Es _____. (his)

7. Son nuestras sillas. Son _____. (ours)

8. Es mi reloj. Es _____. (mine)

B. Whose is it? First use the <u>possessive adjective</u>, then use the <u>possessive pronoun</u>. **2.4 + 2.5**
(*The verb <u>tener</u> means "to have." 2.2)

1. <u>Yo tengo</u> un carro. *Es **mi** carro (it is **my** car)* . *Es **mío** (it is **mine**)* .

2. <u>Tú tienes</u> dos bicicletas. *Son **tus** bicicletas* . *Son **tuyas*** .

3. <u>María tiene</u> un perro. *Es **su** perro* . *Es **suyo*** .

4. <u>Tenemos</u> muchas Biblias. *Son **nuestras** Biblias* . _____.

5. <u>Yo tengo</u> una casa._____. _____.

6. <u>Usted tiene</u> un hermano._____. _____.

7. <u>Él tiene</u> una computadora._____. _____.

8. <u>Ustedes tienen</u> muchos amigos._____. _____.

Answers: B. 4. Son nuestras Biblias. Son nuestras. 5. Es mi casa. Es mía. 6. Es su hermano. Es suyo. 7. Es su computadora. Es suya. 8. Son sus amigos. Son suyos.

C. *¿Qué tienes tú?* Talk about something yours. Say you **have** it. Then say it is **yours**.
Example: <u>Yo tengo una Biblia. Es mía.</u>   <u>Yo tengo un lápiz. Es mío.</u>

Yo tengo _____. _____.

2.6 INTERROGATIVE WORDS

Question words in Spanish take an accent mark on the strong sounding vowel and are preceded with an upside down question mark. (The same thing happens with exclamation marks.)

¿Qué?	*What?*	**¿Cuál?**	*Which?/Which one?*
¿Cuándo?	*When?*	**¿Cuánto/a(s)?**	*How much?/How many?*
¿Dónde?	*Where?*	**¿Quién?**	*Who?/Whom?*
¿Adónde?	*To where?*	**¿Cómo?**	*How?*
¿De dónde?	*From where?*	**¿Por qué?**	*Why?* *porque - because*

These words are usually at the beginning of the question and are followed by the verb.

¿Qué es?	*What is it?*	**¿Cuánto** cuesta?	*How much does it cost?*
¿Dónde está María?	*Where is María?*	**¿Cuál** libro es?	*Which book is it?*

¿Por qué estás feliz? *Why are you happy?*   - **Porque** tengo vida en Jesús. *Because I have life in Jesus.*

A. Translate.

1. ¿Dónde están mis libros? _____

2. ¿Quién es tu primo? _____

3. ¿Cómo son tus padres? (describe them) _____

4. ¿Quién es tu pastor? _____

5. ¿Cuántas sillas hay aquí? _____

These "question words" seek out information. It is according to what information you want to obtain which will determine the correct interrogative word for your question.

B. Look at chart 2.6, and determine which question word you would use to find out the information given.

1. a place   ___*¿ Dónde?*___

2. a person   _____

3. a thing   _____

4. an amount   _____

5. which thing   _____

6. to where   _____

7. how   _____

8. a time or day   _____

9. a reason (why)   _____

C. Fill in the first blank with a family member. Then answer the question.
The answer must have the information for the question it is asking.

1. ¿Cómo se llama tu _*hermano*_ ?   —Se llama _____ .

2. ¿Cómo es tu _____ ?   —Es _____ .

3. ¿Dónde vive tu _____ ?   —Vive en _____ .

4. ¿Cuál es la profesión de tu _____ ?   —(Él, Ella) es _____ .

5. Translate the question and answer: *¿Por qué eres alto?* — *Porque mis padres son altos.*

_____

2.7 POSITIVE AND NEGATIVE WORDS

As you know, to make a sentence negative you simply place "*no*" before the verb.
There are other "negative" words that can be used to express negative sentences.
Here is a list of them, along with their affirmative counterparts:
The ones marked with (*) are the most important to know. Memorize them.

*algo	something	*nada	nothing
*alguien	someone	*nadie	no one
*también	also	*tampoco	either, neither
*siempre	always	*nunca/jamás	never/never ever
algún	some (singular/masc.)	ningún	none, not any (sing./masc.)
alguno/a(s)	some	ninguno/a(s)	none, not any
*y/o	and/or	ni…ni	neither…nor

Double negatives are used in Spanish, meaning that if you negate the verb, you must use the negative words. In English one says, "I don't have anything." But in Spanish one must say, "I don't have nothing."

Yo tengo **algo**.	I have **something**.
Yo **no** tengo **nada**.	I **don't** have **anything**. ^{literally} (I don't have nothing)

¿Hay **alguien** aquí?	Is **someone** here?
No hay **nadie** aquí.	There **isn't anyone** here.

It is possible to use the negative word before the verb to negate it instead of the word "no."

Yo **siempre** voy a la iglesia.	I always go to church.
Yo **nunca / jamás** voy al cine.	I **never/never ever** go to the movies.

Yo **también** soy estudiante.	I'm **also** a student.
Yo **tampoco** soy estudiante.	I'm not a student **either.**
Yo **también.**	Me **too.**
Yo **tampoco.**	Me **neither.**

Note: *Alguno* and *ninguno* drop the -o before a masculine, singular noun.

¿Tienes **algún** libro en español?	Do you have **some** book in Spanish?
No, no tengo **ningún** libro en español.	No, I don't have **any** book in Spanish.

Fill in the blank with an affirmative or a negative word. (Use chart **2.7**)

1. Tengo un lápiz __*y*__ una pluma. (*I have a pencil **and** a pen.*)

      No tengo __*ni*__ un lápiz __*ni*__ una pluma. (*I have **neither** a pencil **nor** a pen.*)

2. No hay _____ en casa. (*There is **no one** at home.*)

      Hay _____ en casa. (*There is **someone** at home.*)

3. Yo _____ estoy en mi casa. (*I'm **always** at home.*)

      Yo _____ estoy en mi casa. (*I'm **never** at home.*)

4. Hay _____ aquí. (*There is **something** here.*)

      No hay _____ aquí. (*There is **nothing** here.*)

5. ¿Hay **algún** estudiante en la clase? (*Is there **any** student in the class.*)

      No, no hay _____ estudiante en la clase. (*No, there is **not any** student in the class.*)

6. Make your own negative sentence: _____

DID YOU KNOW? The "youth" group (*grupo de jóvenes*) in some countries can cover the ages of young people up through their early 30's since they are still considered "*joven.*" The younger group that we call "youth group" in the U.S. is sometimes called "el grupo de adolescentes."

Cultural Note
MARCO BARRIENTOS

Marco Barrientos was born in Mexico City in 1963. He is an artist, writer, communicator, international conference speaker, and performer of contemporary Christian music. He travels extensively with his band (Marco Barrientos Band) throughout the Spanish-speaking world.

Marco has been nominated twice to the Latin GRAMMY® Awards, for his Live Albums *Viento+Fuego* and *Transformados*, the latter being one of the most relevant Christian albums of 2011. Because of his passion and commitment to communicate a message of hope and freedom through his music, Marco has become one of the most beloved Latin Christian artists. He has recorded 48 albums in a successful career that spans almost three decades. The following is the chorus to one of his well-known songs.

NO HAY NADIE COMO TÚ (*There is no one like You*)

No hay nadie como Tú,	*There is no one like You*
No hay nadie como Tú,	*There is no one like You*
Precioso y glorioso,	*Precious and glorious*
Tan bello y tan hermoso.	*So beautiful and so marvelous**

Authors: ©Marco Barrientos & Luis Barrientos, all rights reserved. Used by permission.
(The complete song is in the Praise and Worship section in the back.)
* Translation in English by M. Barrientos.

Corito

JESÚS ES MÍO (*Jesus is mine*) **2.5**

Mío, mío, mío, Jesús es mío	*Mine, mine, mine, Jesus is mine*
Mío en la tristeza,	
Mío en la alegría	*Mine in sadness, mine in happiness*
Mío mío, mío, Jesús es mío.	
Mío para siempre. Amén, amén.	*Mine forever, amen*
-Tuyo	*Yours*
-Nuestro	*Ours*

Traditional song from *Cancionero Latinoamericano*.

Written Work

Write the Spanish Bible verse for this lesson. Repeat it several times, and learn it.

_____

_____

A. Fill in the blank with the correct conjugated form of the verb _TENER._ **2.3**

_1._ Pedro _____ *tiene* _____ cuatro abuelos.

_2._ Mis padres _____ una casa en Guadalajara.

_3._ Tú _____ una computadora Mac.

_4._ El Presidente _____ 55 años.

_5._ Nosotros _____ mucho dinero.

_6._ El café _____ mucha cafeína.

B. Write the number of how many. **2.1**

_1._ Tengo _____ hermanos.

_2._ Tengo _____ primos.

_3._ Mi mamá tiene _____ hermanos.

_4._ Mis padres tienen _____ hijos.

C. Write the family vocabulary that is described. **2.1**

_1._ El hijo de mi hija es mi _____

_2._ Los padres de mi madre son mis _____

_3._ La hermana de mi padre es mi _____

_4._ La hija de mis tíos es mi _____

_5._ El hijo de mis padres es mi _____

D. What are all the different meanings for _"sus casas"_? **2.5**

_1._ _Las casas de él_ _____

_2._ _____

_3._ _____

_4._ _____

_5._ _____

_6._ _____

E. Write the question word. Don't forget the question marks and accents. **2.6**

1. What? _____

2. Who? _____

3. When? _____

4. Why? _____

5. Which? _____

6. Where? _____

F. Translate, then make it affirmative. **2.7**

1. No hay nadie en la iglesia. _There is no one in the church._
   Hay alguien en la iglesia

2. No tengo nada en mi carro. _____

   _____

3. Nunca tengo dinero. _____

   _____

G. Pick 8 family members and pick an adjective to describe them. **1.2 + 2.1**

Example: _Mi Tía Ligia es chistosa._

1. _____

2. _____

3. _____

4. _____

5. _____

6. _____

7. _____

8. _____

H. ¿Cómo eres tú? Describe yourself.

_____

_____

_____

_____

I. Translate:

1. The class has 22 students. _____

_____

2. My brother-in-law is 47 years old. _____

_____

3. We have his backpack. _____

_____

4. ¿Do you (plural) have our Bibles? _____

_____

5. The books are mine. _____

_____

6. I don't have your (informal) chairs. _____

_____

7. Where is your (formal) church? _____

_____

8. I have many friends in my Bible class. (B.5) _____

_____

Reading (*Lectura*)

¿Cómo es Dios? La Biblia nos dice[tells us] que Dios es amor, es paz y es nuestro refugio. Nuestro Padre celestial tiene un gran[great] amor por nosotros. ¿Qué es Dios para ti[for you]?

Dios es. . . _____

Grande means big. If you shorten it to *gran* and place it before the noun, it means *great*.

Lesson 3
Time, Weather, Dates, & Holidays

Time Phrases / Telling Time / Questions About Time / Days of the Week / Months /
Dates / Holidays / Seasons / Weather / Contractions *al* and *del* /
10 - 1000 / Dates with Years / *¿Cuánto cuesta?*

Lección 3

3.1 ¿QUÉ HORA ES? | *TIME PHRASES*

¿Qué hora es?	*What time is it?*	**la hora**	*the hour*
Es la una.	*It's one o'clock.*	**el minuto**	*the minute*
Son las dos.	*It's two o'clock.*	**los segundos**	*the seconds*
Son las tres.	*It's three o'clock.*	**la reunión**	*the meeting*
la mañana*	*the morning*	**el trabajo**	*the job*
la tarde	*the afternoon*	**de, desde**	*from*
la noche	*the night*	**a, hasta**	*to, until*
cuarto	*¼ (hour)*	**por**	*during, through*
media	*½ (hour)*	**más tarde**	*later*
Es mediodía.	*It's noon.*	**a tiempo**	*on time*
Es medianoche.	*It's midnight.*	**ahora**	*now*

***Mañana** means *tomorrow*. **La mañana** means *morning*.

Son las ocho <u>de</u> la mañana	*It's 8:00 in the morning (8:00 a.m.)*
<u>por</u> la mañana	*during the morning*
Es la una <u>de</u> la tarde	*It's 1:00 in the afternoon (1:00 p.m.)*
<u>por</u> la tarde	*during the afternoon*
Son las diez <u>de</u> la noche	*It's 10:00 in the evening (10:00 p.m.)*
<u>por</u> la noche	*during the evening*

El reloj.

NOTE: For a specific time use "***de***." For no specific time use "***por***."
Examples: *I work at 10 a.m.* = Trabajo a las diez <u>de</u> la mañana.
I work during the morning. = Trabajo <u>por</u> la mañana.

3.2 TELLING TIME

The verb *SER* is used with telling time. Use "***es***" with one o'clock. "***Son***" is used with all the other hours.

1:00	Es la una.
2:00	Son las dos.
6:00	Son las seis.

When you add minutes, use "**y**."

1:05	Es la una y cinco.
2:10	Son las dos y diez
5:20	Son las cinco y veinte

> **Did you know?**
>
> Military (24 hr.) time is used in many Hispanic countries.

For 15 minutes, say "**cuarto**". For 30 minutes, say "**media**".
(You can also say the minutes as "quince" and "treinta" but it's less common.)

When it is past the ½ hour, some countries will say it is the next hour **minus** the minutes.
Go to the next hour and take away minutes. Use "**menos**."

6:50	Son las siete menos diez.	(Son las seis y cincuenta.)
8:45	Son las nueve menos cuarto.	(Son las ocho y cuarenta y cinco.)
12:55	Es la una menos cinco.	(Son las doce y cincuenta y cinco.)

TO EXPRESS TIME

verb ser	article	hour	add or subtract	minutes
Es/Son	**la/las**	**una/dos…**	**y/menos**	**cinco/diez …**

¿Qué hora es? _____

Vamos a practicar - Say the time, then write it out.

1. 7:05 _*Son las siete y cinco.*_____

2. 9:20 _____

3. 11:15 _____

4. 1:30 _____

5. Noon _*Es mediodía.*_____

6. Midnight _____

7. 12:30 p.m. _*Son las doce y media de la tarde.*_____

8. 6.35 a.m. _____

9. 2:15 p.m. _____

10. 10:45 p.m. _____

3.3 QUESTIONS ABOUT TIME

¿A qué hora?   *At what time?*   **¿Cuándo?**   *When?*

To ask a question about time, you need the preposition "*a*" (at).

¿A qué hora es la reunión? —La reunión es a **las 9:00 de la mañana.** *The meeting is at 9:00am.*
¿Cuándo es la clase? —La clase de español es a **las 6:00 de la tarde.** *Spanish class is at 6:00pm.*

To say *"from"* this time *"to"* that time: Use **de** and **a**. *(From … to …)* Example: **De** las 8:00 **a** las 9:00.

Note: "*desde*" and "*hasta*" can be used, which also mean "*from*" and "*to*".
Example: La clase es **desde** las 8:00 de la mañana *hasta* las 5:00 de la tarde.

Write the answer, then ask someone. (Make sure you use "*a*" in the answer.)

1. ¿A qué hora es la clase de español? _*La clase de español es a las cuatro de la tarde*_

2. ¿A qué hora es el servicio de la iglesia?_____

3. ¿A qué hora es tu trabajo? _*Mi trabajo es desde las* _____ *hasta las* _____
   (State the hours of your job/work.)

domingo	*Sunday*	el día	*day*
lunes	*Monday*	la semana	*week*
martes	*Tuesday*	los días de la semana	*weekdays*
miércoles	*Wednesday*	el fin de semana	*weekend*
jueves	*Thursday*	todos los días	*all the days, every day*
viernes	*Friday*	cada	*each*
sábado	*Saturday*	cada domingo	*each (and every) Sunday*
hoy	*today*	este/esta	*this*
mañana	*tomorrow*	este lunes, esta semana	*this Monday/this week*

*Days of the week and months are not capitalized in Spanish.

A. Answer.

1. ¿Qué día es hoy? *Hoy es. . .* _____

2. ¿Qué día es mañana? _____

3. ¿Si hoy es sábado, qué día es mañana? _____
*Si = if (yes=sí with the accent)

4. ¿Si hoy es jueves, qué día es mañana? _____

5. ¿Cuál es tu día favorito de la semana? _____

6. Fill in: lunes _____ , miércoles, _____ , _____

TALKING ABOUT DAYS

When you talk about events scheduled on certain days of the week, in English we say "on Friday." In Spanish you simply say "*el viernes.*" If you want to say, "on Fridays," in Spanish you make it plural with the article, "*los viernes.*"

B. Fill in the blank.

1. La fiesta es *el sábado* . *The party is <u>on Saturday.</u>*

2. Vamos (we go) a la iglesia _____ . *We go to church <u>on Sundays.</u>*

Note: Cada domingo.   *Each Sunday.*   Todos los domingos.   *Every Sunday.*

To express the **day and time**, first say the day(s) and follow it with the time. Make sure you include the articles. ¿Cuándo es la reunión?   —La reunión <u>es</u> **el lunes <u>a</u> las 9:00 de la mañana.**

Este/esta :   These are the masculine and feminine forms of "*this.*"

Masculine nouns: <u>Este</u> sábado, <u>este</u> lunes, <u>este</u> mes, <u>este</u> año.

Feminine nouns: <u>Esta</u> semana, <u>esta</u> reunión, <u>esta</u> señora.

C. Translate: The meeting is this Saturday at 11:00 am.

3.5 LOS MESES DEL AÑO | *MONTHS OF THE YEAR*

enero	*January*	**mayo**	*May*	**septiembre**	*September*
febrero	*February*	**junio**	*June*	**octubre**	*October*
marzo	*March*	**julio**	*July*	**noviembre**	*November*
abril	*April*	**agosto**	*August*	**diciembre**	*December*

3.6 HOW TO SAY DATES

¿Qué día es hoy? *What day is today?* | **¿Cuál es la fecha de hoy?** *What is today's date?*

Start with the day, then the month, then the year.
In Hispanic countries, when the date is written, the day is first.
6/1/07 is January 6th, 2007. (expressing years in Spanish will be covered in 3.12)
A. When is Diego's birthdate? 8/3/85 _____.

Did you know?

Many think "5 de mayo" is Mexico's Independence Day, but it is not. Mexico's Independence is celebrated on September 16. The celebration of *Cinco de Mayo* is the day Napoleon's forces were defeated in Northern Mexico and the French retreated.

How to say dates:

El ___(date)___	de ___(month)___
El cuatro	**de julio**
El siete	**de marzo**

Important: ***primero* = *first*.** It is used for the 1st day instead of *uno*. Example: El primero de enero - *Jan. 1st*.

B. 1. ¿Cuál es la fecha de hoy? _____

2. ¿Cuál es la fecha de mañana? _____

3. ¿Cuándo es tu cumpleaños? _____

4. ¿Cuándo es Navidad? _____

5. ¿Cuándo es el Día de San Valentín? _____

3.7 LOS DÍAS FERIADOS | *HOLIDAYS*

Año Nuevo	*New Year's*	**el cumpleaños**	*the birthday*
Día de los Reyes	*Day of the Maggi*	**el 5 de Mayo**	*May 5th*
Día de San Valentín	*Valentine's Day*	**¡Felicitaciones!**	*congratulations!*
Semana Santa	*Holy Week*	**los regalos**	*gifts*
La Pascua (de resurrección)	*Easter*		
Día de la Madre	*Mother's Day*	**la fecha**	*the date*
Día del Padre	*Father's Day*	**el mes**	*the month*
Día del Trabajador	*Labor Day*	**el año**	*the year*
Día de la Independencia	*Independence Day*		
Día de Acción de Gracias	*Thanksgiving Day*		
La Navidad	*Christmas*	**del = de + el**	
La Nochebuena	*Christmas Eve*		

¡Feliz Cumpleaños!

3.8 LAS ESTACIONES | *SEASONS*

la primavera	*spring*
el verano	*summer*
el otoño	*autumn*
el invierno	*winter*

 **Did you know?** The countries in South America have the opposite seasons of the U.S. since they are on the other side of the equator. For example, Argentina is cold in June and July, while hot during Christmas!

¿Cuáles meses están en cada estación?
(*Which months are in each season?*)

Una flor de primavera.

1. ¿Cuáles son los meses de la primavera? _____

2. ¿Cuáles son los meses del verano? _____

3. ¿Cuáles son los meses del otoño? _____

4. ¿Cuáles son los meses del invierno? _____

3.9 EL TIEMPO | *WEATHER*

Hispanic countries use the Celsius system. 25°–30° C is very nice weather (77°–86° Fahrenheit).

¿Qué tiempo hace?	*What's the weather?*
hace calor	*it's hot*
hace fresco	*it's cool*
hace buen tiempo	*it's nice weather*
hace mal tiempo	*it's bad weather*
hace frío	*it's cold*
hace viento	*it's windy*
hace sol	*it's sunny*
llueve	*it's raining/it rains*
nieva	*it's snowing/it snows*

Hace sol en la playa.

mucho/poco	*a lot/a little*	**siempre/nunca**	*always/never*

¿Qué tiempo hace en junio? Siempre hace mucho calor.

1. ¿Qué tiempo hace hoy? _____

2. ¿Qué tiempo hace en la primavera? _____

3. ¿Qué tiempo hace en el verano? _____

4. ¿Qué tiempo hace en el otoño?_____

5. ¿Qué tiempo hace en el inverno? _____

3.10 LAS CONTRACCIONES | *CONTRACTIONS*

There are only 2 contractions in Spanish. One is with the preposition *de*, the other is with the preposition *a*. When they are each followed by *el*, they contract. Any other combination will not contract.

de + el = *del*	a + el = *al*

Hoy es el Día **del** Padre.   *Today is Father's Day.*
El Día **de la** Madre es en mayo.   *Mother's Day is in May.*

Yo voy **al** supermercado.   *I'm going to the super market.*
La clase es **a las** 6:00 **de la** tarde.   *The class is at 6:00 in the afternoon.*

Remember: The contraction is with the article *el* , not the pronoun *él*.
Este libro es **del** señor López. - *This book belongs to Mr. López.*
Este libro es **de él**. - *This book belongs to him.* (No contraction.)

Did you know?

In many Hispanic countries, with numbers, the period is used where we use a comma, and vice versa.

1.000 = one thousand

0,5 = 5 tenths

3.11 LOS NÚMEROS | *NUMBERS 10 - 1000*

10	diez	200	doscientos	101	ciento uno
20	veinte	300	trescientos	102	ciento dos
30	treinta	400	cuatrocientos	115	ciento quince
40	cuarenta	500	quinientos	128	ciento veintiocho
50	cincuenta	600	seiscientos	167	ciento sesenta y siete
60	sesenta	700	setecientos	254	doscientos cincuenta y cuatro
70	setenta	800	ochocientos	573	quinientos setenta y tres
80	ochenta	900	novecientos	1.986	mil novecientos ochenta y seis
90	noventa	1.000	mil	2.004	dos mil cuatro
100	cien	2.000	dos mil	100.000	cien mil
				150.000	ciento cincuenta mil

To learn to say the years, we must learn the numbers up to a thousand.

3.12 HOW TO SAY DATES WITH YEARS

El ___(date)___	de ___(month)___	de ___(year)___ .
El primero	**de julio**	**de dos mil siete.**
El siete	**de marzo**	**de mil novecientos ochenta y tres.**
El veintidós	**de septiembre**	**de dos mil quince.**

A. Answer:

1. ¿Qué fecha es hoy? (What is today's date?) _____

2. ¿Cuál es la fecha de tu nacimiento[date of birth]? _____

3. ¿Cuál es la fecha de nacimiento de tu… hijo/a, madre/padre, esposo/a? _____

_____

B. Write the birthdays of different people in class or members of your family.
Ask: *¿Cuándo es su cumpleaños?* (formal) or *¿Cuándo es tu cumpleaños?* (informal)

Nombre *(Susana)*	Cumpleaños *(el 4 de marzo)*

C. Listen to your teacher say different years, and circle them when you hear them.

1972	1689	1999	1787
2007	1946	1874	1876
1965	2005	1663	1500

D. Listen to your teacher and write the number you hear.

_____   _____   _____   _____

_____   _____   _____   _____

E. Listen to your teacher, write the dates you hear:

Example: you will hear: el ocho de diciembre de mil novecientos noventa y uno.
You will write: **8/12/1991** (The day is first, then the month, then the year.)

1. _____   2. _____   3. _____   4. _____

3.13 ¿CUÁNTO CUESTA? | *HOW MUCH DOES IT COST?*

Ask: **¿Cuánto cuesta?** - *How much does it cost?*

$100 $200 $500 $1.000 $20.000 $100.000

una bicicleta   **un carro**   **una moto**   **una casa**

Example: ¿Cuánto cuesta <u>una moto</u>?

—<u>Una moto</u> cuesta _____ dólares.

Cultural Note

EL DÍA DE LOS REYES | *DAY OF THE KINGS*

El Día de los Reyes Magos es el 6 de enero. En la noche, los niños les dejan pasto *leave hay* para los camellos *camels* que llevan a los Reyes *that carry the Wise Men* buscando *looking for* al Niño Jesús.

En la mañana, los niños encuentran un regalo *find a present* que los Reyes les dejan *that they leave them* por agradecimiento *to show their appreciation*. ¡Qué alegría para los niños!

¿Hay una tradición similar en tu cultura? _____

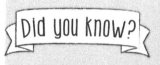 Hispanics celebrate Christmas on the 24th of December with a big evening family meal. The 25th is the day you rest after the celebration. In warmer countries, such as Uruguay and Argentina, where it's summertime, many families go to the beach or shoot fireworks at home.

EL DÍA DE LOS MUERTOS | *DAY OF THE DEAD*

Esta tradición es celebrada *celebrated* en México. Se celebra *it is celebrated* el primero y el dos de noviembre, después *after* de nuestra celebración de Halloween.

Las familias van *go* al cementerio a visitar y a recordar *remember* sus seres queridos *loved ones* que han pasado *have passed* a la otra vida. Allí limpian y decoran *they clean and decorate* sus tumbas. En las casas ponen *they put* altares a los difuntos, *deceased* con su foto y les ofrecen *offer them* sus cosas o comidas *things or foods* favoritas mientras esperan *while they wait* que regrese su espíritu *for their spirit to return* a visitar.

Para un cristiano puede ser difícil *can be difficult* entender esta tradición arraigada *deep-seated* en la cultura y religión mexicana.

Photo by Lupita Cortés

Cultural Note: Holidays in Hispanic Countries

Año Nuevo: In most Hispanic countries there are fireworks in the streets to celebrate New Year's Eve. They are set off in the streets because the houses are made of cement or stone and won't catch on fire.

Día de San Valentín/Día de los enamorados: This is a holiday sometimes called *Día de la amistad*friendship. This way they can celebrate it as a friendship holiday and not just for the "enamorados"in love.

Pascua y Semana Santa: During Holy Week, the schools are closed and most business are too. Many cities will have great processions in the streets as they take their "Cristos" to the people or from one church to the other. People of the Catholic faith will make pilgrimages during this time.

Día de la Independencia: Mexico's Independence Day is September 16, not May 5 (*Cinco de Mayo*) as many believe. May 5 is the day the Mexicans defeated the French in Mexico after Napoleon tried to overtake them (a kind of David and Goliath story). Many countries in Central America celebrate their Independence Day on the same day, September 15, because Central America was unified when it gained its independence from Spain.

Día de todos los Santos: Day that the souls of the beloved deceased will come back to visit their loved ones. Mexico is known for highly celebrating this holiday and they call it, *Día de los Muertos*. It is a time to honor the memory of their loved ones that have passed away. Death is accepted as a part of the circle of life. The family will usually spend time cleaning and decorating the grave of their loved ones. This is not a time of sadness, however. It's a time to remember and celebrate the lives of the ones they lost.

Navidad: Christmas is not as comercialized as it is in the United States. Many Hispanic Christians think it is wrong for parents to teach a child that there is a Santa Claus, since it takes away from Jesus being the reason for the season. In fact, many children are told that Baby Jesus has brought them their present. On Christmas Eve, *Noche Buena*, they will attend mass and have a late night family meal.

Las Posadas/Las Purísimas: A very traditional Christmas celebration that lasts for 9 days to symbolize the days Mary and Joseph traveled to Bethlehem. A group will go to a house and ask for "lodging" at the Inn. This group will have a Mary and a Joseph leading the group. They will be turned away two times, but on the third they will be invited to stay at the home at which time the doors are opened and everyone is invited in to celebrate with food and a *piñata*.

Día de los Reyes: January 6th, the 12th day of Christmas, is day of the Epiphany. This day celebrates the journey of the Wise Men that traveled from afar, to visit baby Jesus and bring Him gifts. Children will leave water and hay for the camels before going to bed, and wake in the morning finding a gift. For children, this day is as exciting as Christmas.

Cultural Note: Words from a Missionary
WHAT DID YOU DO TO HELP YOURSELF LEARN SPANISH?

1. "I went to all the small stores in the neighborhood to speak to the owners, increase vocabulary and make friends."

2. "I carried a dictionary with me all the time and jotted down new words and phrases I learned."

3. "I used Spanish as much as I could during the day, and reviewed vocabulary and grammar every night."

4. "I had to give myself permission to make mistakes for the sake of communicating."

5. "I laughed at my mistakes."

Coritos

ESTE ES EL DÍA (*This is the Day*)

Este es el día, este es el día	*This is the day*
Que el Señor nos dio,	*That the Lord gave us*
Que el Señor nos dio	
Me gozaré, me gozaré,	*I will rejoice*
Y me alegraré, y me alegraré.	*I will be glad*

Este es el día que el Señor nos dio,
Me gozaré y me alegraré.

Este es el día, este es el día, que el Señor nos dio.

¡Gloria a Dios!

Anonymous translation.

TE ALABO EN LA MAÑANA (*Praise Him in the morning*)

Cristo, Cristo,	
te alabo en la mañana,	*I praise you in the morning*
te alabo a mediodía.	*I praise you at the noon time*
Cristo, Cristo,	
te alabo al ponerse el sol.	*I praise you when the sun goes down*

Anonymous translation.

Written Work

Write the Spanish Bible verse for this lesson. Repeat it several times, and learn it.

_____

_____

A. Fill in the blanks with the correct word having to do with time. **3.1, 3.2 and 3.3.**

Word bank: *la, hora, qué, a, son*

1.   ¿A _____ hora es el programa de televisión?

2.   _____ las 7:30 de la mañana.

3.   ¿Es _____ 1:15 de la tarde?

4.   La clase de español es _____ las 6:00.

5.   ¿Qué _____ es?

> ## REMEMBER   on = el / los   every = cada

B. Write out the days of the week. **3.4**

_____   _____   _____

_____   _____   _____

_____

C. On what days do you do these things?

1. Trabajar *work*.   *El lunes, el. . .* _____

2. Ir *go* a la iglesia. _____

3. Ver *see* una película *movie*. _____

4. Dormir tarde *sleep late*. _____

5. Ir al supermercado _____

D. Answer with a day(s).

1. ¿Qué día es hoy? Hoy es _____

2. ¿Qué día es mañana?   Mañana es _____

3. ¿Qué día fue *was* ayer *yesterday*? Ayer fue_____

4. ¿Qué días trabajas? _____

_____

5. ¿Qué días no trabajas?_____

_____

E. Write out the months of the year. **3.5**

_____	_____	_____
_____	_____	_____
_____	_____	_____
_____	_____	_____

F. What is the weather like where you live? **3.5, 3.8 and 3.9**

El mes	La estación	¿Qué tiempo hace?
septiembre		
julio		
octubre		
marzo		
enero		
abril		
diciembre		

G. Write the day and month: **3.6**

1. Navidad. *El veinticinco de diciembre*

2. Año Nuevo. _____

3. El Día de la Independencia. _____

H. Say the number, then write it out. **3.11**

1.   25 _____

2.   76 _____

3.   100 _____

4.   148 _____

5.   570 _____

6.   1852 _____

I. Say then write out these dates. **3.5, 3.6 and 3.12**

1. July 4, 1776. *El cuatro de julio de mil setecientos setenta y seis.*

2. October 12, 1492. _____

_____

3. December 7, 1941. _____

_____

4. January 1, 1999. _____

_____

5. Tu cumpleaños. _____

_____

6. Hoy. _____

_____

I. Translate: *En el nombre del Padre, del Hijo y del Espíritu Santo. Amén.* **3.10**

_____

Lesson 4
It's All About Verbs!

More Classroom Vocabulary / Verbs / What do you like? *GUSTAR* / Indirect Object Pronouns /Prepositions and Objects After Prepositions / *Para* vs. *Por* / Vocabulary of Things You Can Have / Descriptive Adjectives / Idiomatic Expressions with *TENER*

Buenos Aires, Argentina

Lección 4

Ama a tu prójimo como a ti mismo. Levítico 19:18
Love your neighbor as yourself. Leviticus 19:18

4.1 MÁS FRASES PARA LA CLASE | *MORE PHRASES FOR CLASS*

Me gusta(n)	*I like it (them)*	díganme	*tell me (Uds.)*
No me gusta(n)	*I don't like it (them)*	siéntense	*sit down (Uds.)*
¿Qué te gusta?	*What do you like? (informal)*	los amigos	*friends*
¿Cómo se dice...?	*How do you say...?*	no sé	*I don't know*
Se dice...	*One says...*	el nombre	*name (first)*
¿Qué significa?	*What does it mean?*	el apellido	*last name*
¿Cómo se escribe?	*How do you spell?*	con	*with*
escuchen	*listen (Uds.)*	a	*at, to*
repitan	*repeat (Uds.)*	de	*of, from*
hablemos	*let's talk*	en	*in, on, at*
digan...	*say...*		

4.2 LOS VERBOS | *VERBS*

ser	*to be*	hacer	*to do / to make*	compartir	*to share*
hablar	*to speak*	trabajar	*to work*	esperar	*to wait*
cantar	*to sing*	mirar	*to watch*	preparar	*to prepare*
ir	*to go*	ir de compras	*to go shopping*	vender	*to sell*
llamar	*to call*	bailar	*to dance*	beber	*to drink*
viajar	*to travel*	enseñar	*to teach*	descansar	*to rest*
correr	*to run*	aprender	*to learn*	limpiar	*to clean*
estudiar	*to study*	salir	*to go out*	ver	*to see*
cocinar	*to cook*	visitar	*to visit*	tomar	*to take, to drink*
dormir	*to sleep*	nadar	*to swim*	testificar	*to witness*
soñar	*to dream*	ganar	*to win, to earn*	orar	*to pray*
escribir	*to write*	jugar	*to play*	alabar	*to praise*
leer	*to read*		*(game or sport)*	predicar	*to preach*
manejar	*to drive*	tocar	*to play*		
caminar	*to walk*		*(musical instrument)*	Yo también.	*Me too.*
comer	*to eat*	charlar, platicar	*to chat*	mucho	*a lot*
vivir	*to live*	conversar	*converse*	poco	*a little*

Me gusta + infinitivo = *I like to + infinitive*
Yo quiero + infinitive = *I want to + infinitive*
Yo puedo + infinitive = *I can + infinitive*
Yo necesito + infinitive = *I need to + infinitive*

Me gusta correr.	*I like to run.*
Yo quiero descansar.	*I want to rest.*
Yo puedo cocinar.	*I can cook.*
Necesito ir a la iglesia.	*I need to go to church.*

¿Qué **te gusta**? *What do **you like**?* Example answer: —Me gusta <u>leer y viajar</u>. *I like to read and to travel.*

1. Me gusta _____

2. What do you **want to do**? Yo quiero _____

3. What **can you do**? Yo puedo_____

4. What do you **need to do**? Yo necesito _____

The verb *"gustar"* means *"to be pleasing to."* It does not have the same literal meaning as in English when "<u>to like</u>" is used. Because of this it has a different construction.

Me gusta - *I like it* - literally means *"it is pleasing to me."* It can be used with verbs:

Me gusta comer tacos.	*I like to eat tacos*
Me gusta jugar al fútbol.	*I like to play soccer.*
Me gusta viajar.	*I like to travel.*
Me gusta llamar a mi amiga.	*I like to call my friend.*
No me gusta manejar.	*I don't like to drive.*

A. ¿Qué te gusta o no te gusta hacer? *What do you like or not like to do?* Choose from below.

(No) Me gusta..._____.

hablar español	llamar a mi mamá	orar a Dios
ir a la iglesia	correr en la mañana	tomar fotos
tocar la guitarra	cocinar bistecs[steaks]	aprender español
estudiar en la noche	escribir cartas[letters]	charlar con amigos
dormir ocho horas	manejar mucho	alabar a Cristo
leer la Biblia	vivir en mi ciudad[city]	ir en un viaje misionero[go on a mission trip]
caminar mucho	trabajar mucho	hablar por teléfono
nadar[swim] en el océano	jugar al fútbol	hacer la tarea
comer hamburguesas	mirar televisión/películas[movies]	viajar a Latinoamérica
cantar coritos	compartir a Jesús	preparar un estudio bíblico

When *gustar* is used with a noun, expressing you like something, there are two conjugations.
1. Singular - **gusta**   2. Plural - **gustan**.

Me gusta.	*I like it. (It is pleasing to me.)*
Me gustan.	*I like them. (They are pleasing to me.)*

Me <u>gusta</u> el restaurante.	*I like the restaurant. (The restaurant is pleasing to me.)*
Me <u>gustan</u> los tacos.	*I like the tacos. (The tacos are pleasing to me.)*

B. Using the chart below, say what things you like or not. **¿Qué te gusta? ¿Qué no te gusta?**

(No) Me gusta(n)…_____

la escuela	los niños	los tacos
la tarea	la iglesia	la música
las computadoras	la biblioteca	las enchiladas
los libros	los perros / los gatos	la playa

The verb **gustar** uses indirect object pronouns, since it literally means "something is pleasing to someone." The indirect object answers the question; "to whom" or "for whom."
These are all the indirect object pronouns.

Indirect Object Pronouns	Singular		Plural
1st person (yo)	**me**	(nosotros)	**nos**
2nd person familiar (tú)	**te**	(ustedes)	**les**
2nd person formal (usted)	**le**		
3rd person (él, ella)	**le**	(ellos, ellas)	**les**

Me gusta.   *I like it.*   **Nos** gusta.   *We like it.*
Te gusta.   *You like it.*   **Les** gusta.   *You (plural) like it.*
Le gusta.   *You (formal) like it.*   **Les** gusta.   *They like it.*
Le gusta.   *He/She likes it.*

As you can see, *le gusta* can have 3 different meanings. If the meaning is not clear, you will have to clarify using "*a*" followed by the person (indirect object).

Le gusta →
    le gusta <u>a usted</u>   *(to you)*
    le gusta <u>a él</u>   *(to him)*
    le gusta <u>a ella</u>   *(to her)*

Les gusta also has 3 different meanings. If it is not clear, you must clarify:

Les gusta →
    les gusta <u>a ustedes</u>   *(to you-plural)*
    les gusta <u>a ellos</u>   *(to them)*
    les gusta <u>a ellas</u>   *(to them-feminine)*

me gusta, *te gusta* and *nos gusta* don't need to be clarified, but can be added to emphasis.

   a mí *to me*   **a ti** *to you (informal)*   **a nosotros** *to us*

¿Te gusta viajar?   —Sí, **a mí** me gusta mucho viajar.   *(Yes, I like to travel a lot.)*
¿**A ustedes** les gusta correr?   —Sí, **a nosotros** nos gusta correr.   *(Yes, we like to run.)*
¿Y **a María** le gusta viajar?   —No, **a ella** no le gusta viajar.   *(No, she doesn't like to travel.)*

A. Matching. Make the connection.

   a mí   le gusta
   a ti   les gusta
   a usted   me gusta   Draw lines to connect.
   a él   te gusta
   a ella   les gusta
   a nosotros   les gusta
   a ustedes   le gusta
   a ellos   nos gusta
   a ellas   le gusta

B. Fill in blank with the correct *Indirect Object Pronoun*.

1. A nosotros _____ *nos* _____ gusta hablar en español.

2. A ellos _____ gusta tomar fotos.

C. Write what each picture shows that they like or don't like to do. Use the charts in 4.2 & 4.3.

1. A las chicas les gusta

_____ *nadar* _____

2. A Marisa le gusta

_____

3. A Diego le gusta

_____

4. A Felipe le gusta

_____

5. A David le gusta

_____

6. A María le gusta

_____

7. A nuestro pastor le gusta

_____

8. A nosotros nos gusta

_____

9. A Cristina le gusta

_____

10. A Dieguito le gusta

_____

11. A Miguel le gusta

_____

12. A ellas les gusta

_____

D. ¿Qué les gusta o no les gusta? *What do they like or not like?* Finish the sentences.

1. A mis padres les gusta _____

2. A mi mejor amigo/a no le gusta _____

3. A los cristianos les gusta _____

4. A nosotros nos gusta _____

5. A los niños no les gusta _____

There are several prepositions in Spanish. The most common ones are:

a	to, at	**con/sin**	with/without		*"on" certain day(s),
de	of, from, about	**por**	during, through, for, by		is translated as
en	in, at, on	**para**	for, in order to		"el" or "los"

Prepositions are not always translated the same as in English and students of Spanish sometimes get confused as to when to use which ones. Sometimes the only way to learn them is to remember the phrases in which they are used. Pay close attention to them in these examples.

La clase es **a** las cinco **de** la tarde *los lunes **en** la iglesia.
*The class is **at** 5:00 **in** the afternoon *on Mondays **at (in)** the church.*

El libro **de** mi amigo.	*My friend's book.*
Me gusta hablar **con** mi novio/a.	*I like to talk **with** my boyfriend/girlfriend.*
Tengo clase **por** la tarde.	*I have class **during** the afternoon.*
Para quién es la pluma?	***For** whom is the pen?*
Para mi profesora.	***For** my professor. (**Para** ella. = **For** her.)*

A. Fill in blank with correct preposition: Tengo clase _____ (with) mi hermana

_____ (at) las 8:30 _____ la noche _____ (on) jueves _____ (at) la universidad.

PRONOUNS AFTER A PREPOSITION

When you say *con ella*, the pronoun *ella* follows the preposition. Most pronouns don't change after a preposition. Only *Yo* and *Tú* have special forms after a preposition.

Yo changes to **mí. Tú** changes to **ti.**	
All other pronouns remain the same.	

Pronouns after a Preposition	
mí	**nosotros**
ti	**ustedes**
él, ella, usted	**ellos, ellas**

El dinero es para **ti.**	*The money is for **you.***
La Biblia es para **mí.**	*The Bible is for **me.***

Remember: Other than *yo* and *tú*, no other pronouns change after a preposition.

El señor canta con **ellos.**	*The man sings with **them.***
Yo viajo con **ustedes.**	*I travel with **you (plural).***
Los libros son para **nosotros.**	*The books are for **us.***
Jorge estudia español con **él** y con **ella.**	*Jorge studies Spanish with **him** and with **her.***

"with me" and "with you" have a special form in Spanish.	
conmigo = *with me*	**contigo** = *with you*

Me gusta trabajar **contigo.**	*I like to work **with you.***
A ti te gusta salir **conmigo.**	*You like to go out **with me.***
A Ud. le gusta compartir a Jesús **conmigo.**	*You (formal) like to share Jesús **with me.***
A mí me gusta mirar la televisión **contigo.**	*I like to watch television **with you.***

B. Write the correct pronoun after the preposition.
¿Para quién es....? *(Who is it for?)* Example: El libro es para _____*él*_____ (Victor).

1. El lápiz es para _____. (Alicia)

2. El teléfono es para _____. (us)

3. La Biblia es para _____. (you-informal)

4. Te gusta hablar _____. (with me)

5. El libro es de _____. (you- formal)

6. Las sillas son de _____. (you-plural)

7. Me gusta ir a la iglesia _____. (with you-informal)

4.6 *PARA* VS. *POR*

These 2 prepositions are the most confusing for English speakers because they both can be translated as "for." Look at the uses of these two prepositions.

PARA
A. When something is FOR, or intended for someone or something.
Las Biblias son **para** los padres.   *The Bibles are **for** the parents.*
Los libros son **para** la clase.   *The books are **for** class.*

B. Destination of a place or time.
Mañana viajo **para** México.   *Tomorrow I travel **for (to)** México.*
La tarea es **para** el lunes.   *The homework is **for** Monday.*

C. To express "IN ORDER TO DO" something. It will be followed by the infinitive.
La pluma es **para** escribir.   *The pen is **for** writing. (In order to write.)*
La Biblia es **para** leer.   *The Bible is **for** reading. (In order to read.)*

> **Did you know?**
>
> In many Hispanic families, children live with their parents until they marry.

POR
A. Through or along.   El gato entra **por** la ventana.   *The cat comes in **through** the window.*
B. In exchange for.   Pagué $15 **por** el vestido.   *I paid $15 **for** the dress.*
C. On behalf of.   Lo hago **por** ti.   *I do it **for** you.*
D. By transportation or means. Voy a Canadá **por** tren.   *I'm going to Canada **by** train.*
                                   Hablamos **por** teléfono.   *We talk **by** phone.*
E. Duration of time.   Siempre estudio **por** 2 horas.   *I always study **for** 2 hours.*

Fill in the blank with either *POR* or *PARA*:

1. El dinero es _____ la iglesia y es _____ comprar Biblias.

2. El sábado voy^(I'm going) _____ Honduras _____ avión^(plane).

3. Voy a Panamá_____ 3 semanas.

4. Jesús pagó^(paid) el precio^(price) _____ nuestros pecados^(sins).

Answers: 1. para / para 2. para / por 3. por 4. por

REVIEW OF THE VERB *TENER*

Yo	**tengo**	nosotros/as	**tenemos**
tú	**tienes**	Uds.	**tienen**
él / ella / Ud.	**tiene**	ellos/ellas	**tienen**

Tengo la paz de Cristo.
I have the peace of Christ.

4.7 COSAS COMUNES | *COMMON THINGS*

una casa	*a house*	un reloj	*a watch, clock*	el dinero	*money*
un apartamento	*an apartment*	un perro	*a dog*	la salud	*health*
un auto, carro, coche	*a car*	un gato	*a cat*	la felicidad, alegría	*happiness*
una camioneta	*a truck*	un pájaro	*a bird*		
una moto	*a motorcycle*	una carta	*a letter*	la tristeza	*sadness*
una bicicleta	*a bicycle*	un radio	*a radio*	la libertad	*liberty, freedom*
una computadora	*a computer*	una cartera	*a purse*		
un teléfono (celular)	*a cell phone*	una billetera	*a wallet*	la salvación	*salvation*
una televisión, un televisor	*a television*	un trabajo	*a job*	la paz	*peace*
		un problema	*a problem*	el amor	*love*

mucho/a= *a lot of*
muchos/as = *many*
muy = *very*

No tengo <u>mucho</u> dinero.
(**Mucho/a(s)**) is used before <u>nouns</u>.)

Yo tengo un carro <u>muy</u> viejo.
(**Muy** is used before <u>adjectives</u>.)

4.8 DESCRIPTIVE ADJECTIVES

nuevo/a	*new*	gran	*great (used before the noun)*	malo/a	*bad*
viejo/a	*old*	pequeño/a	*small*	rápido/a	*fast*
grande	*big*	bueno/a	*good*	lento/a	*slow*

A. Fill in the blank with the correct form of *TENER*.

1. Yo _____ una moto grande.

2. Nosotros _____ buena salud.

3. Ella _____ un apartamento en el centro[downtown].

4. Ud. _____ un carro muy rápido.

B. ¿Qué tienes? *What do you have?*
Example:　Yo **tengo** dos perros grandes.　　Yo **no tengo** una casa nueva.
　　　　　Yo **tengo** muchos problemas.　　Yo **no tengo** un radio en mi carro.

Tell someone what you have or don't have.　Name many things.
　　　1.　Yo tengo. . .　　　　　2.　Yo no tengo. . .

Note: With things you can't count, generally the article will not be used. Example:　Yo **tengo** libertad.

el calor	heat	**el hambre**	hunger	**la prisa**	haste/hurriedness
el frío	cold	**la sed**	thirst	**el estrés**	stress
el sueño	sleepiness	**el miedo**	fear	**mucho, mucha**	a lot (very)

Note: These are nouns, so they are things you <u>have</u>.
(Use *mucho* with masculine nouns and *mucha* with feminine nouns.)

Yo **tengo hambre.** Is literally, *I **have hunger**.* (*Even though it means **I'm hungry**.*)

Yo **no tengo** hambre, pero **tengo mucha** sed.   I ***am not*** hungry, but I ***am very*** thirsty.

A. Fill in the 1ˢᵗ blank with the correct form of *TENER*, then the 2ⁿᵈ blank with a feeling or condition.

1. Marita _____*tiene*_____ _____*frío*_____ (*is cold*)

2. Roberto y Francisco _____ _____ (*are sleepy*)

3. Nosotros _____ mucha _____ (*are thirsty*)

4. Tú _____ mucho _____ (*are very stressed*)

B. Tell what feelings or conditions you have.

Ahora (now) yo tengo _____ y _____.

C. ¿Qué tienen ellos?   *What do they have?*

1. _____   2. _____   3. _____

4. _____   5. _____   6. _____

D. Use each one of the expressions in the 4.9 chart and finish the sentence with a partner.

Yo tengo calor... *en el verano. / cuando hace mucho calor.*

Yo tengo sueño...   Yo tengo frío...   Yo tengo miedo...   Yo tengo prisa...   Yo tengo sed...

Cultural Note

 **Did you know?**

<u>No Más Violencia, a Message from God</u> is a movement that began in Argentina in 1997 when Christians embarked on going into violent places in the cities. Two of these places are schools and stadiums. After many years this movement is affecting lives in several countries. Training is provided to churches, teaching Biblical principles that enable God's people to reach into the community with concrete actions. Transformation begins, and lives are changed through the power of the Gospel.

NMV believes that peace is not the absence of violence, but the presence of God in the heart of the peoples, cities, states and nations. To read more about *No Más Violencia*, go to **nmvglobal.org**.

The violence on the Mexico-United States border, especially related to drug wars, has claimed the lives of approximately 60,000 people from 2006 to 2012. This, unfortunately, has lowered drastically the number of churches doing missions and ministry in that area. Pray for this land and people.

Coritos

YO TENGO UN AMIGO QUE ME AMA (*I have a friend that loves me*)

Yo tengo un amigo que <u>me ama</u>, me ama, me ama. Yo tengo un amigo que me ama. Su nombre es Jesús.	*I have a friend who <u>loves me</u>*
Que me ama, que me ama, Me ama, sí, con tierno amor, Que me ama, que me ama, Su nombre es Jesús.	*That loves me, loves me* *Yes, with tender love* *His name is Jesus*
Tú tienes un amigo que <u>te ama</u>... Tenemos un amigo que <u>nos ama</u>...	*You have a friend who <u>loves you</u>* *We have a friend who <u>loves us</u>*

Traditional song from *Cancionero Latinoamericano*.

DIOS BUENO ES (*God is so Good*)

Dios bueno es, Dios bueno es, Dios bueno es, Bueno es mi Dios.	*God is good* *Good is my God*
Dios me ama a mí, Dios me ama a mí, Dios me ama a mí,	*God loves me*
Él me ama a mí.	*He loves me*

Anonymous translation.

Reading (*Lectura*)

Read about Lucas. Read it once slowly to understand it. Then read it out loud 2 - 3 times. The more you read it, try not to translate every word in your head but to picture it and comprehend as you read.

Vocabulario:

ciudad - *city*
curso - *course*
departamento - *apartamento*
lomitos y papas fritas - *steak sandwich and french fries*

programador de informática - *computer programmer*
relativamente - *relatively*
Primera Iglesia Bautista - *First Baptist Church*
más jóvenes que - *younger than*

Hola. Me llamo Lucas, tengo veintiún años y soy de Argentina. Vivo en la ciudad de La Plata.

Soy estudiante en la Universidad Nacional. Estudio medicina. Me gustan mis cursos, especialmente la clase de anatomía.

Los lunes, martes, miércoles y jueves tengo clases. Los fines de semana no tengo clase. Me gusta pasar los fines de semana con mis amigos. Nos gusta ir al cine y salir a comer. También me gusta mucho tocar la guitarra.

Yo vivo en un departamento con un amigo. Tengo una bicicleta para ir a la universidad y para ir al trabajo. Soy cocinero en un restaurante pequeño. Soy rápido para hacer los lomitos y papas fritas.

Me gusta mucho mi ciudad. Mi familia vive aquí también. Tengo tres hermanos, son más jóvenes que yo. Mi mamá es maestra y mi papá es programador de informática.

Los domingos me gusta ir a la iglesia. Soy miembro de la Primera Iglesia Bautista de La Plata. Nuestro pastor se llama Jorge Arce. Es una iglesia relativamente grande. Me gusta mucho vivir en Argentina. Dios es bueno con nosotros.

1. ¿Cuántos años tiene Lucas? _____

2. ¿Dónde vive? _____

3. ¿Cuál curso le gusta más? _____

4. ¿Qué le gusta hacer con sus amigos? _____

5. ¿Cuántos hermanos tiene? _____

6. ¿Cuál es la profesión de sus padres? _____

Written Work

Write the Spanish Bible verse for this lesson. Repeat it several times, and learn it.

_____

_____

A. What do you do in these places? Write all the verbs that correspond. **4.2**

1. En la clase. *escuchar, escribir, aprender, hablar. . .*

2. En la iglesia. _____

3. En la playa. _____

4. En la biblioteca. _____

5. En el restaurante. _____

6. En tu carro. _____

B. Translate to English: **4.4**

1. A mi cuñado le gusta viajar a Centroamérica. _____

_____

2. Me gusta vivir en las montañas. _____

3. A mí no me gusta ir al hospital. _____

4. ¿Te gusta la comida china? _____

5. A mis primos les gusta testificar. _____

6. Nos gusta estudiar español en nuestra clase. _____

_____

C. Finish the sentence with a verb in the infinitive form. **4.2 and 4.4**

1. A mi profesora le gusta _____

2. A nosotros nos gusta _____

3. A mi iglesia le gusta _____

4. A mi madre le gusta _____

5. A mi hermano/a le gusta _____

D. Fill in the blank with the correct indirect object pronoun. *(me, te, le or les)* **4.4**

1. A mi pastor _____ *le* _____ gusta predicar.

2. A Liliana y Cristina _____ gusta estudiar inglés.

3. A Shakira _____ gusta cantar y bailar.

4. A mí _____ gusta hablar en español.

5. A ti _____ gusta testificar.

E. Translate to Spanish: **4.4 and 4.7**

1. I have her new pen. _____

2. They have my old computer. _____

3. I like to go out with my friends. _____

4. I like to read books, but she likes to watch television. _____

_____

F. Fill in the blank with the correct preposition *POR* or *PARA*. **4.6**

1. El pájaro entró[entered] en la casa _____ la ventana.

2. Mañana voy [I go] al aeropuerto y viajo _____ Europa.[Europe]

3. Pagué[I paid] quinientos dólares _____ este viaje[trip] a Florida.

4. Me gusta mucho caminar _____ el parque.

5. Aprendo[I learn] español _____ hablar de Cristo a mis vecinos.[neighbors]

Now fill in the blank with the correct preposition. *(a, de, en, con, sin, conmigo, contigo)* **4.5**

6. _____ [in] mi clase _____ [of] español conversamos _____ [for] 2 horas.

7. Yo quiero ir _____ [to] la iglesia _____ [in order to] alabar a mi Dios.

8. No puedo hablar _____ [with] él, por que él no habla _____.[with me]

G. Idiomatic expressions with *Tener*: (conjugate TENER in the first blank) **4.9**

1. En el verano[summer] yo_____ mucho _____.

2. En el invierno ella _____ mucho _____.

3. Si no como en todo[all] el día, yo _____ _____.

4. Necesito agua, _____ mucha _____.

5. La secretaria _____ _____ is sleepy.

6. Mañana él toma[takes] un examen, él _____ _____.

H. Translate. **4.9**
I'm cold. I'm scared. I'm hot. I'm thirsty and hungry. I'm in a hurry. I'm sleepy.

_____

_____

I. What do I want to do? What can I do? What do I need to do? **4.2**
Write sentences using the 3 phrases…_Yo quiero, Yo puedo, Yo necesito._
Example: _Yo necesito estudiar español a las 3:00 de la tarde._

1. _____

2. _____

3. _____

J. Write about some of your family members. Give their name, what they are like and what they like to do.
Example: _Mi hermana se llama Cindy. Ella es muy amable y simpática. A ella le gusta estudiar francés._

1. _____

_____

2. _____

_____

3. _____

_____

4. En Navidad, a mi familia le gusta _____

_____

5. En Día de Acción de Gracia nos gusta_____

_____

6. En una fiesta de cumpleaños, a los invitados les gusta _____

_____

Lesson 5
Clothes & Colors

Clothes and Color Vocabulary / Conjugation of *LLEVAR* / Regular *-ar* verbs / Common Phrases Followed by Infinitives / Conjugation of Regular *-ar* verbs / personal "*a*" / *ME, TE, NOS*; Direct and Indirect objects / Irregular verbs *IR & DAR* / Demonstrative Adjectives and Pronouns: *Este, Ese, Aquel* / Review of Numbers

Cuzco, Perú

Lección 5

5.1 LA ROPA | *CLOTHING* (the word *ROPA* will never be plural)

el vestido	*dress*	los pantalones	*pants*
el traje	*suit*	los pantalones cortos	*shorts*
el cinturón	*belt*	los bluyines, jeans	*jeans*
la corbata	*tie*	pequeño	*small*
la camisa	*shirt*	mediano	*medium*
la blusa	*blouse*	grande	*large*
la falda	*skirt*	largo/a	*long*
la chaqueta	*jacket*	cómodo/a	*comfortable*
el suéter	*sweater*	el ropero, el armario	*closet*
la camiseta	*t-shirt*	caro/a	*expensive*
el abrigo	*coat*	barato/a	*inexpensive/cheap*
la bufanda	*scarf*	gratis	*free (of cost)*
el sombrero	*hat*	llevar	*to wear/to take with you*
los zapatos	*shoes*	Yo llevo	*I am wearing*
las zapatillas	*tennis shoes*	Él/Ella lleva	*He/She is wearing*
las botas	*boots*	así	*like this, like so*
las sandalias	*sandals*		
el traje de baño	*bathing suit*	¿Qué llevas tú?	*What are you wearing?*
los anteojos, lentes	*glasses*	¿Qué lleva él/ella?	*What is he/she wearing?*
el reloj	*watch*	¿Cuánto cuesta?	*How much does it cost?*
el collar	*necklace*	¿Qué talla necesita?	*What size do you need?*
el anillo	*ring*	¿Cuánto calza?	*What size shoe do you wear?*

¿Qué hay en la foto?

A. 　　B. 　　C.

Foto **A.** Hay una chica. Ella lleva ___*un vestido largo*___. **B.** Hay tres chicos . . . **C.** . . .

5.2 LOS COLORES | *COLORS*

anaranjado	*orange*	amarillo	*yellow*	café, marrón	*brown*
blanco	*white*	negro	*black*	verde	*green*
azul	*blue*	rojo	*red*	morado, violeta	*purple*
celeste	*light blue*	rosado	*pink*	gris	*grey*

Important: Colors are adjectives, so make sure they agree with the noun they are modifying.

Example: Llevo un **suéter blanco**, una **camisa roja** y unos **pantalones azules**.

¿Qué llevas tú? *What are you wearing?*　　—**Yo llevo** _____.

(Name the articles of clothing you and others are wearing and the color.)

LLEVAR is a regular *-ar* verb, this means it follows a pattern in the conjugation. Each conjugation has a different ending. The *-ar* is dropped to leave the **stem** or **root** of the verb. Then an ending is added according to the person or subject.

The regular endings for *-ar* verbs.

singular		plural	
yo	**-o**	nosotros/as	**-amos**
tú	**-as**		
él, ella, Ud.	**-a**	ellos, ellas, Uds.	**-an**

With the regular verb *LLEVAR*

llevar → llev - ar → llev- is the stem

singular		plural	
yo	llev**o**	nosotros/as	llev**amos**
tú	llev**as**		
él, ella, Ud.	llev**a**	ellos, ellas, Uds.	llev**an**

Did you know?

Words referring to food and clothing can differ from one country to another. For example, "abrigo" is coat, but in Argentina they call it a "campera."

Yo llevo una camisa amarilla. - *I wear (I am wearing) a yellow shirt.*
Ella lleva un vestido negro. - *She wears (she is wearing) a black dress.*
Nosotros llevamos pantalones cortos. - *We wear (we are wearing) shorts.*

A. Fill in the blank with the correct conjugation of *llevar*.

1. Mi hermano _____ *lleva* _____ unos lentes.

(1)

2. Ella _____ un abrigo negro.

3. Sr. Díaz, usted _____ un traje elegante.

4. La profesora y yo _____ zapatos tenis.

5. ¿Tú _____ lentes de contacto?

6. Yo _____ unos zapatos cómodos.

(2)

7. ¿ _____ ustedes abrigos?

8. Los chicos no _____ sus camisas.

B. Fill in the correct form of the color in parenthesis.

1. Él lleva una corbata _____ (*blue*)

2. Nosotros llevamos pantalones _____ (*brown*)

(3)

3. Mis zapatillas son _____ (*white*)

If in a class, each student can stand, and other students can say what each person is wearing. Use colors and make them agree in number/gender.
Or you can look through a clothes catalog and say what different people are wearing.

Answers: A. 2. lleva 3. lleva 4. llevamos 5. llevas 6. llevo 7. llevan 8. llevan B. 1. azul 2. cafés/marrones 3. blancas

5.4 REGULAR -*AR* VERBS (some you will recognize from LESSON 3)

with your mouth
hablar	*to talk, speak*
charlar, platicar	*to chat, converse*
conversar	*to converse*
preguntar	*to ask*
cantar	*to sing*
llamar	*to call*
explicar	*to explain*
orar	*to pray*
predicar	*to preach*

with your eyes
mirar	*to look, to watch*

with your ears
escuchar	*to listen*

with your hands
trabajar	*to work*
preparar	*to prepare*
ayudar	*to help*
usar	*to use*
tocar	*to touch, to play an instrument*

with your mind
amar	*to love*
estudiar	*to study*
olvidar	*to forget*
desear	*to wish, to desire*

other actions
viajar	*to travel*
caminar	*to walk*
llevar	*to take, to wear*
ganar	*to win*
formar	*to form*
llegar	*to arrive*
pasar (tiempo)	*to pass (spend time)*
comprar	*to buy*
pagar	*to pay*
enseñar	*to teach*
bailar	*to dance*
tomar	*to take, to drink*
cambiar	*to change*
necesitar	*to need*
presentar	*to present*
esperar	*to wait for, to hope*
buscar	*to look for*
entrar	*to enter*
terminar	*to finish*
descansar	*to rest*
aceptar	*to accept*
alabar	*to praise*

yo puedo + infinitive	*I can + infinitive*
yo necesito + infinitive	*I need to + infinitive*
yo tengo que + infinitive	*I have to + infinitive*
yo quiero + infinitive	*I want + infinitive*

5.5 COMMON PHRASES FOLLOWED BY INFINITIVE VERBS

Learn these phrases to be able to express what you can or need to do.

1. <u>What can you do?</u> Say "Yo puedo" and add a verb.
Example: "**Yo puedo** hablar español."   *I can speak Spanish.*
Tell someone what you can do: Yo puedo _____

2. <u>What do you need to do?</u> Say "Yo necesito" and add a verb.
Example: "**Yo necesito** preparar la comida."   *I need to prepare the meal.*
Tell someone what you need to do: Yo necesito _____

3. <u>What do you have to do?</u> Say, "Yo tengo que" and add a verb.
Example: "**Yo tengo que** descansar."   *I have to rest.*
Tell someone what you have to do: Yo tengo que _____

4. <u>What do you want to do?</u>   Yo quiero _____

Spanish with a Mission | For Ministry, Witnessing and Mission Trips

5.6 CONJUGATION OF -AR VERBS IN THE PRESENT TENSE

Regular -ar verbs are conjugated just like *LLEVAR*. Add the ending to the stem or root of the verb.

hablar → *habl - ar* → *habl-* is the stem

singular		plural	
Yo	habl**o**	nosotros/as	habl**amos**
tú	habl**as**		
él, ella, Ud.	habl**a**	ellos, ellas, Uds.	habl**an**

Tú hablas con el pastor.
You speak with the pastor.

Present tense, as in *"Yo hablo"* can mean "I speak", or "I am speaking." For this reason, sometimes it can be used to refer to the immediate future. Example: Hablo a las 3:00. *I'm speaking at 3:00.*

A. Conjugate the *-ar* verb in the correct form.
Each one of these verbs is conjugated like *llevar* and *hablar*. They are all regular *-ar* verbs.

1. mirar Ella _____*mira*_____ la televisión.

2. cantar Nosotros _____ los coritos.

3. escuchar Yo _____ la música latina.

4. viajar Ellos _____ a México mañana.

5. comprar Usted _____ los zapatos negros.

6. predicar El Pastor _____ en la iglesia.

7. descansar Yo _____ en la noche.

8. necesitar Tú _____ hablar con Dios.

9. alabar Las señoras _____ a Dios.

B. ¿Qué hacen ellos? *What are they doing?*

1. Susana

_____

2. El empleado

_____

3. El señor

_____

4. Ellos

_____

5. Rosa

_____

6. Los estudiantes

_____

English is usually structured in this order: **subject - verb - object**
Examples: Jorge listens to Mary.   Jorge listens to the music.

The structure of Spanish is much more flexible than English.
In Spanish the *subject* can be placed at the end and the *object* can start the sentence or be placed in some other part of the sentence. To keep this from being confusing, a preposition *"a"* goes in front of the direct object when it is a PERSON.

EXAMPLE: <u>Jorge</u> escucha **a** <u>María</u>.   <u>Javier</u> mira **a** <u>su primo</u>.
               Subject   *Object*   *Subject*   *Object*

The "personal *a*" is not needed when the direct object is a thing because the context is understood, and it will not be confused with the subject.

<u>Jorge</u> escucha <u>la música</u>.   <u>Javier</u> mira <u>la película</u>.
_{Subject}   _{Object}   _{Subject}   _{Object}

Note: The *personal a* is used with animals when they are family pets.

Example: Yo busco **a** mi perro.   *I look for my dog.*

The exception: You do not need the *personal a* after the verb *tener*.
Example: Yo tengo tres hijos.   *I have 3 children.*

Fill in the blank. Does it need the *personal a ...* or not?

1. Yo llamo _____*a*_____ mi mamá por teléfono.

2. Tú miras _____ la televisión.

3. Nosotros escuchamos _____*al*_____ (el) profesor.

4. Uds. compran _____ las chaquetas.

5. Ellos necesitan _____ Dios.

6. Tengo _____ un hermano.

7. ¿Aceptas _____ Jesucristo?

8. Ella busca _____ su perrito.

9. Yo toco _____ (el) piano.

10. El ama _____ su esposa.

REMEMBER   **a + el = al**

Did you know?

Garage Sales don't really exist in Latin America as they do in the U.S. There are *"ferias americanas"* or stores where used clothing and other goods are sold, similar to our Thrift stores.

Answers: 1. a 2. X 3. al 4. X 5. a 6. X 7. a 8. a 9. X 10. a

A Direct Object Pronoun takes the action directly from the verb. It is the *object* of the *verb*.

Examples: I sing the song. (What do I sing?... the song.)
I=subject   sing=verb   the song=direct object

You play the guitar. (What do you play?... the guitar.)
You=subject   play=verb   the guitar=direct object

A. Name the subject, verb and direct object in each of these sentences.

1. Él mira la televisión. Subject=____*él*____ Verb=____*mira*____ direct object =____*televisión*____

2. Marisa compra una blusa. Subject=_____ Verb=_____ direct object =_____

3. El pastor escucha la musica. Subject=_____ Verb=_____ direct object =_____

The direct object can be people, for example: <u>me</u>, <u>you</u> or <u>us</u>.
Example: I see you.   I=subject   see=verb   you=direct object.

"You need us."   What is the subject? _____ verb?_____ direct object?_____

In Spanish, if the direct object is "me," "you" or "us," use the direct object pronouns *"me," "te"* or *"nos."*
*Not *YO, TÚ* or *NOSOTROS*…these are **subject** pronous.

These are direct object pronouns. They must go <u>before</u> the verb when it is conjugated.

me - *me / to me*	[1st person singular]
te - *you / to you* (tú form)	[2nd person singular familiar]
nos - *us / to us*	[1st person plural]

Yo **te** amo. *I love **you**.*
José **me** ayuda.   *Joe helps **me**.*

Ella **nos** presenta.   *She presents/introduces **us**.*
Yo **te** alabo, Dios.   *I praise **you**, God.*

"Me," "te" and *"nos"* can also be Indirect Object Pronouns. *Indirect objects* answer the question **to whom** or **for whom,** in reference to the verb.

Example: *La profesora* **te** habla.   *The professor talks **to you**.*

B. Fill in the blank with the correct direct or indirect object.

1. Mario _____*me*_____ habla. (*Mario speaks **to me**.*)

2. Yo _____ espero. (*I wait for **you**.*)

3. El Señor Jesús _____ ama. (*The Lord Jesus loves **us**.*)

4. Rosa _____ prepara la ensalada. (*Rosa prepares **for you** the salad.*)

5. El pastor _____ enseña. (*The pastor teaches **us**.*)

6. Mis padres _____ compran zapatos nuevos. (*My parents buy **me** new shoes.*)

Answers: 2. te 3. nos 4. te   5. nos 6. me

5.9 IRREGULAR VERBS

A verb that is not conjugated in a "regular pattern" is called an **irregular** verb. Sometimes the verb is irregular because the ending is different. Sometimes the verb is irregular because the stem changes. Sometimes it is irregular because both stem and ending change. *SER* is an irregular verb, so is *ESTAR*. We will begin learning more irregular verb conjugations. Most irregular verbs are very common and highly used verbs so they are important to memorize. The best way to learn an irregular verb conjugation is by repetition.

5.10 CONJUGATION OF THE IRREGULAR VERBS *IR* AND *DAR*

Two very common verbs are the verbs *IR* (to go) and *DAR* (to give). These two verbs are similar to the irregular conjugation of *ESTAR*. Since they are irregular, repeat, and learn them.

IR- to go

singular		plural	
yo	**voy**	nosotros/as	v**amos**
tú	**vas**		
él, ella, Ud.	v**a**	ellos, ellas, Uds.	**van**

Yo **voy** a la iglesia los domingos.   *I go to church on Sundays.*
Ellos **van** a clase los miércoles.   *They go to class on Wednesdays.*

DAR- to give

singular		plural	
yo	**doy**	nosotros/as	d**amos**
tú	d**as**		
él, ella, Ud.	d**a**	ellos, ellas, Uds.	d**an**

Yo te **doy** las Biblias.   *I give you the Bibles.*
Mis padres me **dan** amor.   *My parents give me love.*

A. Fill in the blank with the correct conjugation of the verb **IR** or **DAR**.

1. Tú _____*vas*_____ a la escuela conmigo.

2. Mario me _____ una fiesta para mi cumpleaños.

3. Nosotros _____ dinero para el viaje misionero.

4. Las señoras _____ a El Salvador.

5. Yo _____ a la casa de Rodolfo.

6. Los perros me _____ mucho miedo.

7. El jefe[boss] nos _____ mucho trabajo.

8. Uds. _____ a clase.

B. Tell someone where you go on each day of the week.

C. Tell someone what God gives you. *Dios me da...*

Answers: A. 1.vas 2.da 3.damos 4.van 5.voy 6.dan 7.da 8.van

Did you know?

The Mayan language is still spoken in southern Mexico and Guatemala. "Baktun," the first *telenovela* (soap opera) in the Mayan language, was filmed in 2013 to help keep the language and customs alive in the younger generation.

We learned in Lesson 3 that "este/esta" mean "this." *Este* is masculine; *esta* is feminine. There are plural forms as well. Each one must agree with the noun it modifies.

Here are the 4 ways to say "this" / "these." (When you are close to the object.)

demonstrative adjective THIS/THESE	masculine	feminine
singular	este	esta
plural	estos	estas

Yo necesito <u>esta</u> bufanda.   *I need <u>this</u> scarf.*

There are 4 ways to say "that" / "those." (When the object is not so close to you.)

demonstrative adjective THAT/THOSE	masculine	feminine
singular	ese	esa
plural	esos	esas

Ella compra <u>esas</u> sandalias.   *She buys <u>those</u> sandals.*

There are 4 ways to say "that over there" / "those over there." (When object is farthest away.)

demonstrative adjective THAT OVER THERE / THOSE OVER THERE	masculine	feminine
singular	aquel	aquella
plural	aquellos	aquellas

Yo puedo mirar <u>aquel</u> reloj.   *I can see <u>that</u> clock <u>over there</u>.*

A. Fill in the blank with the correct demonstrative adjective.

(1)

1. these - ___*Estos*___ pantalones largos.

2. this - _____ blusa azul.

3. those - _____ botas cafés.

4. that over there - _____ corbata roja.

(2)

5. that - _____ falda negra.

6. these - _____ lentes de contacto.

7. that - _____ traje de baño blanco.

(3)

8. that over there - _____ suéter amarillo.

9. this - _____ abrigo gris.

Answers: 2. Esta 3. Esas 4. Aquella 5. Esa 6. Estos 7. Ese 8. Aquel 9. Este

B. The demonstrative adjective can take the place of the noun to avoid repetition. It then becomes a demonstrative pronoun.
Example: Tengo <u>estos zapatos</u>. *I have <u>these shoes</u>.* → Tengo <u>estos</u>. *I have <u>these</u>.*

1. Me gusta ese vestido.   ___*Me gusta ese.*___

2. Yo quiero comprar esta corbata. _____

3. Miguel necesita aquel sombrero. _____

C. Each demonstrative form also has a **NEUTER** gender (a form not specific to masculine or feminine). Use the following demonstrative pronouns when you do not know what it is, or when talking about something abstract.

ESTO = THIS (thing) ¿Qué es <u>esto</u>? *What is <u>this</u>?*
ESO = THAT (thing) <u>Eso</u> es bueno. *<u>That's</u> good.*
AQUELLO = THAT (thing) OVER THERE ¿Ves <u>aquello</u>? - *Do you see <u>that over there</u>?*

5.12 REVIEW NUMBERS | ¿CUÁNTO CUESTA? | HOW MUCH DOES IT COST?

Name different articles of clothing and name the price.

¿Cuánto cuesta(n)? **$20 $25 $40 $50 $75 $100**
How much does it/do they cost?

Examples: Un abrigo <u>cuesta (singular)</u> _____ dólares.
                    Unos vestidos <u>cuestan (plural)</u> _____ dólares.

*Unos vestidos de flamenco.
Sevilla, España*

caro = *expensive*	**barato** = *inexpensive*

Reading *(Lectura)*

Vocabulary:

el centro comercial	*mall*
me encanta	*I love*
precios	*prices*
tiendas	*stores*
liquidación	*sale/ liquidation*
todavía	*still*
todos	*all, everyone*
pasar tiempo	*spend time*

Hola, me llamo Liliana. Los sábados siempre voy al <u>centro comercial</u> con mis amigas. <u>Me encanta</u> ir de compras y buscar buena ropa con <u>precios</u> baratos.

Este sábado necesito comprar una corbata para mi papá. El domingo es Día del Padre y quiero darle[give to him] una corbata elegante para[in order to] usar con su traje.

Me gusta mucho cuando las <u>tiendas</u> tienen <u>liquidaciones</u>. Compro mucha ropa cuando no está muy cara.

El domingo viajan mis abuelos a nuestra casa. Ellos son viejos pero muy activos. Mi abuelo <u>todavía</u> trabaja en una compañía grande y mi abuela es ama de casa. Son muy amables y siempre están contentos. Mi abuela y mi mamá cocinan para <u>todos</u>. A mi papá y a mi abuelo les gusta la buena comida y pasar tiempo con la familia.

Reading questions:

1. ¿Dónde le gusta ir a Liliana con sus amigas? _____

2. ¿Qué tiene que comprar para su papá? _____

3. ¿Cuál celebración hay el domingo? _____

4. ¿Quiénes viajan a su casa el domingo? _____

5. ¿Cómo son sus abuelos? _____

Cultural Note

JESÚS ADRIAN ROMERO

Jesús A. Romero is a Mexican author, singer, composer and pastor. J.A.R. is a well known and loved Christian artist who travels extensively throught Latin America. He is the founder of *Vástago Producciones* which promotes Spanish Christian music and concerts. He currently is the pastor of Vastago Epicentro Church in Arizona. Jesús A. Romero sings this song, about God's presence, as a duet with Marcela Gándara (lesson 9).

TÚ ESTÁS AQUÍ (*You are here*)

Mi corazón puede sentir tu presencia	*my heart can feel your presence*
Tú estás aquí, tú estás aquí.	*You are here*
Puedo sentir tu majestad.	*I can feel your majesty*
Tú estás aquí, tú estás aquí.*	*You are here*

- Written by Jesús Adrian Romero & Michael Rodríguez.
*The complete song is found in the Praise and Worship section in the back of the book.

Coritos

SI EL ESPÍRITU DE DIOS SE MUEVE EN MÍ (*If the spirit of God moves in me*)

Si el espíritu de Dios se mueve en mí,	*If the spirit of God moves in me*
yo <u>canto</u> como David.	*I'll sing like David*
Si el espíritu de Dios se mueve en mí,	
yo <u>canto</u> como David.	
Yo <u>canto</u>, yo <u>canto</u>, yo <u>canto</u> como David.	

- <u>Alabo</u>	*I praise*
- <u>Oro</u>	*I pray*

- Traditional song from *Cancionero Latinoamericano.*

Written Work

Write the Spanish Bible verse for this lesson. Repeat it several times, and learn it.

_____

_____

A. Write all the clothes items that apply. **5.1**

1. Cuando hace frío, yo llevo _____

2. Cuando llueve, llevamos _____

3. Cuando hace mucho calor usamos _____

4. Cuando trabajo, llevo _____

5. En la primavera uso _____

B. TABLE TO CONJUGATE - Write the present tense conjugations that are missing. **5.6**
Write the meaning to the left of the verb.

Verb	yo	tú	él, ella, Ud.	nosotros	ellos/Uds.
cantar			canta		
escuchar					escuchan
viajar		viajas			
comprar				compramos	
esperar	espero				
ayudar			ayuda		
estudiar					
necesitar		necesitas		necesitamos	
orar					
predicar	predico				
trabajar					trabajan
tocar			toca		

C. Conjugate the verb in parenthesis.

1. Víctor _____ (viajar) cada^each Navidad a México.

2. Yo _____(cocinar) los domingos a mediodía.

3. Nosotros _____(cantar) en la iglesia.

4. Mi jefe^boss _____ (caminar) a su casa.

5. Uds. _____ (trabajar) con sus amigos.

6. Tú _____ (terminar) la lección.

7. Adela _____ (hablar) francés.

8. La profesora _____ (enseñar) español en la iglesia.

9. Yo _____ (escuchar) al pastor.

10. Los chicos _____ (mirar) mucha televisión.

D. According to the sentence, does it need a personal **a** or not? **5.7**

1. Yo compro ____X____ tres Biblias.

2. El niño mira ____a____ sus padres.

3. Guillermo espera _____ el autobús.

4. José Carlos visita _____ su abuela.

5. Uds. estudian _____ las lecciones.

6. Virginia ama _____ su esposo.

E. Fill in the blank with the correct direct object pronoun. **5.8**

1. God loves me: Dios _____ ama.   *2.* God loves you: Dios _____ ama.

3. God loves us: Dios _____ ama.

F. Fill in the blank with the correct conjugation of *IR* or *DAR.* **5.10**

1. Dios nos _____ mucha paz.

2. Esteban _____ a la conferencia con el pastor.

3. Uds. _____ a Honduras en junio.

4. Yo te _____ una computadora nueva.

5. Nuestro pastor nos _____ ayuda^help.

6. ¿Tú _____ al banco mañana?

G. Translate. **5.1 and 5.11**

1. ¿Cuánto cuestan estos pantalones negros?

_____

2. ¿Cuánto cuesta esta camisa verde?

_____

3. A mí no me gusta eso para ti.

_____

4. Aquella iglesia tiene alguien que toca la guitarra muy bien.

_____

H. Pasaje Bíblico | Bible passage
Salmo 31:14-16

English:
[14]But I trust in you, LORD; I say, "You are my God."
[15] My times are in your hands;
deliver me from the hands of my enemies,
from those who pursue me.
[16] Let your face shine on your servant; save me in your unfailing love.

Spanish:
[14] Pero yo, SEÑOR, en ti confío, y digo: «Tú eres mi Dios.»
[15] Mi vida entera está en tus manos;
líbrame de mis enemigos y perseguidores.
[16] Que brille tu faz sobre tu siervo; y sálvame, por tu gran amor.

Write the Spanish equivalent:

1. I trust in you. _____

2. You are my God. _____

3. My life is in your hands. _____

4. Let (may) your face shine on your servant. _____

5. Save me. _____

Lesson 6
Restaurant, food & drink

Food and Agriculture Vocabulary / REGULAR -er and -ir Verbs / Overview of -ar, -er, and -ir Verbs / QUERER / Direct Object Pronouns "lo, la, los, las" / Verbs that are Irregular in the YO form - HACER, PONER, SALIR, VALER, TRAER, OÍR, VER, TRADUCIR / SABER vs. CONOCER

Buenos Aires, Argentina

Lección 6

No sólo de pan vive el hombre, sino de toda palabra que sale de la boca de Dios.
San Mateo 4:4

Man does not live on bread alone, but on every word that comes from the mouth of God.
Matthew 4:4

6.1 LA COMIDA | *FOOD*

¡Vamos a comer!	*Let's eat!*	el plato	*the plate*	el mesero	*waiter*
¡A la mesa!	*To the table!*	el vaso	*glass*	la mesera	*waitress*
Buen provecho.	*Enjoy your food.*	la taza	*cup*	la cuenta	*the bill*
el desayuno	*breakfast*	el tenedor	*the fork*	la propina	*the tip*
el almuerzo	*lunch*	el cuchillo	*the knife*	delicioso/a	*delicious*
la cena	*dinner*	la cuchara	*the spoon*	rico/a	*yummy*
la merienda	*snack*	la servilleta	*the napkin*	fresco/a	*fresh*
un poco (de)	*a little (of)*	el mantel	*tablecloth*	sano/a	*healthy*

una hamburguesa   una ensalada   un sandwich   un bistec con   una sopa/un guiso
y papas fritas   papa al horno

CARNES | *MEAT*

la carne de res	*beef*	el pollo	*chicken*	el atún	*tuna*
las chuletas (de cerdo)	*(pork) chops*	el chorizo	*sausage*	el jamón	*ham*
los mariscos	*seafood*	el pescado	*fish*	el tocino	*bacon*
los camarones	*shrimp*	el bistec	*steak*	el pavo	*turkey*

VEGETALES/VERDURAS | *VEGETABLES*

la lechuga	*lettuce*	el maíz	*corn*	el pepino	*cucumber, pickle*
el tomate	*tomato*	la papa, patata	*potato*	el brócoli	*broccoli*
la zanahoria	*carrot*	la espinaca	*spinach*	los guisantes	*peas*
la cebolla	*onion*	el apio	*celery*	las habichuelas	*green beans*
la calabaza	*pumpkin*	el repollo	*cabbage*	el aguacate	*avocado*

FRUTAS | *FRUITS*

la manzana	*apple*	la banana	*banana*	la piña	*pineapple*
la naranja	*orange*	el plátano	*banana, platain banana*	el limón	*lemon*
el durazno	*peach*	las uvas	*grapes*	la cereza	*cherry*
las fresas	*strawberries*	el melón	*melon*	la toronja	*grapefruit*
la sandía	*watermelon*	la ciruela	*plum*	la pera	*pear*

OTRAS COMIDAS | *OTHER FOODS*

el arroz	*rice*	el yogur	*yogurt*	la mantequilla de maní	*peanut butter*
los frijoles	*beans*	el queso	*cheese*	la jalea, la mermelada	*jelly*
la pasta	*pasta*	las aceitunas	*olives*	el pan (tostado)	*(toasted) bread*
los huevos	*eggs*	las palomitas	*popcorn*	el cereal	*cereal*
la miel	*honey*	la avena	*oatmeal*	los panqueques	*pancakes*

BEBIDAS | *DRINKS*

el agua	*water*	el jugo (de naranja)	*(orange) juice*
el té	*tea*	una soda, gaseosa	*carbonated drink*
el café	*coffee*	el hielo	*ice*
la leche	*milk*	el agua con gas	*soda water*
el vino	*wine*	el agua mineral	*bottled water*
la cerveza	*beer*	el licuado	*shake, smoothie*

CONDIMENTOS | *CONDIMENTS*

la sal	*salt*	el edulcorante	*sweetener*	el aceite	*oil*
la pimienta	*pepper*	la mayonesa	*mayonaise*	el vinagre	*vinegar*
el azúcar	*sugar*	la mostaza	*mustard*	la crema	*cream*
la mantequilla	*butter*	el ajo	*garlic*	el aderezo	*salad dressing*

POSTRES | *DESSERTS*

dulce	*sweet*	las galletas	*cookies*
la torta, el queque	*cake*	el helado	*ice cream*
el pastel	*pie, cake*	el chocolate	*chocolate*
los dulces, caramelos	*candy*	la vainilla	*vanilla*
el flan	*egg custard*	el dulce de leche	*caramel*

Talk about what you like or don't like. *Me gusta(n)…, no me gusta(n)…* remember to say *gustan* for plural.
Example: Me <u>gusta</u> el arroz, <u>no me gustan</u> los frijoles.

1. ¿Qué te gusta? _____
2. ¿Qué no te gusta? _____
3. ¿Qué te gusta comer para el desayuno? _____
4. ¿Qué te gusta comer para el almuerzo? _____
5. ¿Qué te gusta comer para la cena? _____
6. ¿Qué ensalada te gusta preparar? _____
7. ¿Cuál te gusta más, el helado de chocolate o el de vainilla? _____
8. ¿Cuáles son tus frutas favoritas? _____

Name the ingredients in. . .
¿Cuáles son los ingredientes de…? un sandwich, una ensalada de frutas, una sopa de vegetales

6.2 AGRICULTURE MISSIONS EXTENDED VOCABULARY (OPTIONAL)

la agricultura	*agriculture*	la vaca/el toro	*cow/bull*
la granja, la finca	*farm*	la cabra, (el chivo)	*goat, (kid)*
el campo	*field*	el gallo/la gallina	*rooster/hen*
cavar	*to dig*	el chancho, cochino, puerco, cerdo	*pig*
sembrar, plantar	*to plant*		
las semillas	*seeds*	los pollos	*chicken*
la cosecha	*the crop*	el pato	*duck*
cosechar	*to harvest*	el conejo	*rabbit*
el azadón	*hoe*	el caballo	*horse*
la tierra	*dirt, ground*	el burro	*donkey*

6.3 REGULAR -ER AND -IR VERBS

comer	to eat	vivir	to live
leer	to read	escribir	to write
creer	to believe	abrir	to open
comprender	to comprehend	compartir	to share
correr	to run	existir	to exist
beber	to drink	recibir	to receive
aprender	to learn	cumplir	to fulfill, complete
vender	to sell	cubrir	to cover
responder	to answer, respond	decidir	to decide
romper	to break, to tear	sufrir	to suffer
ver	to see (yo veo, tú ves…)		

Yo puedo + infinitive	I can …	Me gusta + infinitive	I like to …
Yo necesito + infinitive	I need to…	Me gustaría + infinitive	I would like to …

The endings for -er verbs are just like the -ar verbs, except they will have an -e instead of an -a in the ending. Here is the conjugation of the regular verb COMER.

comer → com - er → **com-** is the stem.

yo	com**o**	nosotros/as	com**emos**
tú	com**es**		
él, ella, Ud.	come	ellos, ellas, Uds.	com**en**

Ella no come dulces.
She doesn't eat candy.

Regular -ir verbs are just the same as the -er verbs except for the *nosotros* form.

vivir → viv - ir → **viv-** is the stem

yo	viv**o**	nosotros/as	viv**imos**
tú	viv**es**		
él, ella, Ud.	viv**e**	ellos, ellas, Uds.	viv**en**

¿Vives en Panamá?
Do you live in Panama?

Note: For the verbs *LEER / CREER* drop the -er and keep the first -e in the stem.
Example: Leo, lees, lee, leemos, leen.
The verb *VER* keeps the -e in the *YO* form. *(yo veo)*

Fill in the blank with the correct form of the verb given.

1. Yo _____*creo*_____ (creer) en Dios.

2. Tú _____ (comer) jalapeños.

3. Nosotros _____ (aprender) en la clase de español.

4. Los estudiantes no _____(comprender) el problema.

5. Dios siempre _____ (cumplir) sus promesas.

6. Yo _____ (escribir) muchos e-mails.

7. Yo sé que[that] Dios _____ (existir).

Answers: 2. comes 3.aprendemos 4. comprenden 5. cumple 6. escribo 7. existe

> ## Did you know?
> Spicy food is consumed in just a few Hispanic countries.

Look at all the endings for the 3 types of regular verbs.

	-ar	-er	-ir
yo	**-o**	**-o**	**-o**
tú	**-as**	**-es**	**-es**
él, ella, Ud.	**-a**	**-e**	**-e**
nosotros	**-amos**	**-emos**	**-imos**
ellos, ellas, Uds.	**-an**	**-en**	**-en**

With this chart, you can conjugate any REGULAR Spanish verb.

STEM + ending = conjugation

	PREPARAR	BEBER	RECIBIR
yo	**preparo**	**bebo**	**recibo**
tú	**preparas**	**bebes**	**recibes**
él, ella, Ud.	**prepara**	**bebe**	**recibe**
nosotros	**preparamos**	**bebemos**	**recibimos**
ellos, ellas, Uds.	**preparan**	**beben**	**reciben**

A. What are these people doing? ¿Qué hacen? (Use "quick list" of verbs in Appendix I.)

1. El niño _____   **2.** Ramón_____   **3.** Paola_____

4. Ella _____   **5.** Los chicos_____   **6.** El niño _____

B. Ask someone: Answer with the same verb that is in the question.

1. ¿Dónde vives? _Yo vivo en Dallas._____

2. ¿Qué comida preparas para la cena? _____

3. ¿Necesitas comprar ropa nueva? ¿Qué necesitas comprar? _____

4. ¿Qué música escuchas? _____

5. ¿Dónde trabajas? ¿Cuántas horas trabajas? _____

6. ¿Vas a la iglesia todos los domingos? _____ _____

7. ¿Lees muchos libros? ¿Lees el periódico^newspaper? _____ _____

8. ¿Te gusta recibir muchos regalos^gifts en tu cumpleaños? _____

The conjugation of the verb *QUERER* (to want) has the regular *-er* endings, but, is an irregular verb because the stem of the verb *(quer-)* changes in some of the conjugations of the present tense. The *-e* will change to *-ie*. For example, the *yo* form is **quiero**.

Yo quiero - I want	This can be followed by a <u>noun</u> or a <u>verb.</u>

Yo quiero <u>una computadora nueva.</u>   *I want <u>a new computer.</u>*
Yo quiero <u>un vaso más grande.</u>   *I want <u>a bigger glass.</u>*

A. ¿Y Ud.? ¿Qué quiere para su cumpleaños?   Yo quiero _____

algo *something*	**Yo quiero algo.** *I want something.*
nada *nothing*	**No quiero nada.** *I don't want anything.*

The verb *querer* can also be used with another verb to express that you want to do something. The first verb, *querer*, is conjugated. The second verb is NOT conjugated, it will be in the infinitive form.

Yo quiero <u>leer</u> toda la Biblia.   *I want to <u>read</u> the whole Bible.*
Yo quiero <u>comer</u> pollo.   *I want to <u>eat</u> chicken.*

B. ¿Y Ud.? ¿Qué quiere comer? _____

The stem of the verb *querer* changes to *quier-* in all but the *nosotros* form. The verb *tener* also has the same stem changes. These verbs are called **e → ie** verbs. They are best learned by repetition.

	singular		plural
Yo	qu**ie**ro	nosotros/as	qu**e**remos
tú	qu**ie**res		
él, ella, Ud.	qu**ie**re	ellos, ellas, Uds.	qu**ie**ren

Did you know?

In Spanish if you tell some one *"Te quiero"* it means "I love you," not "I want you." *"Te quiero mucho"* means "I love you so much." It is used as much or more than "te amo." *"Te amo"* is a more serious "I love you."

Él **quiere** un carro nuevo.   *He **wants** a new car.*
Ellas **quieren** comida mexicana.   *They (fem.) **want** mexican food.*
Jack **quiere hablar** español.   *Jack **wants to speak** Spanish.*
Yo **quiero ser** misionero/a.   *I want **to be** a missionary.*

C. Finish the sentence using *querer + infinitive* to express what they want to do:

Mis amigos _____

D. ¿Qué más quieres? Pick from the list below to say what you or someone you know wants or doesn't want to do. Example: *Yo quiero una casa grande. Yo no quiero trabajar.*

una casa grande	más tiempo con mi familia	estudiar más
un millón de dólares	una Biblia en español	ir de compras^{go shopping}
un carro nuevo	hacer la tarea ^{homework}	ir en un viaje misionero
ser médico	comer en un restaurante	limpiar^{clean} mi casa
trabajar más	viajar mucho	ver^{see/watch} televisión

Yo (no) quiero _____

Name students in your class...or members of your family. _____ (no) quiere _____

6.6 THIRD PERSON DIRECT OBJECT PRONOUNS | *LO, LA, LOS, LAS*

You have learned that *ME, TE, NOS* are 1st and 2nd person direct object pronouns (5.8). The 3rd person direct object pronouns take the place of "him", "her", "it" and their respective plural "them." These pronouns can refer to <u>people</u> or <u>things</u>.

Direct object pronouns	masculine	feminine
singular	**lo** (him / it)	**la** (her / it)
plural	**los** (them)	**las** (them)

Remember: The **direct object** is a noun that directly takes the action of the verb.
A **direct object pronoun** takes the place of the **direct object noun** and keeps us from having to repeat when it has already been mentioned, especially when answering questions.
Example: Did you read **the book**? —Yes, I read **it.**
The **direct object pronoun** must be placed <u>before</u> the conjugated verb.

Yo leo el libro. - *I read the book.*
I (YO) =subject   read (LEO) =verb   the book (EL LIBRO)=direct object
YO **LO** LEO. - *I read it.* - *It* takes the place of "book."

Tú ves la casa. - *You see the house.*
You (TÚ) =subject   see (VES) =verb   the house (LA CASA)=direct object
TÚ **LA** VES. - *You see it.* - *It* takes the place of "house."

Nosotros vemos a Esteban y David. - *We see Esteban and David.*
We (NOSOTROS)=subject   see (VEMOS)=verb   Esteban & David=direct object
NOSOTROS **LOS** VEMOS. - *We see **them**. - **Them** takes the place of "Esteban and David."

I see **Jorge**. → I see **him**. → Yo **lo** veo. (*veo* is an irregular *YO* form because the *-e* is not dropped)
I see **María**. → I see **her**. → Yo **la** veo.

I see **Jorge** and **María**. → I see **them**. → Yo **los** veo.
I see **Juana** and **María**. → I see **them.** (females) → Yo **las** veo.

Note: *lo/la* can also refer to *USTED, los/las* can also refer to *USTEDES.* You can specify with, "*a Ud.*" or "*a Uds.*" in the sentence.   Yo **lo** veo **a Ud.** *I see you.* (formal)   Yo **los** veo **a Uds.** *I see you.* (plural)

Yo preparo **los tacos**. ⟶ Yo **los** preparo. (*I prepare the tacos.* ⟶ *I prepare them.*)
Yo tengo **el libro**. ⟶ Yo **lo** tengo. (*I have the book.* ⟶ *I have it.*)
Ella quiere **la ensalada**. ⟶ Ella **la** quiere. (*She wants the salad.* ⟶ *She wants it.*)
Ellos comen **las enchiladas**. ⟶ **Las** comen. (*They eat the enchiladas.* ⟶ *They eat them.*)

A. To have or want something. Fill in the blank with the correct direct object pronoun.

1. Yo tengo <u>una casa</u>. Yo ____*la*____ tengo. (*I have it.*)

2. Yo quiero <u>un carro</u>. Yo _____ quiero. (*I want it.*)

3. Yo tengo <u>unas plumas</u>. Yo _____ tengo. (*I have them.*)

4. Yo quiero <u>unos libros</u>. Yo _____ quiero. (*I want them.*)

When the direct object is a person, remember the personal "*a*" is placed before that person. Read the sentence, determine which is the direct object and replace it with the correct pronoun.

5. Yo veo <u>a los niños</u>. Yo _____ veo.

6. Yo recibo <u>las cartas.</u> ^{letters} Yo _____ recibo.

7. Yo veo a <u>José y a María</u>. Yo _____ veo.

8. Yo necesito <u>a Dios</u>. Yo _____ necesito.

9. Yo preparo <u>las enchiladas</u>. Yo _____ preparo.

10. Tú cantas <u>la canción</u>. Tú _____ cantas.

B. Rewrite the sentence replacing the direct object with the correct pronoun.

1. María recibe <u>la Biblia</u>. ___*María la recibe.*___

2. Roberto lee <u>los libros</u>. _____

3. Los niños comen <u>las hamburguesas</u>. _____

4. Nosotros escuchamos <u>al pastor</u>. _____

C. Direct object pronouns are used mostly in questions/answers. This way you do not have to repeat what you are talking about when you answer.

Example: Do you see the book? Yes, I see <u>it</u>. Make sure the answer is in the *YO* form.

1. ¿Quieres <u>el libro</u>? ___*Sí, lo quiero.*___

2. ¿Quieres la pluma? _____

3. ¿Compras las Biblias? _____

4. ¿Comes los frijoles? _____

Answers: A. 2. lo 3. las 4. los 5. los 6. las 7. los 8. lo 9. las 10. la   B2. Roberto los lee. 3. Los niños las comen.
4. Nosotros lo escuchamos. C.2. Sí, la quiero. 3. Sí, las compro. 4. Sí, los como.

Note: See Appendix VI for information on double object pronoun.

6.7 VERBS IRREGULAR IN THE *YO* FORM

There are some verbs that are regular in the present tense endings <u>except</u> for the *YO* form. You must learn the *YO* form by repetition and memorization.

hacer	*to do*	oír	*to hear*
poner	*to put*	venir	*to come*
salir	*to go out*	traducir	*to translate*
valer	*to be worth*	saber	*to know (knowledge)*
traer	*to bring*	conocer	*to know/to be familiar with*

HACER - to do / to make

yo	**hago**	nosotros/as	**hacemos**
tú	**haces**		
él, ella, Ud.	**hace**	ellos, ellas, Uds.	**hacen**

The verb *hacer* is used in questions to ask what someone is doing. —*¿Qué haces?*

PONER - to put

yo	**pongo**	nosotros/as	**ponemos**
tú	**pones**		
él, ella, Ud.	**pone**	ellos, ellas, Uds.	**ponen**

Pongo la sal en la mesa.
I put the salt on the table.

SALIR - to go out

yo	**salgo**	nosotros/as	**salimos**
tú	**sales**		
él, ella, Ud.	**sale**	ellos, ellas, Uds.	**salen**

Salgo con mis amigos.
I go out with my friends.

VALER - to be worth

yo	**valgo**	nosotros/as	**valemos**
tú	**vales**		
él, ella, Ud.	**vale**	ellos, ellas, Uds.	**valen**

Valgo mucho.
I am worth a lot.

TRAER - to bring

yo	**traigo**	nosotros/as	**traemos**
tú	**traes**		
él, ella, Ud.	**trae**	ellos, ellas, Uds.	**traen**

Traigo una ensalada.
I am bringing a salad.

OÍR - to hear (this verb changes the -*i* to a -*y* between 2 vowels)

yo	**oigo**	nosotros/as	**oímos**
tú	**oyes**		
él, ella, Ud.	**oye**	ellos, ellas, Uds.	**oyen**

¿Oyes la música?
Do you hear the music?

VENIR - to come (this is an e → ie verb that has an irregular *YO* form) like TENER

yo	**vengo**	nosotros/as	**venimos**
tú	**vienes**		
él, ella, Ud.	**viene**	ellos, ellas, Uds.	**vienen**

Vengo de clase.
I am coming from class.

TRADUCIR - to translate

yo	**traduzco**	nosotros/as	**traducimos**
tú	**traduces**		
él, ella, Ud.	**traduce**	ellos, ellas, Uds.	**traducen**

Traduzco para ellos.
I translate for them.

Conjugate correctly the verb in parenthesis.

1. Yo te _____. (oír)

2. Yo _____ la comida para[for] la fiesta. (traer)

3. Yo _____ de la clase a las 11:00. (salir)

4. Yo _____ la tarea todos los días. (hacer)

6.8 *SABER* VS. *CONOCER*

Both of these verbs mean "to know." But there is a difference. *Saber* means to know something as a fact or to have knowledge about it, as through study. *Conocer* means to know/to be familiar with someone or a place.

SABER - to know (knowledge or information)

yo	**sé**	nosotros/as	**sabemos**
tú	**sabes**		
él, ella, Ud.	**sabe**	ellos, ellas, Uds.	**saben**

CONOCER - to know / to be familiar with

yo	**conozco**	nosotros/as	**conocemos**
tú	**conoces**		
él, ella, Ud.	**conoce**	ellos, ellas, Uds.	**conocen**

1. SABER

Yo <u>sé</u> donde vive el pastor.   *I know where the pastor lives.*
Yo <u>sé</u> la información.   *I know the information.*
Yo no <u>sé</u>.   *I don't know.*

You can also use *saber* + infinitive verb to say what you "know how to do."
Mi hermano <u>sabe</u> nadar.   *My brother <u>knows how</u> to swim.*

2. CONOCER

Yo <u>conozco</u> al Presidente.   *I know the President.*
Yo <u>conozco</u> Houston.   *I know (am familiar with) Houston.*

> **Did you know?**
>
> In Peru, the guinea pig is considered a delicacy. It's called "cuy."

Fill in the blank with the correct verb **saber** or **conocer**, and conjugate it accordingly.

1. Yo _____ cuándo es el campamento[camp].

2. Yo _____ a los miembros de la iglesia.

3. Tú _____ cantar muy bien.

4. Mis primos _____ Los Ángeles.

5. Yo no _____ tocar el piano.

> **REMEMBER**
>
> **No sé = I don't know**

Finish the sentences for yourself: Yo sé (+ inf) _____

Answers: 1. sé   2. conozco 3. sabes 4. conocen 5. sé

Cultural Note

COMIDAS DEL MUNDO HISPANO

If not familiar with these, you can look them up on the internet for more information or the recipe.

Hispanic Desserts: flan, arroz con leche, panes dulces, churros

flan

arroz con leche

panes dulces

México: pozole, ponche, tacos al pastor, menudo, caldo

Guatemala: pepián

El Salvador: pupusas

Nicaragua: gallo pinto, mondongo

Honduras: carne asada

Argentina & Uruguay: empanadas, mate, dulce de leche, el asado

Perú: lomo saltado, chicha morada

Chile: ceviche, el asado, mote con huesillo

España: paella, tortilla española, tapas, jamón serrano

Colombia & Venezuela: arepas

Puerto Rico: mofongo, arroz con gandules

Cuba: lechón asado, moros y cristianos

República Dominicana: sancocho

plátanos fritos

menudo

pupusas

gallo pinto y carne asada

empanadas

el asado

mate

paella

Did you know? Tex-Mex is a term that is used for the mixture of cultures that happened with Mexico and Texas. Most Tex-Mex food from southern U.S. is not found in Mexico or is very altered since the ingredients are not the same as the ones found in Mexico.

Recipe: Ask a Hispanic or look on the internet for a recipe of a traditional food from a Hispanic country that you would like to make. You can copy it here and share it with the class.
Note: Food vocabulary varies among Hispanic countries.

Name of Dish_____

Country _____

_____

_____

_____

_____

_____

_____

_____

_____

_____

_____

_____

Coritos

CRISTO ME AMA (*Jesus loves me*)

Cristo me ama, bien lo sé.	*Jesus loves me this I know*
Su palabra me hace ver.	*His Word makes me see*
Que los niños son de aquel.	*That the children belong to Him*
Quien es nuestro amigo fiel.	*Who is our faithful friend*
Sí, Cristo me ama.	*Yes, Jesus loves me*
Sí, Cristo me ama.	
Sí, Cristo me ama.	
La Biblia dice así.	*The Bible says so*

Letra, Anna B. Wagner, traducción. Música, William B. Bradbury. Himnario Bautista.

QUIERO CANTAR UNA LINDA CANCIÓN *(I want to sing a beautiful song)*

Quiero cantar una linda canción	*I want to sing a beautiful song*
De un hombre que me transformó.	*about a man who transformed me*
Quiero cantar una linda canción	*I want to sing a beautiful song*
De aquel que mi vida cambió.	*About He who changed my life*
Es mi amigo, Jesús.	*He is my friend, Jesus*
Es mi amigo más fiel	*He is my most faithful friend*
Él es Dios, Él es Rey,	*He is God, He is King*
Es amor y verdad.	*He is love and truth*
Solo en Él encontré	*Only in Him I found*
Esa paz que busqué.	*That peace that I searched*
Solo en Él encontré	*Only in Him I found*
La felicidad.	*Happiness*

Traditional song from *Cancionero Latinoamericano*.

Written Work

Write the Spanish Bible verse for this lesson. Repeat it several times, and learn it.

_____

_____

A. ¿A qué hora comes el desayuno? ¿el almuerzo? ¿la cena? ¿la merienda?
Example: Yo como el desayuno a las ocho de la mañana. **6.1**

_____

_____

B. Answer with <u>Vocabulary Words</u>. **6.1**

1. What things go on a set table? _____

2. What are the healthiest meats? _____

3. ¿Cuáles vegetales/frutas son verdes? _____

4. ¿Cuáles vegetales/frutas son rojas o anaranjadas? _____

5. What are the healthiest drinks?_____

C. TABLE TO CONJUGATE - Write the present tense conjugations that are missing. **6.3 and 6.4**

Verb	yo	tú	él, ella, Ud.	nosotros	ellos/Uds.
leer	leo				
correr					corren
escribir			escribe		
olvidar		olvidas			
decidir				decidimos	
enseñar	enseño				
creer					creen
sufrir				sufrimos	
ver	veo	ves			
abrir			abre		

1. Nosotros _____ (creer) en Cristo.

2. El señor López _____ (escribir) su nombre.

3. Yo _____ el carro en el garaje. (poner)

D. TABLE TO CONJUGATE - Write the present tense conjugations that are missing. **6.5 and 6.7**

Verb	yo	tú	él, ella, Ud.	nosotros	ellos/Uds.
poner	pongo			ponemos	
salir			sale		
conocer		conoces		conocemos	
hacer		haces			hacen
saber			sabe		
oír	oigo				oyen
traducir				traducimos	
querer		quieres		queremos	

1. Yo _____*traduzco*_____ la conversación. (traducir)

2. Yo _____ la tarea. (hacer)

3. Yo no _____ nada. (saber)

4. Yo _____mucho y tú _____ mucho también. (valer)

5. Mi amigo _____ el mensaje.^message (oír)

6. Ustedes _____ mucho trabajo. (hacer)

7. Yo _____ a mi abuela. (ver)

8. Dios _____ todo.^everything (saber)

E. Write a sentence with each of these verbs: **6.3 and 6.4**

1. recibir - *Usted recibe a Jesucristo.*

2. leer - _____

3. correr - _____

4. escribir - _____

5. decidir - _____

6. saber - _____

7. conocer - _____

8. creer - _____

9. enseñar - _____

10. vender - _____

F. Finish the sentence with verbs, be sure you conjugate correctly. **6.3**

1. En mi casa, yo _____

2. En la iglesia, el pastor _____

3. En la iglesia, nosotros _____

4. En mi trabajo, yo _____

5. En la clase, yo _____

6. En la clase, la profesora _____

7. En el supermercado, tú _____

8. En un viaje misionero, los voluntarios _____

G. Finish the sentence with a noun or a verb to go in the blank. (#2 and #4 are verbs) **6.5**

1. Mis amigos quieren un/una _____

2. Mi pastor quiere _____

3. Mi profesor/a quiere un/una _____

4. Nosotros queremos _____

H. Fill in the blank with the correct form of *QUERER*. **6.5**

1. Yo _____ ir a la iglesia.

2. Los animales en el zoológico _____ comer.

3. El niño _____ jugar al béisbol.

4. ¿ _____ tú mirar una película (*movie*)?

5. Silvia _____ conocer al Presidente.

6. Nosotros _____ beber agua con limón.

I. Replace the direct object in the first sentence with the correct pronoun. **6.6**

Me, te, lo, la, nos, los or las.

1. I see <u>David</u>.   Yo veo <u>a David</u>.   Yo ____*lo*_____ veo.

2. You hear <u>them</u>.   Tú _____ oyes.

3. I play the guitar. Yo toco <u>la guitarra</u>. Yo _____ toco.

4. Jesus loves <u>me</u>. Jesús _____ ama.

5. Jesus loves <u>you</u>. Jesús _____ ama.

6. Ana prepara <u>las enchiladas</u>. Ana _____ prepara.

7. ¿Wycliffe traduce <u>las Biblias</u>? Sí, Wycliffe _____ traduce.

8. ¿Conoce Ud. a <u>los voluntarios</u>? No, no _____ conozco.

J. Choose *SABER* or *CONOCER* in the following sentences and conjugate. **6.8**

1. Ustedes _____ a mi tío.

2. Yo no _____ tocar el piano.

3. Nosotros _____ cómo usar la computadora.

4. Mi hermano _____ México y Europa.

5. María, ¿ tú_____ cuál es la capital de Nicaragua?

6. ¿Tú _____ a aquel señor?

Lesson 7
The Home, Nature, Sports & Activities

Home and Construction Vocabulary / Home activities / Present Progressive / Stem-changing verbs -e → -ie, -o → -ue, -e → -i / *Preguntar* vs. *Pedir* / Sports and Activities / Informal Future *IR* + *A* + INFINITIVE / Pronoun Placement for Infinitives and Gerunds / Nature Vocabulary

Lago Titicaca, Perú/Bolivia

Lección 7

Quiero vivir en la casa de mi Señor todos los días de mi vida. Salmo 27:4
I will live in the house of the Lord all my days. Psalm 27:4

7.1 LA CASA | *THE HOUSE*

la **puerta**	*door*	el **suelo, piso**	*floor*
la **ventana**	*window*	el **techo**	*roof*
la **pared**	*wall*	la **chimenea**	*chimney*

LA SALA | *THE LIVING ROOM*

el **sofá**	*sofa*	la **lámpara**	*lamp*
el **cuadro**	*wall picture*	los **estantes**	*shelves*
las **cortinas**	*curtains*	el **sillón**	*arm chair*
la **televisión**, el **televisor**	*television*	la **alfombra**	*rug*

EL COMEDOR | *DINING ROOM*

la **mesa**	*table*	los **platos**	*dishes*	el **florero**	*flower vase*
las **sillas**	*chairs*	los **vasos**	*glasses*	el **mantel**	*tablecloth*

LA COCINA Y EL LAVADERO | *KITCHEN AND LAUNDRY ROOM*

la **estufa**	*stove*	el **fregadero**, la **pileta**	*sink*	el **microondas**	*microwave*
el **horno**	*oven*	el **lavaplatos**	*dishwasher*	el **refrigerador**	*refrigerator*
la **plancha**	*iron*	la **lavadora**	*washing machine*	los **gabinetes**	*cabinets*

EL DORMITORIO/LA RECÁMARA | *BEDROOM*

el **cuarto**, la **habitación**	*room*	la **cama**	*bed*	el **ropero**	*closet*
la **recámara**, el **dormitorio**	*bedroom*	la **almohada**	*pillow*	la **manta, cobija**	*blanket*
la **mesita de noche**	*night stand*	las **sábanas**	*sheets*	la **llave**	*key*

EL BAÑO | *BATHROOM*

la **bañera**, la **tina**	*bathtub*	la **ducha**	*shower*	el **champú**	*shampoo*
el **inodoro**	*toilet*	la **toalla**	*towel*	el **cepillo de dientes**	*toothbrush*
el **lavamano**	*bathroom sink*	el **jabón**	*soap*	el **espejo**	*mirror*

1  2  3

EL PATIO | *BACK YARD*

el **jardín**	*garden*	**afuera**	*outside*	el **garaje**	*garage*
los **árboles**	*trees*	el **césped**	*lawn*	la **piscina, alberca**	*pool*
los **arbustos**	*bushes*	las **flores**	*flowers*	la **cerca**	*fence*

TO DESCRIBE ROOMS OR THINGS IN YOUR HOUSE

amplio/a	*roomy*	**está organizado/a**	*it's organized*	**está limpio/a**	*it's clean*
claro/a	*bright*	**cómodo/a**	*comfortable*	**está sucio/a**	*it's dirty*

Ask someone or answer for yourself (use adjectives to describe).

1. ¿Cómo es tu casa? _____

2. ¿Qué hay en tu sala? _____

3. ¿Qué hay en tu comedor? _____

4. ¿Qué tienes en tu cocina? _____

5. ¿Qué tienes en tus dormitorios? _____

6. ¿Qué tienes en tu baño? _____

7. ¿Qué hay en tu jardín? _____

> **Did you know?**
>
> "Primer piso" which means "first floor" is actually the 2nd floor in Hispanic countries. "Planta baja" is the first floor.

7.2 HOME ACTIVITIES

limpiar	*to clean*	**cocinar**	*to cook*
limpiar el piso	*clean the floor*	**organizar**	*to organize*
lavar platos	*wash dishes*	**hacer la cama**	*to make the bed*
lavar ropa	*to wash clothes*	**jardinear**	*to garden*

Where do you do these activities? Answer using the verbs above.

Examples: ¿Dónde limpias?   —Yo limpio en mi casa.
            ¿Dónde haces la cama?   —Yo hago la cama en mi habitación.

1. ¿Dónde lavas los platos? _____

2. ¿Dónde lavas la ropa? _____

3. ¿Dónde cocinas? _____

4. ¿Dónde miras la televisión? _____

5. ¿Dónde limpias el piso? _____

7.3 CONSTRUCTION EXTENDED VOCABULARY (OPTIONAL)

construir	*to construct, build*	**las herramientas**	*tools*	**el andamio**	*scaffold*
clavar	*to nail*	**el martillo**	*hammer*	**los tornillos**	*screws*
levantar	*to raise*	**los clavos**	*nails*	**el cemento**	*cement*
romper, quebrar	*to break*	**la sierra, el serrucho**	*saw*	**la arena**	*sand*
medir	*to measure*	**las tenazas**	*pliers*	**el hierro**	*iron*
mezclar	*to mix*	**el pegamento**	*glue*	**la pala**	*shovel*
reparar, arreglar	*to repair, fix*	**la madera**	*wood*	**el alambre, el cable**	*wire*
ayudar	*to help*	**la pintura**	*paint*	**la escoba**	*broom*
el destornillador	*the screwdriver*	**la brocha**	*paint brush*	**barrer**	*to sweep*
la carretilla	*wheelbarrow*	**la basura**	*trash*	**¡Cuidado!**	*Careful!*

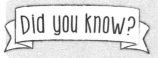 **Did you know?** Most Hispanic countries use the metric system. One *KILO* is about 2.2 pounds.

The **present participle** in English is made by adding -ing to the verb form. (Example: eating) In Spanish, the" gerundio" is made by adding *-ando* or *-iendo* to the stem of the verb, depending if it is an *-ar, -er* or *-ir* verb. Every verb has only one present participle.

-*ar* verbs *-ando*	-*er* verbs *-iendo*	-*ir* verbs *-iendo*
cantar - **cantando**singing	comer - **comiendo**eating	vivir - **viviendo**living
viajar - **viajando**traveling	vender - **vendiendo**selling	escribir - **escribiendo**writing
mirar - **mirando**looking	beber - **bebiendo**drinking	recibir - **recibiendo**receiving

Here are a few irregulars:

leer - **leyendo** reading	oír - **oyendo** hearing	morir - **muriendo** dying
creer - **creyendo** believing	dormir - **durmiendo** sleeping	repetir - **repitiendo** repeating

The present participle (called "*gerundio*") is used to express what you "are doing" at the moment. The present participle is preceded by the verb *ESTAR* as the auxiliary verb (conjugation in 1.6). This is called the **present progressive: *ESTAR* + present participle (-ndo).**

Yo estoy **trabajando.** *I am **working.***   Usted está **comiendo.** *You (formal) are **eating.***
Tú estás **cantando.** *You are **singing.***   Nosotros estamos **orando.** *We are **praying.***
Él está **hablando.** *He is **talking.***   Uds. están **viajando**. *You (plural) are **traveling**.*

Ella está cocinando.   Él está lavando los platos.   Está limpiando.   Está haciendo la cama.

Answer the questions by filling in the blank with the present participle.

1. ¿Qué <u>estás haciendo</u>? *What <u>are you doing</u>?*

—Yo estoy _____*leyendo*_____ y _____

2. ¿Y tus amigos, qué están haciendo?

—Ellos están _____ y_____

3. ¿Qué está haciendo el/la profesor/a? —Él/ella está _____

4. ¿Qué está haciendo tu hermano/a? —Está _____

5. ¿Qué están haciendo los estudiantes? —Están _____

Irregular verbs ("e → ie" verbs like "querer")

As with the verb *QUERER*, there are other verbs that go through the same stem change of **e → ie**. The change takes place with the "-e" that is directly before the ending.

* They all change EXCEPT the *nosotros* form. Here is a list of *e → ie* stem-changing verbs:

qu**e**rer	to want	v**e**nir	to come
p**e**nsar	to think	c**e**rrar	to close
ent**e**nder	to understand	p**e**rder	to lose
s**e**ntir	to feel	com**e**nzar	to begin, to commence

PENSAR - to think

yo	**pienso**	nosotros/as	**pensamos**
tú	**piensas**		
él, ella, Ud.	**piensa**	ellos, ellas, Uds.	**piensan**

¿Piensas ir esta noche?
Are you thinking about going tonight?

ENTENDER - to understand

yo	**entiendo**	nosotros/as	**entendemos**
tú	**entiendes**		
él, ella, Ud.	**entiende**	ellos, ellas, Uds.	**entienden**

No lo entiendo.
I don't understand it.

SENTIR - to feel

yo	**siento**	nosotros/as	**sentimos**
tú	**sientes**		
él, ella, Ud.	**siente**	ellos, ellas, Uds.	**sienten**

Lo siento mucho.
I am very sorry.

VENIR - to come (has an irregular *YO* form)

yo	**vengo**	nosotros/as	**venimos**
tú	**vienes**		
él, ella, Ud.	**viene**	ellos, ellas, Uds.	**vienen**

¿Vienes a mi casa?
Are you coming to my house?

A. Ask someone: (Write their answers; possible answers are given below.)

1. ¿Entiendes francés? _____

2. ¿A qué hora cierran los bancos? _____

3. ¿Tú sientes el frío? _____

4. ¿Qué piensas hacer^what are you thinking of doing mañana? _____

5. ¿Qué días vienes a clase? _____

6. ¿Cuándo comienza el servicio? _____

7. ¿Pierdes tus llaves^keys? _____

8. ¿Qué quieres hacer el sábado? _____

1. No, no entiendo el francés. 2. Los bancos cierran a las 6:00. 3. Sí, siento el frío. 4. Pienso estudiar.

5. Vengo a clase los lunes. 6. El servicio comienza a las 11:00 de la mañana. 7. Sí, pierdo mis llaves. 8. Yo quiero ___infinitive___.

Stem changing ("o → ue" verbs)

The change takes place with the "o" (or "u") that is directly before the ending.

poder	to be able to	recordar	to remember	u → ue	
dormir	to sleep	volver	to return	jugar	to play

PODER - to be able to (This verb is used to express that you "can" do something.)

yo	**puedo**	nosotros/as	**podemos**
tú	**puedes**		
él, ella, Ud.	**puede**	ellos, ellas, Uds.	**pueden**

Ignacio puede cocinar.
Ignacio can cook.

JUGAR - to play

yo	**juego**	nosotros/as	**jugamos**
tú	**juegas**		
él, ella, Ud.	**juega**	ellos, ellas, Uds.	**juegan**

David juega al fútbol.
David plays soccer.

B. 1. Mi madre _____ (poder) hablar francés.

2. Yo _____ (dormir) ocho horas todas las noches.

3. ¿Tú _____ (recordar) el año 1999?

4. ¿A qué hora _____(volver) a tu casa todos los días?

5. ¿Qúe deportes^{sports} _____ (jugar) ellos?

> **Did you know?**
>
> During the 2008 U.S. elections the phrase, "¡Sí se puede!" was used. It was translated as "Yes, we can!"

Stem changing ("e → i" verbs)

A number of verbs change *e → i*. The change takes place with the "e" that is directly before the ending.

pedir	to ask for	servir	to serve	bendecir	to bless
decir	to say	seguir	to follow, continue	maldecir	to curse

*Remember that they all change EXCEPT the *nosotros* form.

PEDIR - to ask for

yo	**pido**	nosotros/as	**pedimos**
tú	**pides**		
él, ella, Ud.	**pide**	ellos, ellas, Uds.	**piden**

Ellos piden bendiciones.
They ask for blessings.

*Notice that *DECIR* and *SEGUIR* also have an irregular *YO* form.

DECIR - to say (conjugated like *bendecir* - to bless)

yo	**digo**	**bendigo**
tú	**dices**	**bendices**
él, ella, Ud.	**dice**	**bendice**
nosotros	**decimos**	**bendecimos**
ellos, Uds.	**dicen**	**bendicen**

Dios bendice a su pueblo. *God blesses His people.*

SEGUIR - to follow, continue

yo	**sigo**
tú	**sigues**
él, ella, Ud.	**sigue**
nosotros	**seguimos**
ellos/Uds.	**siguen**

Yo sigo a Jesús. *I follow Jesus.*

C. What would you ask for?

1. Tengo hambre - Pido _comida_

2. Tengo sed - Pido_____

3. Tengo frío - Pido_____

D. Translate:

1. Nosotros seguimos a Cristo._____

2. Mi mamá me dice que me ama._____

3. Dios me bendice todos los días. _____

7.6 PREGUNTAR VS. PEDIR

Both *PEDIR* and *PREGUNTAR* mean to **ask**. The difference is: *PEDIR* means to **ask for** something. *PREGUNTAR* is **to ask a question**.

Los estudiantes preguntan mucho en clase. - *Students ask a lot in class.*

Yo te pregunto si conoces al Presidente. - *I ask you if you know the President.*

Ella pide un café. - *She asks for a coffee.*

Ellos me piden un favor. - *They ask me for a favor.*

Fill in the blank with either *PREGUNTAR* or *PEDIR*.

1. En el restaurant ellos _____ papas fritas.

2. Maura me _____ a dónde voy.

3. El niño _____ helado de chocolate.

1. piden 2. pregunta 3. pide

7.7 LOS DEPORTES Y LAS ACTIVIDADES | *SPORTS AND ACTIVITIES*

hacer ejercicio	*to do exercise*	**nadar**	*to swim*
el fútbol	*soccer*	**montar a caballo**	*to ride a horse*
el fútbol americano	*football*	**ir a la playa**	*to go to the beach*
el béisbol	*baseball*	**acampar**	*to go camping*
el básquetbol, baloncesto	*basketball*	**esquiar**	*to ski*
el golf	*golf*	**video juegos**	*video games*
el voleibol	*volleyball*	**me encanta + Infinitive**	*I love to _____*
el tenis	*tennis*		
la cancha	*field, court*		
el campo de deportes	*sports field*	**afuera**	*outside*
el balón, la pelota	*ball*	**adentro**	*inside*
		al aire libre	*outside*
¿Quiere(n) jugar... ?	*Do you (plural) want to play...?*		

Use the verb *jugar* or *practicar* to talk about sports.
Ask someone:

1. ¿Te gusta el fútbol, o el fútbol americano?_____

2. ¿Qué te gusta jugar?_____

3. ¿Qué puedes hacer?_____

4. ¿Qué te encanta[love] hacer?_____

Did you know? Not only is soccer the number one sport in Hispanic countries, but there are more National Associations affiliated with the World Cup than with the United Nations.

A simple way to express the future is to use the verb IR + A + Infinitive.
It is equivalent to the phrase "Going to…" as used in English.
Review the conjugation of *IR - to go*.

IR- to go

yo	**voy**	nosotros/as	**vamos**
tú	**vas**		
él, ella, Ud.	**va**	ellos, ellas, Uds.	**van**

The word "e-mail" is understood and used in most Hispanic countries, even though the correct way to say it is "correo electrónico."

Yo **voy** a estudiar.	*I'm going to study.*
Tú **vas** a estudiar.	*You're going to study.*
Él **va** a estudiar.	*He is going to study.*
Nosotros **vamos** a estudiar.	*We are going to study.*
Ellos **van** a estudiar.	*They are going to study.*

Yo **voy a hablar** con mi amigo.	*I'm going to talk with my friend.*
Nosotros **vamos a leer** la Biblia.	*We are going to read the Bible.*
¿**Va a viajar** usted mañana?	*Are you going to travel tomorrow?*
Ellos **van a ir** a Colorado.	*They are going to go to Colorado.*

A. Fill in the blank with the correct conjugation of *IR*.

1. Yo _____ a escribir un e-mail (correo electrónico).

2. Mis primos _____ a dormir toda la noche.

3. Mi hermano _____ a cantar en el coro de la iglesia.

B. Tell what <u>you</u> are going to do this summer. Use vocabulary from 7.7 or verbs from "Quick list".

Este verano yo voy a _____ y _____....

C. Write a sentence with the words given, telling what each will do in the future.

1. El pastor / predicar / el domingo. *The pastor will preach on Sunday.*

   El pastor va a predicar el domingo.

2. Yo / trabajar / el lunes. *I'm going to work on Monday.*

   _____

3. Alicia / limpiar / su cocina. *Alicia is going to clean her kitchen.*

   _____

Note: The phrase, "Vamos + a + infinitive" can also mean, "*Let's ___.*" Vamos a cantar. → *Let's sing.*

Direct and indirect object pronouns must come before a conjugated verb in the sentence. (5.8)

Yo leo <u>el libro.</u> Yo **lo** leo. *(I read <u>the book.</u> I read **it**.)*
Yo leo <u>la Biblia.</u> Yo **la** leo. *(I read <u>the Bible.</u> I read **it**.)*

When the verb is an **infinitive** or **present participle** (*-ndo*) , the pronoun may be tagged on.

¿Qué hace Dios? —Cambiar**te**.   *What does God do?* —*Change* **you**.
¿Qué estás haciendo en tu habitación?   —Limpiándo**la**.
What are you doing in your room?   —*Cleaning* **it**.

When there is a VERB PHRASE used in a sentence. (This means the predicate or verb of the sentence is composed of more than one verb.) It will consist of a verb that is conjugated, and another one that is likely in the infinitive or the present participle. Here are examples of verb phrases:

  1. Yo **necesito ver.** *(**I need to see.**)*   *2.* Ella **continúa estudiando**. *(She **continues studying.**)*

In #1, *NECESITAR* is conjugated. *VER* is not conjugated, it is in the infinitive form.
In #2, *CONTINUAR* is conjugated, *ESTUDIAR* is not conjugated, it is the present participle.
Remember when 2 verbs are together, only conjugate the first verb, the second one stays in the infinitive or gerund. (The exceptions are the "perfect" compound tenses, one of which is found in 8.7)

When *object pronouns* (me, te, lo, la, le, nos, los, las, les) are used in a sentence with a VERB PHRASE, they can be tagged on the end of the infinitive and gerund verb forms. Verb phrases ending with the infinitive, such as: <u>ir + a + infinitive</u>, can have the pronoun placed before the conjugated verb, or tagged on to the infinitive. It is the speaker's <u>choice</u> and they both have the <u>same meaning</u>.

Example: *"The pastor is going to visit you,"* can be said both of the following ways. (It is a speaker's option.) Both of these sentences mean, ***The pastor will visit you.***

El pastor **te** <u>va a visitar.</u> = El pastor <u>va a visitar**te**.</u>

The same can be done with verb phrases that end with a **present participle** (*-ndo*). The Present Progressive (7.4) has a conjugated verb AND a present participle. *"The professor is teaching me."* Can be said both ways:

El profesor **me** <u>está enseñando.</u> El profesor está <u>enseñándo**me**.</u>*will need accent mark.

The following sentences have verb phrases either with an infinitive or with a present participle. The speaker has a choice to place the pronoun before the conjugated verb, or tag it on to the infinitive or present participle. One of the options is given to you, write the other option.

Meaning: 1. Patricia is speaking to us. 2. The professor is going to help me.

1. Patricia **nos** <u>está hablando.</u>   *Patricia está hablándonos.*

2. El profesor **me** <u>va a ayudar.</u>   _____

Note: See Appendix VI for information on double object pronoun.

las montañas	*mountains*	**el cielo**	*the sky*
el río	*river*	**el sol**	*sun*
el lago	*lake*	**la luna**	*moon*
la tierra	*earth/dirt*	**las estrellas**	*the stars*
arriba (de)	*above/on top (of)*	**debajo de**	*below/underneath*

Voy a dormir afuera debajo de las estrellas.   *I'm going to sleep outside under the stars.*

Reading *(Lectura)*

Hola, mi nombre es Cristina y mañana voy a tener un día espectacular. Mi familia y yo pensamos ir a un parque a pasar el día. Voy a jugar al fútbol y al béisbol, pero no puedo jugar al béisbol muy bien. A medio día vamos a tener un picnic con mucha comida. Vamos a comer sándwiches de pollo, y de jamón y queso, también nos gusta comer mucha fruta.

Después vamos a ir al campo^country a visitar a mis tíos que viven en un rancho y vamos a montar a caballos. Nos gusta mucho hacer actividades al aire libre y divertirnos^have fun juntos^together en familia.

El próximo^next fin de semana vamos a acampar^to camp en las montañas cerca de un río. Quiero nadar en el río y dormir afuera bajo la luna y las estrellas. Me encanta^I love mirar el cielo en la noche, hablar con Dios y pedirle^ask him for sus bendiciones^His blessings.

1. ¿Qué van a jugar en el parque?_____

_____

2. ¿Qué van a comer en el picnic?_____

_____

3. ¿Qué van a hacer en el campo?_____

_____

4. ¿Qué van a hacer el próximo fin de semana? _____

_____

Coritos

ADENTRO, AFUERA, ARRIBA, ABAJO (*I'm inright, outright, upright, downright*)
*(Get faster every time you sing it. Hand motions are in the section of **Children's Songs** in the back)*

Adentro, afuera, arriba, abajo
Qué feliz estoy.

*I'm inright, outright, upright
downright, happy all the time*

Pues Cristo me salvó y mi corazón limpió.

Well, Christ saved me and My heart he cleaned

Adentro, afuera, arriba, abajo,
Qué feliz estoy.

Anonymous translation.

MI DIOS ES TAN GRANDE (*My God is so Great*)

Mi Dios es tan grande,
tan fuerte y potente,
No hay nada que Él no puede hacer.

*My God is so great
so strong and so mighty
There is nothing he cannot do*

Los montes son de Él
los ríos son de Él
las estrellas son de Él también.

*the mountains are His
the rivers are His
the stars are His, too*

Mi Dios es tan grande
tan fuerte y potente
no hay nada que Él no puede hacer.

Machu Picchu, Perú

Anonymous translation.

MI DIOS PUEDE SALVAR (*My God is Mighty to Save*)

Cristo puede mover montes
Solo Dios puede salvar,
mi Dios puede salvar.

*Jesus, He can move the mountain
only God can save*

Por siempre autor de salvación
Jesús la muerte^death venció^conquered,
Él la muerte venció.

*forever author of salvation
Jesus conquered death (past tense)*

Full song is in the Praise and Worship section Hillsong©

Written Work

Write the Spanish Bible verse for this lesson. Repeat it several times, and learn it.

_____

_____

A. Write the room that corresponds: **7.1**

1. Hay un sofá en mi _____

2. Hay una cama en mi _____

3. Hay una mesa y seis sillas en mi _____

4. Hay una estufa y microondas en mi _____

5. Hay un inodoro en mi _____

B. Describe your house. Talk about each of your rooms. Living room, bedroom, bathroom, kitchen… What do you have in them? Add descriptive adjectives. **7.1**

Example: En mi **sala** tengo un sofá de color crema[beige], una alfombra bonita y unas cortinas rojas. En mi cuarto tengo …

_____

_____

_____

_____

_____

_____

_____

_____

_____

_____

_____

C. Conjugate the verb into the Present Progressive: **7.4**

Example: COMER   ESCUCHAR

Yo **estoy comiendo**   _____

Tú **estás comiendo**   _____

Él **está comiendo**   _____

Nosotros **estamos comiendo**   _____

Ellos **están comiendo**   _____

D. Write what you are doing on the days of the week. **7.4**

El domingo: _____ *Estoy cantando en la iglesia.* _____

El lunes: _____

El martes: _____

El miércoles: _____

El jueves: _____

El viernes: _____

El sábado: _____

E. TABLE TO CONJUGATE. Write the present tense conjugations that are missing. e → ie **7.5**
Write the meaning to the left of the verb.

Verb	yo	tú	él, ella, Ud.	nosotros	ellos, Uds.
querer			quiere		
cerrar		cierras			cierran
sentir	siento		siente		
pensar				pensamos	
perder	pierdo				pierden
entender				entendemos	
venir	vengo				vienen

F. TABLE TO CONJUGATE. Write the present tense conjugations that are missing. e → i. **7.5**
Write the meaning to the left of the verb.

Verb	yo	tú	él, ella, Ud.	nosotros	ellos, Uds.
pedir		pides			
servir	sirvo				sirven
seguir				seguimos	
decir	digo		dicen		
bendecir		bendices			bendicen

G. TABLE TO CONJUGATE. Write the present tense conjugations that are missing. o → ue. **7.5**
Write the meaning to the left of the verb.

Verb	yo	tú	él, ella, Ud.	nosotros	ellos, Uds.
dormir	duermo		duerme		duermen
poder				podemos	
jugar		juegas			
recordar	recuerdo			recordamos	
volver			vuelve		vuelven

H. Fill in the blank with the correct form of the verb in parenthesis. **7.5**

1. "Lo _____ (sentir)" means *"I'm sorry."*

2. ¿A qué hora _____ (venir) Esteban al colegio?

3. ¿Tú _____ (entender) la lección de español?

4. ¿Uds. _____ (seguir) los mandamientos^commands de Cristo?

5. Yo no _____ (recordar) su nombre.

6. Mis padres _____ (dormir) 8 horas cada noche.

7. Nosotros _____ (jugar) el baloncesto todas las tardes.

8. Ellos _____ (volver) de sus vacaciones el lunes.

I. Write from Vocabulary 7.7

1. ¿Qué deportes te gustan? _____

2. ¿Qué actividades te gusta hacer? _____

J. Informal future with *IR + A +* Infinitive. Fill in the blank with the conjugation of *IR.* Then translate each sentence. **7.8**

1. El señor ____*va*____ a viajar a Monterrey. *The man is going to travel to Monterrey.*

2. Yo no _____ a visitar a Honduras. _____

3. ¿Cuándo _____ a trabajar tú? _____

4. Nosotros _____ a cantar en el coro. _____

5. ¿Ustedes _____ a traer a sus amigos a la iglesia? _____

K. In the first sentence, the pronoun is tagged on to the infinitive. Rewrite the sentence with the pronoun <u>before</u> the conjugated verb, (*IR*). **7.9**

1. Yo <u>voy a estudiar</u> los verbos. → Voy a estudiarlos. ____*Los voy a estudiar.*____

2. Nosotros <u>vamos a visitar</u> a la abuela. → Vamos a visitarla. _____

3. Tú <u>vas a hacer</u> la cama hoy. → Vas a hacerla. _____

4. Mariana <u>va a limpiar</u> su cuarto. → Mariana va a limpiarlo. _____

5. Los católicos <u>van a ver</u> al Papa[Pope]. → Los católicos van a verlo. _____

6. Uds. <u>van a preparar</u> la clase. → Uds. van a prepararlo. _____

L. Salmo 101

[1]"Quiero alabar el amor y la justicia;
quiero, Señor, cantarte himnos;
[2] quiero vivir con rectitud."

Look up the English equivalent:

1. alabar _____

2. justicia _____

3. quiero cantarte himnos _____

_____

4. quiero vivir con rectitud _____

_____

L. Take note of these special words/verbs that can sometimes cause confusion.

1. **Trabajo** (I work) vs. **el trabajo** (the work/job/task)

   Yo <u>trabajo</u> en el hospital.   *I work in the hospital.*

   Quiero <u>un trabajo</u>.   *I want a job.*

2. **Gratis** (free from cost) vs. **libre** (free from bondage)

   La comida es <u>gratis</u>.   *The food is free.*

   Somos <u>libres</u> en Cristo.   *We are free in Christ.*

3. **Estar embarazada** (to be pregnant) vs. **tener vergüenza** (to be embarassed)

   Lucía <u>está embarazada.</u>   *Lucía is pregnant.*

   Tengo mucha <u>vergüenza</u>.   *I'm very embarassed.*

4. **Tiempo** (time in general) vs. **vez** (time in a series)

   El señor tiene mucho <u>tiempo</u> porque no trabaja.   *The man has a lot of time because he doesn't work.*

   Leo mi Biblia muchas <u>veces</u> en la semana.   *I read my Bible many times in the week.*

5. **Tomar** (to take / drink) vs. **llevar** (to take something with you / carry / wear)

   <u>Tomo</u> el autobús. / Me gusta <u>tomar</u> agua.   *I take the bus. / I like to drink water.*

   Mañana <u>llevo</u> a mi papá al médico.   *Tomorrow I take my dad to the doctor.*

6. **Personas** (people you can count) vs. **gente** (people you can't count)

   Hay 5 <u>personas</u> en el grupo.   *There are 5 people in the group.*

   Hay mucha <u>gente</u> en la iglesia.   *There are many people in the church.*

Lesson 8
The Body &
Medical Missions

Body Vocabulary / It Hurts (*DOLER* with Indirect Object Pronoun) /
Extended Medical Vocabulary / Reflexive Verbs and Daily Routines / Past
Participles / Reading of Managua Earthquake / Present Perfect

Lección 8 Tu palabra es una lámpara a mis pies y una luz en mi camino. Salmos 119:105
Your word is a lamp to my feet and a light to my path. Psalm 119:105

8.1 EL CUERPO | *THE BODY*

el pelo	hair	los hombros	shoulders	el dedo del pie	toe
la cabeza	head	el brazo	arm	el corazón	heart
la cara	face	la mano	hand	la garganta	throat
los ojos	eyes	el dedo	finger	los pulmones	lungs
las orejas	ears	la espalda	back	la sangre	blood
los oídos	inner ears	el estómago	stomach	el hueso	bone
la nariz	nose	la pierna	leg	los dientes	teeth
la boca	mouth	el pie	foot	la muela	molar

MÁS FRASES

doler	to hurt, to be painful	el dolor	pain
Me duele	it hurts (me)	Tengo dolor.	I have pain.
Me duelen	they hurt (me)	el dolor de cabeza	headache
¿Qué te duele?	What hurts you?	el dolor de estómago	stomach-ache
¿Qué le duele?	What hurts?(formal)	el/la doctor/a, médico/a	doctor
¿Cómo te sientes?	How do you feel?	el/la enfermero/a	nurse
¿Cómo se siente?	How do you feel? (formal)	el hospital, la clínica	hospital, clinic

8.2 THE VERB DOLER | *"IT HURTS!"*

DOLER means "to hurt" or "to be painful." It is used with the indirect object pronouns, like the verb *GUSTAR.* (4.3) In Spanish you say "something is painful to me." The verb uses the indirect object pronouns to express "to whom" something is painful. If more than one thing hurts, the verb is used in the plural form (-n). **Note:** Doler is a stem-changing *o → ue* verb.

"me duele"= it hurts me "me duelen" = *they hurt me.*

Examples: Me **duele** la cabeza.* = *My head hurts.*
Me **duelen** los pies.* = *My feet hurt.*

*You do not need the possessive article "my" since it is understood that it hurts "you." Just use the article.

Here is the verb with the pronouns:

A Roberto le duele la cabeza.
Roberto tiene dolor de cabeza.

me duele	hurts me
te duele	hurts you
le duele	hurts him / her / you -formal
nos duele	hurts us
les duele	hurts them / you -plural

Ask: ¿Qué te duele? (*What hurts you?*) Or ¿Qué te pasa? (*What's the matter with you?*)

Then answer with the vocabulary words:

1. Me **duele** _____ (head), (throat), (stomach), (back)

2. Me **duelen** _____ (feet), (legs), (fingers), (hands), (eyes)

More parts of the body

la frente	forehead	el muslo	thigh	el cerebro	brain
la mejilla	cheek	la rodilla	knee	el hígado	liver
los labios	lips	el tobillo	ankle	la vesícula	gall bladder
el cuello	neck	el pecho	chest	los riñones	kidneys
el codo	elbow	las uñas	nails	la vejiga	bladder
la muñeca	wrist	la piel	skin	el bazo	spleen
la cintura	waist	los huesos	bones	los músculos	muscles
la cadera	hip	el cráneo	the skull	las venas	veins

Other medical vocabulary

la emergencia	emergency	las muletas	crutches
sala de emergencia	emergency room	la inflamación	inflamation
la clínica	the clinic	la fractura	fracture
el accidente	accident	la radiografía	x-ray
doctor/a, médico/a	doctor	roto/a, quebrado/a	broken
pediatra/psiquiatra	pediatrician/psychiatrist	el yeso	cast
la salud	health	la medicina	medicine
la herida	wound	la receta médica	precription
la inyección	injection	pedir turno	to ask for an appointment
el antibiótico	antibiotic	la farmacia, botica	pharmacy
tomar el pulso	take your pulse	el farmacéutico, boticario	pharmacist
la presión sanguínea	blood pressure	la pastilla, píldora	pill

Symptoms

Me siento mal.	I feel bad.
Estoy enfermo/a.	I am sick.
¿Qué tiene?	What do you have?
la tos	cough
la fiebre	fever
desmayarse	to faint
la congestión	congestion
la inflamación	inflammation
el dolor de cabeza	headache
la náusea	nausea
la presión alta	high (blood) pressure
un catarro, resfrío	a cold
la gripe/gripa	flu

Él tiene mucha tos y fiebre.

Questions (in *usted* form)

¿Cómo se siente? / ¿Qué tiene?	How do you feel? / What do you have?
¿Dónde le duele?	Where does it hurt?
¿Cuánto le duele?	How much does it hurt?
¿Por cuánto tiempo le ha dolido?	For how long has it hurt?
¿Qué medicina ha tomado?	What medicine have you taken?
¿Le pica?	Does it itch?

Role play a visit to the doctor; name illness and symptoms.

8.4 REFLEXIVE VERBS AND DAILY ROUTINES

A reflexive verb means the same person doing the action is receiving the action.
These verbs can be compared to the English use of "myself," "yourself," and others.
In Spanish this is formed by using a pronoun called the REFLEXIVE PRONOUN.

The reflexive pronouns are as follows:

Reflexive Pronouns	Singular	Plural
1st person (yo) / (nosotros)	me	nos
2nd person familiar (tú)	te	
3rd person (él/ella/Ud.) & (Uds.)	se	se

ME, *TE*, and *NOS* are the same as the direct and indirect object pronouns.
The 3rd person singular and plural is *SE*. (Not "le" as in the indirect object pronouns.)
"Se" can go with several different subjects so you need to clarify the subject if it is not clear.
Any verb can become a reflexive verb if it makes sense. Make the verb reflexive by simply adding the corresponding reflexive pronoun to it.
The reflexive pronoun (like the object pronouns) precedes the conjugated verb.
To make negative, place "no" before the reflexive pronoun.

For example: Yo **veo.** = *I see.*   Tú **te ves.** = *You see yourself.*
                         Yo **me veo.** = *I see myself.*   Ella no **se ve.** = *She doesn't see herself.*

To be reflexive, the conjugation <u>must agree</u> with the pronoun, or it will not be reflexive.
The reflexive pronoun matches in the same person as the one who is doing the action of the verb.

Yo **me** veo. (I see **myself.**) The "action" is "reflected" back to that same person. What makes the verb reflexive is the "reflexive pronoun" that accompanies it.

When a verb is REFLEXIVE, the infinitive form will have the reflexive pronoun *SE* tagged on to the end.

LAVAR = *to wash*   LAVARSE = *to wash oneself.*
Yo **lavo** el carro. *I wash the car.*   vs.   Yo **me lavo** la cara. *I wash (on myself) my face.*

LAVARSE is conjugated as follows:

yo	me lavo	nosotros/as	nos lavamos
tú	te lavas		
él, ella, Ud.	se lava	ellos, ellas, Uds.	se lavan

Me lavo las manos. = *I wash (on myself) my hands. (It is not necessary to say "my hands" in Spanish.)*

Here is the conjugation of the reflexive verb **BAÑARSE**. (*To bathe oneself.*)
It is also a "regular" verb like *lavarse,* and follows the pattern of a regular -ar verb.

yo	me baño	nosotros/as	nos bañamos
tú	te bañas		
él, ella, Ud.	se baña	ellos, ellas, Uds.	se bañan

Fill in the blank with the correct reflexive pronoun:

1. Yo _____me_____ baño a las 7:00 de la mañana.   2. Ernesto _____ baña en la noche.

3. Nosotros _____ lavamos las manos.   4. Ellos _____ lavan el pelo con champú.

Many of the daily routines are expressed by reflexive verbs. Here are the most common reflexive verbs:

Reflexive verbs - the subject and the direct object are the same person (oneself)

despertarse (e → ie)	to wake (oneself) up	ponerse	to put on (clothes)
levantarse	to get (oneself) up	quitarse	to take off (clothes)
bañarse	to bathe (oneself)	acostarse (o → ue)	to go to bed, to lie down
lavarse	to wash (oneself)	dormirse (o → ue)	to fall asleep
ducharse	to shower (oneself)	sentirse	to feel (feelings)
irse	to leave (take yourself away)	llamarse	to call oneself (name)

The reason "to wake up" is a reflexive verb is because you can wake someone else up… (yo despierto a mis hijos) , or you can wake up (yo me despierto).

Here is the conjugation of the reflexive verb, *DESPERTARSE* (e → ie) - to wake up.

yo	**me despierto**	nosotros/as	**nos despertamos**
tú	**te despiertas**		
él, ella, Ud.	**se despierta**	ellos, ellas, Uds.	**se despiertan**

A. Fill in the blank with the correct reflexive pronoun. Then write the translation.

1. Ellos ___*se*___ levantan a las 8:00 de la mañana. _*They get up at 8:00 a.m.*_

2. Tú _____ acuestas a las 11:00 de la noche. _____

3. Mario _____ pone el sombrero. _____

4. Yo _____ lavo el pelo todas[all / every] las mañanas. _____

5. Nosotros _____ quitamos los zapatos. _____

6. Ella _____ llama Maribel. _____

B. Luisa and her daily routine:
(1) Todos los días, Luisa **se despierta** a las 6:30 de la mañana. *(2)* **Se levanta** y **se baña** a las 7:00.
(3) Siempre **se lava** el pelo. *(4)* Ella **se pone la** ropa y va a la cocina para desayunar.
(5) Después[afterwards] **se va** al trabajo. *(6)* En la noche, ella **se quita** la ropa y **se pone** la pijama.
(7) Mira un poco de televisión y **se acuesta** a las 10:30 de la noche y **se duerme**.

C. Using above paragraph (the numbered sentences), write about your daily routine using the same verbs:

1. Todos los días, yo ___*me despierto*___ a las _____ de la mañana.

2. _*me*_ _*levanto*_ y _____ _____ a las _____.

3. Siempre _____ _____ el pelo.

4. Yo _____ _____la ropa y voy a la cocina para desayunar.

5. Después _____ _____ al trabajo.

6. En la noche, yo _____ _____la ropa y _____ _____ la pijama.

7. Miro un poco de televisión y _____ _____a las _____de la noche _____ _____.

8.5 LOS PARTICIPIOS | *PAST PARTICIPLES*

Every verb has a past participle. It's important to know the past participle because it has important functions in a language.

First, let's identify the past participle and its functions in English.
The past participle for "**break**" is "**broken**."
You can say, "I have **broken** it," (used as a verb)
You can also say, "It is **broken**." (used as an adjective).

Learn the Spanish past participles. <u>Important:</u> Every verb has only 1 past participle.

For -*ar* verbs: drop the ending and add -**ado.**
For -*er* and -*ir* verbs: drop ending and add -**ido.**

hablar	**hablado** (*spoken*)	cerrar	**cerrado** (*closed*)	vender	**vendido** (*sold*)
lavar	**lavado** (*washed*)	unir	**unido** (*united*)	perdonar	**perdonado** (*forgiven*)
terminar	**terminado** (*finished*)	comer	**comido** (*eaten*)	fracturar	**fracturado** (*fractured*)

A. Write the past participle of these regular verbs.

1. lavar _____*lavado*_____ (*washed*)

2. vender _____ (*sold*)

3. dormir _____ (*asleep*)

4. preparar _____ (*prepared*)

5. amar _____ (*loved/beloved*)

6. servir _____ (*served*)

> **Did you know?**
>
> Many Hispanics will go to "healers" that are called *curanderos* when doctors are not available or affordable.

Here are some irregular past participles. Learn them by repetition.

hacer	**hecho** (*done*)	ver	**visto** (*seen*)	leer	**leído** (*read*)
escribir	**escrito** (*written*)	volver	**vuelto** (*returned*)	decir	**dicho** (*said*)
romper	**roto** (*broken, torn*)	abrir	**abierto** (*open*)	morir	**muerto** (*dead*)

Past participles can be used as adjectives. You must make them agree with the noun the same as all adjectives. One of the first past participles you learned was *CANSADO* from the verb *CANSAR* which means *to get tired*.

I am tired. Yo estoy **cansado.**   *She is tired.* Ella está **cansada.**
<u>Cansado</u> must agree in gender and number. Ellos están **cansados.**

Los pantalones están <u>lavados.</u>	*The pants are <u>washed</u>.*
La tarea está <u>terminada.</u>	*The homework is <u>finished</u>.*
El libro está <u>abierto.</u>	*The book is <u>open</u>.*
La iglesia está <u>unida.</u>	*The church is <u>united</u>.*
Los profesores están <u>preparados.</u>	*The profesors are <u>prepared</u>* (*ready*).

Note: The verb "*estar*" is used with the past participle to express a condition or state.

>
> **Did you know?**
>
> According to encyclopedia.com, 40% of families in Latin America have insufficient income for essential needs.

B. Fill in the blank with the correct form of the past participle, using the verb in parenthesis. (Some are irregular.)

1. Las enchiladas están_____*servidas*_____ (servir)
The enchiladas are served.

2. La casa está _____*vendida*_____(vender)
The house is sold.

3. Los vestidos están _____(hacer)
The dresses are made.

4. Ella es mi esposa _____ (amar)
She is my beloved wife.

5. La farmacia está _____ (cerrar)
The pharmacy is closed.

6. Su brazo está _____ (fracturar)
His/ Her arm is fractured.

7. El libro está _____(terminar)
The book is finished.

8. El gato está _____ (morir)
The cat is dead.

9. La clínica está _____(abrir)
The clinic is open.

10. Por la sangre de Cristo estamos _____ (perdonar)
By the blood of Christ we are forgiven.

Reading (*Lectura*)

El 23 de diciembre de 1972 a medianoche, un terremoto^earthquake destruyó^destroyed Managua, la capital de Nicaragua. Todos los edificios cayeron^fell, incluso^including hospitales, bancos y escuelas. Cinco mil (5.000) personas murieron,^died veinte mil (20.000) personas fueron heridas^were injured y 250.000 quedaron^were left sin casa, electricidad ni agua.

Photo by Jack Matlick.

Did you know? In less than 7 years, Nicaragua suffered a devastating earthquake that destroyed its capital city, Managua **and** went through a horrific Civil War. They are now the poorest Hispanic country. Yet, interestingly, Managua is the safest Capital City in Central America.

Once you have learned the past participles, you can use them to say you "have done" something. On a medical mission trip this verb tense can be used to know what the patient "has done" or what medicine they "have taken." The present perfect can also be used to talk about the past. In fact, some areas of Spain use the Present Perfect instead of the simple past.

To form the present perfect: use the present tense of the auxiliary verb **HABER** + **past participle**. The auxiliary verb **HABER** is like the English auxiliary **HAVE**, as in "I **have** gone." This is the present tense conjugation of **haber**:

yo	**he**	nosotros/as	**hemos**
tú	**has**		
él, ella, Ud.	**ha**	ellos, ellas, Uds.	**han**

Yo <u>he</u> tomado dos aspirinas.
I <u>have</u> taken two aspirins.

The *present perfect* of the verb *HABLAR* is as follows: (auxiliary verb + past participle)

yo **he hablado**	(*I **have spoken***)	nosotros **hemos hablado**	(*we **have spoken***)
tú **has hablado**	(*you **have spoken***)		
él **ha hablado**	(*he **has spoken***)	ellos **han hablado**	(*they **have spoken***)

A. Fill in the blank with the correct form of the auxiliary verb.
1. La profesora _____ enseñado la clase. *2.* Nosotros _____ estudiado la lección.

Here is the verb *COMER* in the <u>present perfect</u>. (Can you conjugate the verb VIVIR in the pres. perf.?)

yo **he comido**	(*I **have eaten***)	nosotros **hemos comido**	(*we **have eaten***)
tú **has comido**	(*you **have eaten***)		
él **ha comido**	(*he **has eaten***)	ellos **han comido**	(*they **have eaten***)

A common way to use the present perfect is to make questions.

¿Has hablado con el pastor? ***Have you** spoken with the pastor?* —Sí, **he hablado** con él.

Note: All pronouns must be placed before the auxiliary verb.

<u>¿Has visto</u> al pastor? *<u>Have you seen</u> the pastor?* —Sí, **lo** he visto. *Yes, <u>I have seen</u> **him**.*

A word used often with the present perfect tense is *YA*, it means **ALREADY**.
Daniel **ya** <u>ha terminado</u> el proyecto. *Daniel **already** <u>has finished</u> the project.*

B. Fill in the blank with the correct form of the auxiliary verb *HABER*. Then tell someone what you have done today.

1. ¿ ____*Has*____ leído la Biblia?
Have you (informal) read the Bible?

2. ¿Qué ____*ha*____ hecho Dios por ti?
What has God done for you?

3. ¿Ya _____ lavado la ropa?
Have they already washed the clothes?

4. ¿Ya _____ ido al doctor tu papá?
Has your father already gone to the doctor?

5. ¿ _____ recibido Ud. la salvación eterna?
Have you (formal) received eternal salvation?

6. ¿ _____ hecho ella el pastel?
Has she made the cake?

7. ¿ _____ tomado Ud. la medicina?
Have you (formal) taken the medicine?

8. ¿Te _____ dolido por mucho tiempo?
Has it hurt you (informal) for very long?

Cultural Note

DANILO MONTERO

Danilo Montero is from Costa Rica. He pastors the Hispanic congregation of *Lakewood Church* in Houston, Texas. Danilo is well known throughout Latin America and many of his songs can be heard in churches. One of his best known praise and worship songs is called *"Eres Todopoderoso"* which means, *"You are Almighty,"* from which many versions have been recorded by other artists, including Portuguese and Korean translations.

ERES TODOPODEROSO *(You are almighty)*

La única razón de mi adoración,	*The only reason for my adoration*
Eres Tú mi Jesús.	*Is you my Jesus*
Mi único motivo para vivir,	*My only motive to live*
Eres Tú mi Señor.	*Is you my Lord*
La única verdad está en ti.	*The only truth is in You*
Eres mi luz y mi salvación.	*You're my light and Salvation*
Mi único amor eres Tú Señor,	*My only love is you Lord*
Y por siempre, te alabaré.	*And forever I will praise you*
Eres todopoderoso,	*You are all powerful*
Eres grande y majestuoso,	*You are great and majestic*
Eres fuerte, invencible,	*You are strong and invincible*
Y no hay nadie como Tú.	*And there is no one like you*

Words and Music: Juan Salinas.

Coritos

YO TE ALABO DE CORAZÓN *(I will praise you with my heart)*

Yo te alabo de corazón	*I praise you with my heart*
Yo te alabo con mi voz.	*I praise you with my voice*
Y si me falta la voz	*and if I don't have my voice*
Yo te alabo con las manos.	*I praise you with my hands (clap hands)*
Y si me faltan las manos	*and if I don't have my hands*
Yo te alabo con los pies.	*I praise you with my feet (stomp feet)*
Y se me faltan los pies	*and if I don't have my feet*
Yo te alabo con el alma.	*I praise you with my soul (put hand over heart)*
Y si me falta el alma	*and if I don't have my soul*
Es que ya me fui con Él	*it's because I've left with Him (point up)*
Es que ya me fui con Él.	

Traditional song from latinoamerican folklore

Written Work

Write the Spanish Bible verse for this lesson. Repeat it several times, and learn it.

_____

_____

A. *DOLER*

Write the correct indirect object pronoun with the verb *DOLER*. **8.2**

1. A Manuel ____*le*____ duele la cabeza.

2. A ti _____ duele el estómago.

3. A Hebe _____ duelen los pies.

4. A mí _____ duele la espalda.

5. A los trabajadores _____ duelen los brazos.

6. A nosotros _____ duelen las manos.

B. WRITE sentences with blanks for reflexive pronouns. **8.4**

1. Mi hermana __*se despierta*_____ (despertarse) temprano.

2. Yo _____ (ponerse) unos pantalones nuevos.

3. Nosotros _____ (irse) a casa.

4. Tú _____ (levantarse) a las 6:00 de la mañana.

5. Marisol _____ (bañarse) temprano.^early

6. Ustedes _____ (dormirse) a las 11:00.

7. Gerardo y Guillermo _____ (acostarse) tarde.^late

8. Usted _____ (lavarse) el pelo.

9. Yo _____ (irse).

10. Carlos _____ (quitarse) el uniforme.

C. Fill in the blank with the correct past participle, make sure you make it agree with the noun it modifies. **8.5**

1. La comida está _____*preparada*_____ (preparar)

The food is <u>prepared</u>.

2. Los niños están _____ (dormir)

The children are <u>asleep</u>.

3. El trabajo está _____ (terminar)

The work is <u>finished</u>.

4. Las preguntas están_____ (contestar)

The questions are <u>answered.</u>

D. Fill in the blank with the correct form of *HABER* for what each person "has done." Remember that the past participle here is being used as a verb, not an adjective, so you do not have to make it agree, this is why it is in its main form.
("*ya*" means "already.")

After you write the correct form of *HABER*, translate the sentence. **8.6**

1. ¿ ____*Has*____ viajado tú a España?

_____

2. David _____ preparado una buena lección bíblica.

_____

3. Cristina _____ aceptado al Señor como su Salvador.

_____

4. El profesor _____ enseñado la clase.

_____

5. Los niños ya se _____ acostado.

_____

6. ¿Tú _____ visto un ángel?

_____

7. Yo _____ vuelto del viaje misionero.

_____

E. The Present Perfect. Answering questions. **8.6**
The information has been given in the question—you may not need to repeat the direct object if it is in the answer, thus using an object pronoun.

¿Has visto **el carro**? - *Have you seen **the car**?*
Sí, **lo** he visto. - *Yes, I have seen **it**.*

¿Has tomado **la medicina**? *Have you taken the medicine?*
Sí, **la** he tomado. - *Yes, I have taken it.*

Answer these questions, make sure you use the direct object pronoun.

1. ¿Has leído <u>la Biblia</u>? _____*Sí, la he leído.*_____

2. ¿Has estudiado <u>la lección</u>? _____

3. ¿Has bebido <u>el café</u>? _____

4. ¿Han visto a <u>los niños</u>? _____

5. ¿Hemos comprado <u>la comida</u>? _____

6. ¿María ha preparado <u>los tamales</u>? _____

F. Translate this Hymn chorus:

Seguir – *to follow*
Atrás - *back*

He decidido seguir a Cristo,
No vuelvo atrás, no vuelvo atrás.

_____

_____

_____

Lesson 9
City & Transportation

City, Transportation, Hotel, Airport and Bank Vocabulary / Prepositions of Space and Location / Commands and Directions / Inviting Someone to an Event / Ud. and Uds. Commands / Pronouns Tagged on to Affirmative Commands/ Negative Commands

Guatemala

Lección 9
Santo, Santo, Santo es Jehová; toda la tierra está llena de su gloria. Isaías 6:3

Holy, holy, holy is Jehova; all the earth is full of his glory. Isaiah 6:3

9.1 LA CIUDAD Y EL PUEBLO | *THE CITY AND TOWN*

la iglesia/catedral	church/cathedral	el mercado	market
la escuela, el colegio	school	el supermercado	supermarket
la universidad	university	el centro comercial	mall or group of stores
la biblioteca	library	el cine	the movie theatre
el orfanatorio, orfanato	orphanage	la panadería	bread store, bakery
		la frutería	fruit store
el hogar de niños	children's home	la verdulería	vegetable store
la plaza	town square	la carnicería	meat store
el cibercafé	cybercafe	la zapatería	shoe store
el parque	park	la gasolinera, estación de servicio	gas station
la tienda	store		
cerca/lejos	close/far	la vecindad, el barrio	neighborhood
Quiero invitarle(s)	I would like to invite you (pl.)	la pulpería	small neighborhood store (C. Amer)
		el kiosco	small neighborhood store (S. Amer)

9.2 EL TRANSPORTE | *TRANSPORTATION*

el carro, coche, auto	car	el avión	plane
la moto	motorcycle	el barco	ship
la camioneta	(pick-up) truck	la lancha, el bote	boat
el camión	(big) truck	el crucero	cruise (ship)
el bus, autobús	bus	el subterráneo, metro	subway
el taxi	taxi	la calle	street
el tren	train	la carretera, autopista	highway
la bicicleta	bicycle	el mapa, plano	map

Un mototaxi

"¿Dónde se compra…? Where does one buy…?"

1. ¿Dónde se compra ropa? _En la tienda de ropa._

2. ¿Dónde se compra carne? _____

3. ¿Dónde se compra pan? _____

4. ¿Dónde se compran fruta y verduras (vegetales)? _____

5. ¿Dónde cuidan^take care a niños? _____

6. ¿Qué haces en una biblioteca? _Leo libros._

7. ¿Qué haces en un parque? _____

8. ¿Qué haces en el cine? _____

9. ¿Qué haces en un supermercado? _____

10. ¿Qué haces en una iglesia? _____

11. ¿Cómo te gusta viajar? _____ ¿Cómo no te gusta viajar? _____

9.3 EN EL HOTEL | *AT THE HOTEL*

la reservación	*reservation*	el jabón	*soap*
el vestíbulo	*lobby*	el papel higiénico	*toilet paper*
el cuarto/habitación	*room*	el camarero, la camarera	*the maid*
la cama	*bed*	el empleado	*the employee (man, clerk)*
las sábanas	*sheets*	la empleada	*the employee (woman, maid)*
las toallas	*towels*	el servicio de cuarto	*room service*
la almohada	*pillow*	la llave	*key*

Necesito una habitación para una noche. *I need a room for one night.*

9.4 EN EL AEROPUERTO | *AT THE AIRPORT*

¿Hay un retraso?	*Is there a delay?*
¿Dónde está mi equipaje?	*Where is my luggage?*
Necesito un boleto (pasaje) a…	*I need a ticket to…*
la aerolínea	*airline*
el equipaje	*luggage*
la maleta, la valija	*suitcase*
la maleta de mano	*carry on baggage*
el boleto	*the ticket*
ida y vuelta	*round trip*
la sección de no fumar	*no smoking section*
el asiento	*seat*
la ventana	*window*
el pasillo	*aisle*
la puerta de embarque	*boarding gate*
la salida	*the exit*

Did you know?

Hispanic countries have great public transportation systems. Mexico, Colombia, Argentina, Peru, Chile, Venezuela and Spain have subways.

9.5 EN EL BANCO | *AT THE BANK*

¿A cuánto está el cambio de moneda?	*What is the exchange rate?*
¿A qué hora abre/cierra el banco?	*At what time does the bank open/close?*
el cambio de moneda/cambio monetario	*currency change*
el cajero automático	*ATM*
el cambio	*change*
los billetes/las monedas	*bills/coins*
el dinero efectivo	*cash*
la cuenta	*account*
los cheques (de viajeros)	*(travelers') checks*
la tarjeta de crédito	*credit card*
la tarjeta de débito	*debit card*

Did you know?

Ecuador, Panama and El Salvador use the U.S. dollar as their official currency.

1. ¿Cuando estás de vacaciones, necesitas hacer reservación de hotel? _____
2. ¿Qué te gusta en un hotel? _____
3. ¿Cuál aerolínea te gusta más? _____
4. ¿Compras boletos de ida y vuelta? _____
5. ¿Prefieres usar cheque, tarjeta de crédito o efectivo? _____

9.6 PREPOSITIONS OF LOCATION

cerca de	*close to*		**detrás de**	*behind*
lejos de	*far from*		**encima de**	*on top of, on*
enfrente de	*in front of*		**debajo de**	*underneath of*
al lado de	*next to, beside*			
junto a	*next to*		**aquí/allí**	*here/there*
entre	*in between*		**acá/allá**	*around here/around there*

Places and Directions

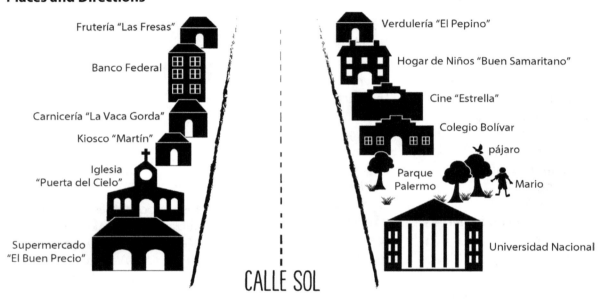

1. ¿Dónde está la iglesia? *Entre el supermercado y el kiosco.*

2. ¿Dónde está el parque? _____

3. ¿Dónde está el hogar de niños? _____

4. ¿Dónde está el cine? _____

5. ¿Dónde está la universidad? _____

6. ¿Qué está al lado de la frutería? _____

7. ¿Dónde está el colegio? _____

8. ¿El supermercado está lejos o cerca de la verdulería? _____

9. ¿Dónde está el pájaro? _____

10. ¿Dónde está Mario? _____

9.7 COMMANDS FOR DIRECTIONS

doble	turn	siga derecho/recto	continue straight	al norte	to the north
pase	pass	la calle	the street	al sur	to the south
vaya	go	a la derecha	to the right	al este	to the east
salga de	go out from, leave	a la izquierda	to the left	al oeste	to the west
cruce	cross	a la esquina	to the corner		

Ask how to get to different places from your home (the star.)

Ask: —¿Cómo llego a <u>la zapatería</u>? *(How do I get to the shoe store?)*

Answer: —Para llegar a <u>la zapatería</u>, salga de la casa, doble a la izquierda y cruce la Calle 2, pase la frutería. La zapatería está a la derecha.

Now you: —¿Cómo llegamos al/a la _____?

—Para llegar^{to get to} al/a la _____ salga de la casa, doble a la derecha/izquierda y . . .

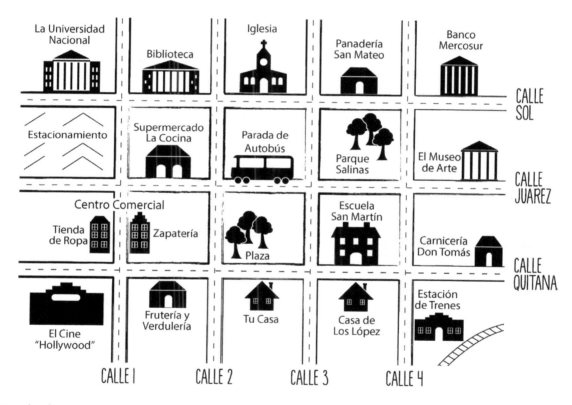

How to invite someone to an event:

1. I want (I would like) to invite you to a special event/program/presentation/service.
Quiero (Me gustaría) invitarle(s) a un evento/programa/presentación/servicio (culto) especial.

2. There's going to be games/ music /food /candy /puppets /balloons /a message.
Va a haber juegos /música /comida /caramelos/ títeres /globos /un mensaje.

3. It's going to be on _____day_____ at _____time_____ at the church / park / plaza.
Va a ser el _____ a la(s) _____ en la iglesia / el parque / la plaza.

4. It's going to be a lot of fun/a blessing. - **Va a ser muy divertido/ una bendición.**

Commands are used to tell someone what to do and are addressed to a person or persons. Simply telling someone, "Have a good day" is a command. Commands in English are a very easy form: *Go, Be, Read, Look*. In Spanish, the commands can be in the *tú, usted or ustedes*, and even the *vos* and *vosotros* form, each with its own ending. The *tú* form is a common form in most of the Latin American countries. But if you want to tell someone what to do and you don't know them well, you should use the *usted* form to show respect.

We will learn the commands in the **Ud.** and **Uds.** forms since these can be used in any situation and in any country.

The *Ud.* command is formed by using the present indicative tense in the *YO* form. This gives you the stem, but the ending will change.

–*ar* verbs, will end with an –*e*.   **–*er* and –*ir* verbs will end with –*a*.**

For example: *VENIR* – to come.
Present Indicative tense for the *yo* form is *VENGO*. (6.7) To make the command form, drop the *–o* and give it the appropriate ending. Since it is an *–ir* verb, the ending will be –*a*.

VENGA aquí.   *Come here.*
Venga is the command in the *Ud.* form for the verb *venir*.

Once you have the *Ud.* command form, all you have to do is add an *–n* to it and you have the *Uds.* form. *VENGAN aquí.* – *(All of you) come here.*

Look at the charts which shows the *Ud.* and *Uds.* command forms.
Remember: All the *Ud.* commands end in *-a* or *-e*.

VERBS THAT ARE REGULAR:

INFINITIVE	PRES. IND. YO	UD. COMMAND	UDS. COMMAND
HABLAR[speak]	HABLO	**HABLE**	**HABLEN**
COMER[eat]	COMO	**COMA**	**COMAN**
VIVIR[vivir]	VIVO	**VIVA**	**VIVAN**
ESTUDIAR[study]	ESTUDIO	**ESTUDIE**	**ESTUDIEN**
LEER[read]	LEO	**LEA**	**LEAN**
ORAR[pray]	ORO	**ORE**	**OREN**
CANTAR[sing]	CANTO	**CANTE**	**CANTEN**
RECIBIR[receive]	RECIBO	**RECIBA**	**RECIBAN**
DOBLAR[turn]	DOBLO	**DOBLE**	**DOBLEN**

1. Tell someone what to do to get closer to God:

   Hable con Dios, Lea la Biblia.

2. Tell someone what to do to learn Spanish: _____

3. Tell someone what to do to be healthy: _____

VERBS IRREGULAR IN THE "YO" FORM

INFINITIVE	PRESENT INDICATIVE *YO*	UD. COMMAND	UDS. COMMAND
SALIR^{go out} VER^{see} HACER^{do or make} TRADUCIR^{translate} SEGUIR^{continue/follow}	SALGO VEO HAGO TRADUZCO SIGO	**SALGA** **VEA** **HAGA** **TRADUZCA** **SIGA**	**SALGAN** **VEAN** **HAGAN** **TRADUZCAN** **SIGAN**

STEM-CHANGING VERBS, the change stays for the command form.

INFINITIVE	PRESENT INDICATIVE *YO*	UD. COMMAND	UDS. COMMAND
VOLVER^{return} TENER^{have} SALIR^{go out}	VUELVO TENGO SALGO	**VUELVA** **TENGA** **SALGA**	**VUELVAN** **TENGAN** **SALGAN**

These next verbs are irregular because the spelling needs to be changed in order to keep the hard –*g* sound, or the hard –*c* sound (like a –k). Also the –*z* has to change to a –*c* when followed by an –*e*. The only verbs affected by this rule are the ones that end with –*car*, -*gar* and -*zar*. According to the pronunciation rules, the spelling is changed to keep the correct sound. Remember that Spanish must be spelled like it sounds.

Jugar, tocar and *comenzar* are good examples.

INFINITIVE	PRESENT INDICATIVE *YO*	UD. COMMAND	UDS. COMMAND
JUGAR^{play} TOCAR^{touch, play instrument} COMENZAR^{begin}	JUEGO TOCO COMIENZO	**JUEGUE** **TOQUE** **COMIENCE**	**JUEGUEN** **TOQUEN** **COMIENZEN**

Here are a handful of irregular commands that are not difficult to learn.

IR → VAYA
SER → SEA
ESTAR → ESTÉ
DAR → DÉ

Vaya con Dios. (**Go** with God / God be with you.)
Sean buenos. (*You all* **be** good.)
Estén en la clase. (**Be** in class.)
Dé su tiempo. (**Give** your time.)

Say and write the commands that one person might tell another.

1. A mother to her son: ___*Limpie su cuarto*___

2. A boss to the employee: _____

3. A teacher to the student: _____

4. A pastor to the church members (use *Uds.*) : _____

5. A teacher to the class (use *Uds.*): _____

9.9 PRONOUNS TAGGED ON TO THE AFFIRMATIVE COMMANDS

Pronouns associated with commands must be tagged on to the end of the command.

Haga **el trabajo.** - *Do **the work**.* → Hágalo. - *Do **it**.* (el trabajo)
Haga **la tarea.** - *Do **the homework**.* → Hágala. - *Do **it**.* (la tarea)

When you tag on the pronoun, you must make sure that the verb is still pronounced the way it is supposed to be pronounced; meaning, the pronoun cannot change the way the verb is pronounced pertaining to the <u>stressed syllable</u>. (According to the accent rules, an accent mark will need to be placed over the stressed syllable to keep the correct pronunciation of the verb.)

Mire la computadora.	*Look at the computer.*	**Mí**rela.	*Look at it.*
Es**tu**die los verbos.	*Study the verbs.*	Es**tú**dielos.	*Study them.*
Diga.	*Tell/say.*	**Dí**game.	*Tell me/Say to me.*

Read the following commands. Then shorten them by changing the *direct object* to a *pronoun*.

Toque <u>el piano.</u> *Play the piano.*   <u>Tóquelo.</u> *Play it.*

1. Tome <u>la medicina.</u> *Take the medicine.* ___*Tómela (Take it)*___

2. Estudie <u>el libro.</u> *Study the book.* _____

3. Reciban <u>la ofrenda.</u> *Receive the offering.* _____

4. Coma <u>los vegetales.</u> *Eat the vegetables.* _____

9.10 NEGATIVE COMMANDS

The *Ud.* and *Uds.* commands form the negative commands by simply placing a **no** before.

No vaya hoy a la escuela.   ***Don't go*** *today to school.*
No venga mañana.   ***Don't come*** *tomorrow.*

If there is a pronoun tagged on, you must separate it and place it before the command when you make it negative.

<u>Positive:</u> Léa**lo.** (Read it.) Estúdie**los.** (Study them.)   <u>Negative:</u> - No **lo** lea. No **los** estudie.

Make negative:
1. Mírelos. *Look at them.* Negative: ___*No los mire.*___ - *Don't look at them.* (No accent mark.)

2. Hágalo. *Do it.* Negative: _____

3. Dígame. *Tell me.* Negative: _____

4. Óiganlo. *Listen to him.* Negative: _____

5. Póngalo en la mesa. *Put it on the table.* Negative: _____

Cultural Note

MARCELA GÁNDARA

Marcela was born in Mexico. She's one of the best known female Christian artists. She knew she wanted to sing for the Lord at a young age and has a powerful testimony. She now lives in Texas. Her song, *Dame tus ojos* says, "Lord give me your eyes I want to see through them. Give me your words, I want to speak… "

DAME TUS OJOS *(Give me your eyes)*

Dame tus ojos, quiero ver
Dame tus palabras, quiero hablar.
Dame tu parecer.

Give me your eyes, I want to see
Give me your words, I want to speak
Give me your thoughts.

Dame tus pies, yo quiero ir
Dame tus deseos para sentir
Dame tu parecer.

Give me your feet, I want to go
Give me your desires to feel
Give me your thoughts.

Dame lo que necesito para ser como tú.
Dame tu voz, dame tu aliento
Todo mi tiempo es para ti.
Dame el camino que debo seguir

Give me what I need to be like you
Give me your voice, give me your breath
All my time is for you
Give me the way I should follow

Dame tus sueños, tus anhelos,
Tus pensamientos, tu sentir.
Dame tu vida para vivir.

Give me your dreams, your deep desires
Your thoughts, your feelings
Give me your life to live

Déjame ver lo que tú ves,
Dame de tu gracia, tu poder
Dame tu corazón,
Déjame ver en tu interior.
Para ser cambiado por tu amor,
Dame tu corazón.

Let me se what you see
Give me your grace, your power
Give me your heart
Let me see inside of you
To be changed by your love
Give me your heart

© Vástago Producciones. Written by Jesús Adrián Romero

Written Work

Write the Spanish Bible verse for this lesson. Repeat it several times, and learn it.

_____

_____

A. What do you do or buy at certain places? **9.1**

1. ¿En la tienda de ropa? _Yo compro ropa   (I buy clothes)_

2. ¿En la panadería? _____

3. ¿En la frutería? _____

4. ¿En la verdulería? _____

5. ¿En la pulpería? _____

6. ¿En el supermercado? _____

7. ¿En la carnicería? _____

8. ¿En la biblioteca? _____

9. ¿En la zapatería? _____

B. Name all the transportations you have ever used: **9.2**

_____

_____

C. Translate the phrases with the prepositions of location: **9.6**

1. cerca de mi casa _____

2. debajo de la mesa _____

3. lejos de mi iglesia _____

4. al lado del supermercado _____

5. entre el cine y el colegio _____

D. Translate these commands: **9.7**

1. Vaya al médico. _____

2. Venga a la reunión. _____

3. Doble a la derecha. _____

4. Doble a la izquierda. _____

5. Siga derecho / recto. _____

6. Tenga un buen día. _____

7. Vengan todos a la iglesia. _____

E. Write out how to get to your supermarket from your house.

Use the vocabulary in **9.7** to give the directions.

_____

_____

_____

_____

Give directions from your house to your church.

_____

_____

_____

_____

Give directions to your friend's or relative's house:

_____

_____

_____

_____

F. The following is handout with the advice to be happy. **9.8**
You are given the verbs, make them into the command for Ud.

1. ___Levántese___ (levantarse) con una sonrisa^smile. (*Get up with a smile.*)

2. ___Cante___ (cantar) una canción en la ducha.

3. _____ (leer) unos versos de la Biblia.

4. _____ (hablar) con el Señor.

5. _____ (decir) "gracias por un nuevo día."

6. _____ (tener) una actitud^attitude positiva.

7. _____ (trabajar) y _____(jugar)

8. _____ (salir) con muchos amigos.

9. _____ (vivir) con mucha pasión.

10. _____ (amar) a Dios.

G. Give several commands, in the Uds. form, that would be commands a parent would give their children.

Estudien mucho. _____

_____

_____

H. You are on a mission trip. Make a list of what you can tell someone you have just met (*Ud.* form) when they ask you what to do to become a Christian.

Lea la Biblia. _____

_____

_____

I. Change the command to the negative. **9.10**

1. Doble a la derecha.^turn to the right _____

2. Vaya a la esquina.^go to the corner _____

3. Dígame.^tell me (be sure you separate the pronoun) _____

4. Hágalo. ^do it _____

Lesson 10
Witnessing

Religious Words and Terms / Books of Bible / Bible Stories Vocabulary / Regular Preterite (Simple Past) Tense / Irregular Preterite (Simple Past) Tense / *HACE* + TIME to Express a Duration of Time / Your Testimony / Phrases for Ministry and Witnessing / Key Bible Verses / Leading Someone to Christ

Lección 10

Vayan y hagan discípulos de todas las naciones, bautizándolos en el nombre del Padre, del Hijo y del Espíritu Santo. San Mateo 28:19

Go and make disciples of all nations, baptizing them in the name of the Father, of the Son and of the Holy Spirit. Matthew 28:19

10.1 VOCABULARIO RELIGIOSO | *RELIGIOUS VOCABULARY*

el testimonio	*testimony*	la Biblia	*Bible*
el poder	*power*	la Palabra de Dios	*God's Word*
poderoso	*powerful*	el versículo	*Bible verse*
la iglesia	*church*	el camino	*the way*
el púlpito	*pulpit*	la verdad	*the truth*
entregar tu corazón	*to give your heart*	digno	*worthy*
el pecado	*sin*	santo	*holy*
el pecador	*sinner*	la esperanza	*hope*
perdonar	*to forgive*	la fe	*faith*
el perdón	*forgiveness*	el Padre	*the Father*
perdonado/a	*forgiven*	el Hijo	*the Son*
la voluntad de Dios	*God's will*	el Espíritu Santo	*Holy Spirit*
el cielo/los cielos	*heaven, the heavens*	Jesucristo	*Jesus Christ*
el ángel	*angel*	bautizar	*to baptize*
tomar una decisión	*to make a decision*	arrepentirse	*to repent*
la invitación	*invitation*	redimido(s)	*redeemed*
el pueblo de Dios	*God's people*	redentor	*redeemer*
Salvador personal	*personal Savior*	la muerte	*death*
la Virgen María	*the virgin Mary*	la sangre	*blood*
Juan el Bautista	*John the Baptist*	derramar	*to shed/spill*
el profeta	*the prophet*	la cruz	*cross*
Satanás/el diablo	*Satan/the devil*	crucificar	*to crucify*
el infierno	*hell*	crucificado	*crucified*
el enemigo	*the enemy*	el don espiritual	*spiritual gift*
vencer	*to conquer, to defeat*	la santa cena	*last supper*
el vencedor	*conqueror*	ser salvo/a	*to be saved*
la victoria	*victory*	la misericordia	*mercy*

These are questions you can ask. Write the translation.

1. ¿Conoces a Jesucristo como tu Salvador personal? _____

2. ¿Eres del pueblo de Dios? _____

3. ¿Quieres hacer la voluntad de Dios? _____

4. ¿Crees que Jesús fue^was crucificado? _____

5. ¿Tienes dones espirituales? _____

6. ¿Crees en la Palabra de Dios? _____

7. ¿Quieres entregar tu corazón a Dios? _____

8. ¿Quieres aceptar a Jesucristo como tu Salvador personal? _____

El Antiguo Testamento | The Old Testament

Génesis	2 Crónicas	Daniel
Éxodo	Esdras	Oseas
Levítico	Nehemías	Joel
Números	Ester	Amós
Deuteronomio	Job	Abdías
Josué	Salmos	Jonás
Jueces	Proverbios	Miqueas
Rut	Eclesiastés	Nahum
1 Samuel	Cantares	Habacuc
2 Samuel	Isaías	Sofonías
1 Reyes	Jeremías	Hageo
2 Reyes	Lamentaciones	Zacarías
1 Crónicas	Ezequiel	Malaquías

The Spanish Bible comparable to the King James version is called "Reina Valera." This was the first printed press Bible in Spanish, printed in 1569. (Thirty-five years before the King James version.)

El Nuevo Testamento | The New Testament

San Mateo	Efesios	Hebreos
San Marcos	Filipenses	Santiago
San Lucas	Colosenses	1 San Pedro
San Juan	1 Tesalonicenses	2 San Pedro
Hechos	2 Tesalonicenses	1 San Juan (* Primero de San Juan)
Romanos	1 Timoteo	2 San Juan (* Segundo de San Juan)
1 Corintios	2 Timoteo	3 San Juan (* Tercero de San Juan)
2 Corintios	Tito	San Judas
Gálatas	Filemón	Apocalipsis

* Example given of how to say first, second and third for books of the Bible.

10.3 HISTORIAS DE LA BIBLIA | *STORIES OF THE BIBLE*

These stories can be downloaded in Spanish free at www.spanishwithamission.com

La creación - Creation **los cielos** - the heavens **la Tierra** - the Earth	**José y la túnica de muchos colores** - Joseph's coat of many colors **los hermanos** – the brothers
Adán y Eva - Adam and Eve **la serpiente**- serpent **el pecado** -sin	**El nacimiento de Jesús** - Birth of Jesus **un pesebre** – manger **la estrella** - star
El arca de Noé - Noah's Ark **la lluvia** - the rain **los animales** - the animals	**Jesús calma la tormenta** – Jesus calms storm **el barco** - boat **el miedo** - fear
David y Goliat - David and Goliath **una honda** - a sling **las piedras** - rocks	**La parábola del hijo perdido /pródigo** - Parable of the Prodigal Son **la herencia** – the inheritance
Daniel en el foso de los leones - Daniel in the Den of Lions **el rey** - the king	**La parábola del buen samaritano** - Parable of the Good Samaritan **herido** - wounded

10.4 REGULAR VERBS IN THE PRETERITE (SIMPLE) PAST TENSE

The simple past tense in Spanish is called the **Preterite**. The Preterite tense is used to express an action, event, or condition seen as completed in the past. Most of the time it expresses actions in the past. The past tense is needed to tell any kind of story, testimony or to communicate what happened. The past tense in Spanish has many irregular forms, just like in English.

Examples: I see - I **saw**;   I go - I **went**;   I think - I **thought**

Vocabulary for talking about the past:

ayer	yesterday	la semana pasada	last week
anoche	last night	el mes pasado	last month
anteayer	day before yesterday	el año pasado	last year
el sábado pasado	last Saturday	hace <u>dos</u> años	two years ago

The regular endings for **-ar** verbs in the preterite tense:

Singular		Plural	
Yo	**-é**	nosotros/as	**-amos**
tú	**-aste**		
él, ella, Ud.	**-ó**	ellos, ellas, Uds.	**-aron**

Preterite tense of the verb *HABLAR* (spoke)

Yo	habl**é**	nosotros/as	habl**amos**
tú	habl**aste**		
él, ella, Ud.	habl**ó**	ellos, ellas, Uds.	habl**aron**

Ayer **hablé** con el médico.   *Yesterday **I spoke** with the doctor.*
Ella les **habló** a todos los niños.   ***She spoke** to all the children.*
Anoche yo **canté** la canción.   *Last night I **sang** the song.*

Note: The *nosotros -ar* conjugated form is the same as the present tense; context will determine understanding.

El sábado pasado le **hablamos** al pastor.   *Last Saturday **we spoke** to the pastor.*

Important: The 3rd person -ó ending is not to be confused with the -o ending in the 1st person present tense. The stress is different and it is <u>important</u> to stress the -ó at the end. Look at where the stress is in these words.

Yo **ha**blo. - *I speak.* (present tense)   Ella ha**bló**. - *She spoke.* (preterite past)

A. Fill in the blank with the correct conjugation of the indicated -*ar* verb.

1. Ayer yo ___*canté*___ en el coro^{choir} de la iglesia. (cantar)

2. La semana pasada José _____ mucho. (trabajar)

3. Nosotros _____ a El Salvador hace 2 años. (viajar)

4. ¿Tú ya^{already}_____ la música? (escuchar)

5. Anoche mis amigos me _____(ayudar).

Answers: 2. trabajó 3. viajamos 4. escuchaste 5. ayudaron

The regular endings for -er AND -ir verbs

yo	-í	nosotros/as	-imos
tú	-iste		
él, ella, Ud.	-ió	ellos, ellas, Uds.	-ieron

With the regular verbs COMER / VIVIR (ate / lived)

yo	comí / viví	nosotros/as	comimos / vivimos
tú	comiste / viviste		
él, ella, Ud.	comió / vivió	ellos, ellas, Uds.	comieron / vivieron

Ayer **comí** con mi mejor amiga. - *Yesterday I ate with my best friend.*
El año pasado **viví** con mis padres. - *Last year I lived with my parents.*

Note: The *nosotros -ir* conjugated form in the preterite is the same as the present tense; context will determine understanding.

With the verbs *LEER* and *CREER*, the *–i* will change to a *–y* in third person singular and plural. Also the *tú* form will have an accent. This is a result of a vowel preceding the endings.

Leí, leíste, leyó, leímos, leyeron
Creí, creíste, creyó, creímos, creyeron

B. Fill in the blank with the correct conjugation of the indicated -er and -ir verb.

1. Ayer Luisa me ___*escribió*___ un correo electrónico. (escribir)

2. Hace 5 años yo _____ a Jesús como mi Salvador. (recibir)

3. Ellos _____ ir a España. (decidir)

4. ¿Ustedes _____ el carro ayer? (vender)

5. ¿ _____ tú con tus amigos anoche? (salir)

Answers: 2. recibí 3. decidieron 4. vendieron 5. Saliste

Many verbs that go through a stem change in the present tense, do not go through a stem change in the preterite, and are conjugated as regular verbs.

pensar	*to think*	**recordar**	*to remember*	**perder**	*to lose*
cerrar	*to close*	**entender**	*to understand*	**volver**	*to return*

C. Fill in the blank with the correct conjugation.

1. En la clase ayer nosotros no ___*entendimos*___ a la profesora. (entender)

2. Yo _____ a casa anoche a las 11:00. (volver)

3. El banco _____ a las 2:00 anteayer. (cerrar)

4. El viernes pasado yo _____ mi teléfono celular. (perder)

5. Anoche nosotros_____el versículo. (recordar)

Using different verbs that have been given to you, finish the sentence.

Ayer yo _____

Note: Reflexive verbs conjugated in the past have the same conjugation but with the reflexive pronoun added. <u>Me lavé</u> el pelo. *I washed my hair.* <u>Me levanté</u> a las 6:00. *I got up at 6:00.*

Many common verbs are irregular in the past tense. Learn these 12 verb conjugations by repetition and memorization. You can see certain patterns:

IR and *SER* have the same conjugations, the meaning will be understood by context. For example, *IR* will usually be followed by "*a.*" Él fue **a** la iglesia. *He went to the church.*

VERB	YO	TÚ	ÉL, ELLA, UD.	NOSOTROS	ELLOS, UDS.
Ir - ser	fui	fuiste	fue	fuimos	fueron

DAR and *VER* are conjugated similarly.

dar	di	diste	dio	dimos	dieron
ver	vi	viste	vio	vimos	vieron

The following verbs have the indicated endings (no accents). The stem changes. Sometimes with a *-u* othertimes with an *-i*. Notice the endings: **-e, -iste, -o, -imos, -ieron.**

tener	tuve	tuviste	tuvo	tuvimos	tuvieron
estar	estuve	estuviste	estuvo	estuvimos	estuvieron
poder	pude	pudiste	pudo	pudimos	pudieron
hacer	hice	hiciste	hizo	hicimos	hicieron
querer	quise	quisiste	quiso	quisimos	quisieron
venir	vine	viniste	vino	vinimos	vinieron

The following verbs have a *-j* in the stem and drop the *-i* in the *ellos/Uds.* form.

decir	dije	dijiste	dijo	dijimos	dijeron
traer	traje	trajiste	trajo	trajimos	trajeron

El sábado pasado **fui** a la tienda.
Dios nos **dio** el Espíritu Santo.
¿**Viste** el programa anoche?
Yo **tuve** que trabajar la semana pasada.
Nosotros **pudimos** correr 10 millas[miles] el fin de semana pasado.

*Last Saturday I **went** to the store.*
*God **gave** us the Holy Spirit.*
***Did you see** the program last night?*
***I had** to work last week.*
***We were able** to run 10 miles last weekend.*

A. Conjugate in the preterite:

1. Anoche tú _____(hacer) la tarea.

2. Ayer él _____ (decir) su nombre.

3. El viernes yo _____ (traer) comida a la fiesta.

B. Write your own creative sentences using these verbs in the past.

1. _____

2. _____

3. _____

HACE + TIME WITH THE PRESENT TENSE

The verb *HACER* is used in a simple way to express how long something has been going on. Remember the verb *HACER* means to make/to do. When used with time, you are literally saying, "it makes this much time" that something has been going on.

The verb *hacer* will always be conjugated in 3rd person singular. – "*hace*"

Example: Express you are living in New Mexico and that you have been living there for 5 years. First state you live/are living there. (the present tense can be used for both of these meanings.)

Yo vivo en Nuevo México. – *I live/am living in New Mexico.*

Now let's add that it has been 5 years that you have been living there.

Yo vivo en Nuevo México **hace cinco años**. - *I have been living in New Mexico **for 5 years**.*

Another example: You have been studying Spanish for 3 months.
Remember you start with the statement of what you are doing. *Yo estudio español.*
Then add for how long. (3 meses).

Yo estudio español **hace tres meses**. - *I have been studying Spanish **for 3 months**.*

A. Write the full sentence to express what has been happening and for how long.

1. Yo soy cristiana. (10 years) *Yo soy cristiana hace diez años.*

2. Yo soy maestro. (20 years) _____

3. Yo trabajo en la iglesia. (6 days) _____

4. María habla con ellos. (30 minutes) _____

Tell a partner what you have been doing and express for how long with *HACE*.

_____

HACE + TIME WITH THE PAST TENSE

HACE + TIME can be used with statements that have a verb in the past tense, in which case will mean "ago". Since the statement is in the past, you are stating how long it has been since that happened. In other words, you are stating how long ago that happened.

Example: Yo fui a Guatemala. – *I went to Guatemala.*
The statement is using the past tense and stating that you went to Guatemala. How long ago did that happen? Let's say it has been 5 years. The same formula of *HACE* + TIME will be used.

Yo fui a Guatemala **hace 5 años**. – *I went to Guatemala **5 years ago**.*

Here are some statements with the verb in the past tense. You are told how long ago it happened. Write the complete sentence.

Example: Tú viste la película *La pasión*. - *You saw the movie The Passion*. (1 year ago)
Tú viste la película *La pasión* hace un año. - *You saw the movie The Passion one year ago.*

B. Write the full sentence to express how long ago it happened.

1. Yo hablé con mi padre. (20 minutes ago) *Hablé con mi padre hace veinte minutos.*

2. Yo vendí mi carro. (6 months ago) _____

3. Yo vi a mi hermano. (4 days ago) _____

10.7 YOUR TESTIMONY (OPTIONAL)

The past tense is important to learn in order to share your testimony of what God did in your life. In lesson 8 you learned the present perfect which translates as "has done." With both of these tenses, you can well express what God has done for you.

The following space is for you to dedicate time writing a short testimony. Ask your teacher or another Spanish speaker to help you. Try to keep it simple and easy to understand which in turn will keep it in simple enough for you to learn it and share it.

_____

_____

_____

_____

_____

_____

_____

_____

_____

_____

_____

_____

_____

_____

_____

_____

_____

_____

_____

10.8 PHRASES FOR MINISTRY AND WITNESSING

Do you believe in God?
¿Cree en Dios?

Do you go to church?
¿Va a la iglesia?

Do you know God loves you?
¿Sabe que Dios le ama?

Can I pray for you?
¿Puedo orar por usted?

Can I pray for your family?
¿Puedo orar por su familia?

I'm going to pray for you in English.
Voy a orar por usted en inglés.

Jesus loves you.
Jesús le ama.

Jesus can help.
Jesús puede ayudar.

Jesus can heal you.
Jesús le puede sanar.

Do you know God can change your life?
¿Sabe que Dios puede cambiar su vida?

If you die today, do you know if you would go to heaven?
¿Si se muriera hoy, sabe si iría al cielo?

Do you know Jesus as your personal Savior?
¿Conoce a Jesús como su Salvador personal?

Do you want to give your heart to Jesus?
¿Quiere darle su corazón a Cristo?
(Go to **10.10** for Bible verses to lead someone to Christ)

Did you know?

According to the current issue of *Operation World*, Guatemala is the most evangelized nation in Latin America, with 20% evangelized.

The Sinners Prayer-
Lord, I know that I'm a sinner.
I confess my sins and I repent.
I ask you to forgive me for my sins.
Lord Jesus, Come into my heart.
Cleanse me and change me.
You are my Lord and my Savior.
I give you my life and surrender to you.
May the Holy Spirit stay in me
And help me do your will for my life.
In Jesus' name, amen.

Señor, sé que soy pecador.
Te confieso mis pecados y me arrepiento.
Te pido que me perdones mis pecados.
Señor Jesús, entra a mi corazón.
Límpiame y cámbiame.
Eres mi Señor y mi Salvador.
Te doy mi vida y me rindo a ti.
Que tu Espíritu Santo se quede en mí,
Y me ayude a hacer tu voluntad para mi vida.
En el nombre de Jesús, amén.

A Blessing:
May the Lord keep you and bless you.
May the Lord make his face shine upon you.
May he have mercy on you and give you peace .

Que el Señor te guarde y te bendiga.
Que el Señor haga resplandecer Su rostro sobre ti.
Que el Señor tenga de ti misericordia y te dé paz.

Here are the translations to some key verses. (NIV - *NVI*) You are encouraged to own a Bilingual Bible so the translation is there as you share any verse or passage from the Bible.

John 3:16
"For God so loved the world, that He gave His only begotten Son, that whoever believes in Him shall not perish, but have eternal life."
Juan 3:16
"Porque tanto amó Dios al mundo, que dio a su Hijo unigénito, para que todo el que cree en él no se pierda, sino que tenga vida eterna."

Romans 5:1
"Therefore, since we have been made right in God's sight by faith, we have peace with God because of what Jesus Christ our Lord has done for us."
Romanos 5:1
"En consecuencia, ya que hemos sido justificados mediante la fe, tenemos paz con Dios por medio de nuestro Señor Jesucristo."

John 13:34-35
[34] "A new command I give you: Love one another. As I have loved you, so you must love one another. [35] By this everyone will know that you are my disciples, if you love one another."
Juan 13:34-35
[34] "Este mandamiento nuevo les doy: que se amen los unos a los otros. Así como yo los he amado, también ustedes deben amarse los unos a los otros. [35] De este modo todos sabrán que son mis discípulos, si se aman los unos a los otros."

1 John 4:10
"This is love: not that we loved God, but that he loved us and sent his Son as an atoning sacrifice for our sins."
1 Juan 4:10
"En esto consiste el amor: no en que nosotros hayamos amado a Dios, sino en que él nos amó y envió a su Hijo para que fuera ofrecido como sacrificio por el perdón de nuestros pecados."

Jeremiah 29:11
"For I know the plans I have for you," declares the LORD, "plans to prosper you and not to harm you, plans to give you hope and a future."
Jeremías 29:11
"Porque yo sé muy bien los planes que tengo para ustedes —afirma el Señor—, planes de bienestar y no de calamidad, a fin de darles un futuro y una esperanza."

Phillipians 4:13
"I can do all things through Christ that gives me strength."
Filipenses 4:13
"Todo lo puedo en Cristo que me fortalece."

1 Corinthians 13:4-7

⁴ "Love is patient, love is kind. It does not envy, it does not boast, it is not proud. ⁵ It does not dishonor others, it is not self-seeking, it is not easily angered, it keeps no record of wrongs. ⁶ Love does not delight in evil but rejoices with the truth. ⁷ It always protects, always trusts, always hopes, always perseveres."

1 Corintios 13:4-7

⁴ "El amor es paciente, es bondadoso. El amor no es envidioso ni jactancioso ni orgulloso. ⁵ No se comporta con rudeza, no es egoísta, no se enoja fácilmente, no guarda rencor. ⁶ El amor no se deleita en la maldad sino que se regocija con la verdad. ⁷ Todo lo disculpa, todo lo cree, todo lo espera, todo lo soporta."

Isaiah 40:31

"But those who hope in the LORD will renew their strength. They will soar on wings like eagles; they will run and not grow weary, they will walk and not be faint."

Isaías 40:31

"Pero los que confían en el Señor renovarán sus fuerzas; volarán como las águilas: correrán y no se fatigarán, caminarán y no se cansarán."

Matthew 6:33

³³ "But seek first his kingdom and his righteousness, and all these things will be given to you as well."

Mateo 6:33

"Más bien, busquen primeramente el reino de Dios y su justicia, y todas estas cosas les serán añadidas."

Psalms 37:4

"Delight yourself in the LORD and he will give you the desires of your heart."

Salmo 37:4

"Deléitate en el Señor, y él te concederá los deseos de tu corazón."

Ephesians 6:10-11

"Finally, be strong in the Lord and in his mighty power. Put on the full armor of God so that you can take your stand against the devil's schemes."

Efesios 6:10-11

¹⁰ "Y ahora, hermanos, busquen su fuerza en el Señor, en su poder irresistible. ¹¹ Protéjanse con toda la armadura que Dios les ha dado, para que puedan estar firmes contra los engaños del diablo."

Matthew 22:37-39

"Jesus replied: "Love the Lord your God with all your heart and with all your soul and with all your mind." This is the first and greatest commandment. And the second is like it: "Love your neighbor as yourself."

Mateo 22:37-39

³⁷ "Jesús le dijo: —"Ama al Señor tu Dios con todo tu corazón, con toda tu alma y con toda tu mente." ³⁸ Éste es el más importante y el primero de los mandamientos. ³⁹ Pero hay un segundo, parecido a éste; dice: "Ama a tu prójimo como a ti mismo."

Proverbs 3:5-6

"Trust in the LORD with all your heart and lean not on your own understanding; in all your ways acknowledge him, and he will make your paths straight."

Proverbios 3:5-6

⁵ "Confía de todo corazón en el Señor y no en tu propia inteligencia. ⁶ Reconócelo en todos tus caminos, y él allanará tus sendas."

Matthew 16:26
"What good will it be for a man if he gains the whole world, yet forfeits his soul? Or what can a man give in exchange for his soul?"

Mateo 16:26

"¿De qué sirve ganar el mundo entero si se pierde la vida? ¿O qué se puede dar a cambio de la vida?"

Matthew 6:24
"No one can serve two masters. Either he will hate the one and love the other, or he will be devoted to the one and despise the other."

Mateo 6:24

"Nadie puede servir a dos amos, porque odiará a uno y querrá al otro, o será fiel a uno y despreciará al otro."

Psalm 46:1-3
"God is our refuge and strength, a very present help in trouble. Therefore we will not fear, though the earth should change and though the mountains slip into the heart of the sea; though its waters roar and foam, though the mountains quake at its swelling pride."

Salmo 46:1-3

"Dios es nuestro refugio y nuestra fuerza; nuestra ayuda en momentos de angustia.
Por eso no tendremos miedo, aunque se deshaga la tierra, aunque se hundan los montes en el fondo del mar, aunque ruja el mar y se agiten sus olas, aunque tiemblen los montes a causa de su furia."

Phillipians 4:8
"Finally, brethren, whatever things are true, whatever things are noble, whatever things are just, whatever things are pure, whatever things are lovely, whatever things are of good report, if there is any virtue and if there is anything praiseworthy—meditate on these things."

Filipenses 4:8

"Por último, hermanos, piensen en todo lo verdadero, en todo lo que es digno de respeto, en todo lo justo, en todo lo puro, en todo lo agradable, en todo lo que tiene buena fama. Piensen en toda clase de virtudes."

10.10 VERSES FOR LEADING SOMEONE TO CHRIST

In the book of Romans, lesson 5, verse 8, it tells us that God loved us so that "when we were in our sin Christ Jesus came to die for us."

En el libro de Romanos, capítulo 5, versículo 8 nos dice que Dios nos amó tanto, que "cuándo éramos pecadores, Jesucristo vino a morir por nosotros."

Romans 3:23
"For all have sinned and fall short of the glory of God,"
This verse tells us that all people have sinned. We have fallen short of God's intended purpose for us. God made us to know Him.... to receive His love and to love Him in return.

Romanos 3:23

"Todos han pecado y están lejos de la gloria de Dios."
Este verso nos dice que todos hemos pecado. Todos nos hemos alejado del propósito que Dios tiene para nosotros. Dios nos creó para conocerlo…para recibir Su amor y amarlo de vuelta.

Romans 6:23
"For the wages of sin is death, but the free gift of God is eternal life in Christ Jesus our Lord."
In sin there is death. We are alive physically but dead spiritually, this means we have no eternal life. We will be separated from God for all eternity. God's free gift is eternal life—life with Him—in the place of sin's payment of death. How can God remain in His holiness and forgive sinners?
Because Jesus, His Son, has paid the price for sin by His death on the cross.

Romanos 6:23
"El pago que da el pecado es la muerte, pero el don de Dios es vida eterna en Cristo Jesús, nuestro Señor."
En el pecado hay muerte. Estamos vivos físicamente, pero muertos espiritualmente, esto significa que no tendremos vida eterna. Seremos separados de Dios por una eternidad. Dios regala vida eterna—vida con Él—en lugar del pago del pecado que es la muerte. ¿Cómo puede Dios mantenerse en Su santidad y perdonar pecadores? Porque Jesús, Su Hijo, ha pagado el precio del pecado con su muerte en la cruz.

How can you receive God's free gift of love and life?
¿Cómo puede recibir este regalo de amor y vida que nos da Dios?

Romans 10:9-10
[9]"That if you confess with your mouth Jesus as Lord, and believe in your heart that God raised Him from the dead, you will be saved; [10] for with the heart a person believes, resulting in righteousness, and with the mouth he confesses, resulting in salvation."
A person receives God's free gift of love and life by placing faith in Jesus Christ. To believe is simply to take God at His word. With our heart (whole believing) we believe that Jesus is God's Son who died for our sin on the cross and arose from the grave to live in us as Savior and Lord.

Romanos 10:9-10
[9]"Si con tu boca confiesas a Jesús como Señor, y con tu corazón crees que Dios lo resucitó, alcanzarás la salvación. [10] Pues con el corazón se cree para alcanzar la justicia, y con la boca se reconoce a Jesucristo para alcanzar la salvación."
Uno recibe el regalo de amor y vida eterna poniendo su fe en Jesucristo. Creer es simplemente tomar las Palabras de Dios como la verdad. Con nuestro corazón (creencia total) creemos que Jesús es el Hijo de Dios quien murió en la cruz por nuestros pecados y resucitó de la tumba para vivir en nostros como Salvador y Señor.

To believe in Jesus will result in confessing that faith with one's mouth.
Creer en Jesús va a resultar en confesar esa fe con la boca.

Do you acknowledge that your are a sinner?
Romans 10:13 - "For whoever will call on the name of the Lord will be saved."
Do you believe by faith that Jesus, God's Son, died for your sin on the cross?
¿Reconoces que eres un pecador?
Romanos 10:13 - "Todos los que invoquen el nombre del Señor, alcanzarán la salvación."
Crees por fe que Jesús, el Hijo de Dios, murió por tus pecados en la cruz?

This verse says that any person who will call upon the name of Jesus, the Lord, shall be saved.
Este versículo dice que cualquier person que lo invoca en el nombre de Jesús, serán salvos.

Will you now confess Him as your Savior and Lord?
¿Lo confiesas hoy como tu Salvador y Señor?

To call means simply to ask in prayer. The verse does not require one to know more... do better... clean up one's life... or in any way try to add to what Jesus has done for us.

Invocarlo simplemente significa pedir en oración. Este versículo no requiere que uno sepa más… haga mejor…limpie su vida…o alguna otra cosa para añadir a lo que Jesús ha hecho por nosotros.

Will you now call upon Jesus to save you from your sin so that you can know God's love and forgiveness?

¿Invocarás ahora a Jesús? A Él que nos salvo de nuestros pecados para que podamos conocer el amor y perdón de Dios.

Pray: "Dear God, I confess that I am a sinner, and I repent. I need to be saved and I need a Savior. I believe by faith that Jesus, is your Son who died on the cross for my sins. I believe He arose from the grave to live as my Lord. I turn from my sin and I ask you, Lord Jesus, to forgive my sin and come into my heart. I trust you and receive you as my Lord and Savior. Thank you, Jesus, for saving me."

Ore: "Señor, confieso que soy pecador, y me arrepiento. Necesito un Salvador y creo por fe que Jesús, tu Hijo, murió en la cruz para ser mi Salvador. Creo que Él resucitó de la muerte para vivir como mi Señor. Le doy la espalda a mis pecados. Te pido, Señor Jesús, que me perdones los pecados y entres a mi corazón. Confío en ti y te recibo como mi Señor. Gracias, Jesús, por salvarme."

When anyone calls on the Lord this way, that person is saved according to God's Word. If you pray for repentance in faith, you are saved. You have God's word on it.

Cuando alguien llama al Señor de esta manera, se salva según la Palabra de Dios. Si oras una oración de arrepentimiento en fe, eres salvo. Tienes la Palabra de Dios.

If you have prayed this prayer to receive Christ as your Lord and Savoir, why not record your decision to follow Jesus? A good place to write this would be inside the cover of your Bible:

Si has orado esta oración para recibir a Cristo como tu Señor y Salvador, por qué no grabar esta decisión de seguir a Jesús? Un buen lugar para escribir lo que sigue es dentro de la tapa de tu Biblia.

Write: "Believing by faith that God loves me and sent His Son, Jesus Christ, to die for my sin and arise from the grave to live in me, I, _____, on this day, _____, repent of my sins and accept Jesus Christ as my personal Lord and Savior. According to the promise of God in Romans 10:13, I have called upon His name and have His word for the assurance of my salvation."

Escribe: "Creo por fe que Dios me ama y mandó su Hijo, Jesucristo, a morir por mis pecados y resucitó de la tumba para vivir en mí. Yo _____, este día _____, me arrepiento de mis pecados y acepto a Jesucristo como mi Señor y Salvador personal. Según la promesa de Dios en Romanos 10:13, yo he invocado Su nombre y tengo Su palabra por la seguridad de mi salvación."

A Blessing you can share with others: May the Lord keep you and bless you. May the Lord make his face shine upon you. May he have mercy on you and give you peace. May he bless your comings and goings; when you rise, and when you lay down. May he bless you in the field, may he bless you in the city. May he bless the work of your hands. May the Lord God Allmighty bless you.

Una Bendición: Que el Señor te guarde y te bendiga. Que el Señor haga resplandecer Su rostro sobre ti. Que el Señor tenga de ti misericordia y te dé paz. Te bendiga tu entrar y tu salir; tu levantar y tu acostar. Te bendiga en el campo, te bendiga en la ciudad. Bendiga la obra de tus manos. Que el Señor Dios todopoderoso te bendiga.

Cultural Note
DANIEL CALVETI

Daniel Calveti was born in Venezuela but now lives in Puerto Rico. He is a contemporary Christian artist since 2004 when he made his first album, though he had been singing and composing since a child. He has been nominated to the Latin GRAMMY® Awards for "Best Christian Album in Spanish" and Premios ARPA for "Composer of the Year." He is an active leader and Minister of Worship in his church where his father pastors, in Caguas, Puerto Rico. *La niña de tus ojos* is a song written about God's love for us. We are the "apple of His eye" which in Spanish is translated as *"niña de sus ojos."* This saying affirms that we are His precious child. "He knew us when no one knew us, and He gave us a name."

LA NIÑA DE TUS OJOS - Daniel Calveti

Me viste a mí, cuando nadie me vio.	*You saw me, when no one saw me*
Me amaste a mí, cuando nadie me amó.	*You loved me, when no one loved me*
Y me diste nombre.	*And you gave me a name*
Yo soy tu niña,	*I'm the apple of your eye*
La niña de tus ojos,	
Porque me amaste a mí.	*Because you loved me*
Me amaste a mí.	*You loved me*
Te amo más que a mi vida,	*I love you more than my life*
Te amo más que a mi vida, más.	

Written Work

Write the Spanish Bible verse for this lesson. Repeat it several times, and learn it.

_____

_____

A. Write the first 4 books of the New Testament (*Nuevo Testamento*): **10.2**

_____   _____

_____   _____

B. Write the titles of 2 of your favorite Bible Stories:

_____

_____

C. TABLE TO CONJUGATE - Write the preterite (past) tense conjugations that are missing. **10.4** and **10.5**

Write the meaning to the left of the verb.

Verb	yo	tú	él, ella, Ud.	nosotros	ellos, Uds.
preguntar	pregunté			preguntamos	
tomar	tomé				
amar					amaron
escribir			escribió		
olvidar		olvidaste			
decidir			decidió		decidieron
* **ir**	fui				
* **leer**					leyeron
sufrir				sufrimos	
vencer		venciste			
* **dar**	di		dio		
* **creer**	creí		creyó		
* **ver**		viste		vimos	
* **hacer**			hizo		
* **decir**	dije				dijeron

*irregular verb

D. Fill in the blank with the correct Preterite form of the verb in parenthesis. **10.4 & 10.5**

1. Ayer yo _____ mi cuarto. (limpiar)

2. Ellos _____ mucho en la clase. (preguntar)

3. Mario me _____ una comida muy deliciosa. (cocinar)

4. ¿ _____ ustedes en México? (vivir)

5. Usted _____ agua en el restaurante. (beber)

6. ¿ Ustedes _____ su tarea ayer? (hacer)

7. José y Verónica _____ el tren por mucho tiempo. (esperar)

8. Nosotros _____ al aeropuerto anoche. (ir)

9. Mi amigo me _____ la verdad. (decir)

10. Tú _____ muy bien el lunes. (cantar)

11. Yo _____ la lección. (leer)

12. Jesús _____ la muerte^death. (vencer)

E. *HACE* + TIME with the **Present** tense. Rewrite the sentence stating how long it has been going on. **10.6**

1. Conozco a Jesucristo (5 years) _____

2. No bebo gaseosas (8 weeks) _____

3. Voy a la Iglesia Nueva Vida (12 years) _____

4. Mario habla por teléfono (40 minutes) _____

5. Translate: I've been watching/ I watch T.V. for 1 hour. _____

_____

HACE + TIME with the **Past** tense. Rewrite the sentence stating how long ago it happened.

6. Fui al supermercado (1 week ago) _____

7. Mi hijo hizo la tarea (15 minutes ago) _____

8. Translate: Carlos ate 2 hours ago. _____

F. Salmo 100 El Señor nos hizo y somos suyos. (*The Lord made us and we are His.*)
Salmo para la acción de gracias.   (*Psalm for giving thanks.*) **9.8**

¹¡**Canten** al Señor con alegría,	**sing**
habitantes de toda la tierra!	
² Con alegría **adoren** al Señor;	**adore**
¡con gritos de alegría **vengan** a su presencia!	**come**
³ **Reconozcan** que el Señor es Dios;	**recognize / acknowledge**
él nos hizo y somos suyos;	
¡somos pueblo suyo y ovejas de su prado!	
⁴ **Vengan** a las puertas y a los atrios de su templo	**come**
con himnos de alabanza y gratitud.	
¡**Denle** gracias, **bendigan** su nombre!	**Give Him / bless**
⁵ Porque el Señor es bueno;	
su amor es eterno y su fidelidad no tiene fin.	

The verbs that are commands are in bold print.
Write down the words you do not know and look up their translation.
(Commands are in Lesson 9.)

_____

_____

_____

G. Write the translation of the following parable and underline the verbs in the Spanish text, then translate and write in English.

Jesús dijo; el reino de los cielos es así: Un comerciante buscó perlas finas. Cuando encontró una de gran valor, fue y vendió todo y la compró.

Mateo 13:45-46 (NVI, *paraphrased*)

_____

_____

_____

_____

Coritos for Children
With Words & Phrases to use with Children

Words and Phrases to Use with Children

COMMANDS IN YOU - *TÚ* (SINGULAR)

Come here - *Ven* / some countries say *Vení* (vos form)
Sit down - *Siéntate*
What do you want? - *¿Qué quieres?*
What do you need? - *¿Qué necesitas?*
What's the matter? - *¿Qué pasa?*
What's the matter with you? - *¿Qué te pasa?*
Where is(are) _____. - *¿Dónde está(n)* _____?
  clothes - *la ropa*
  diapers - *el pañales*
  baby bottle - *la mamadera, la pacha, el biberón*
  bathroom - *el baño*
  to change - *cambiar*

COMMANDS IN YOU- *USTEDES* (PLURAL)

Come here - *Vengan*
Sit down - *Siéntense*
Listen - *Escuchen*
Sing - *Canten*
Read - *Lean*
Learn - *Aprendan*
Repeat - *Repitan*

Did you know?

El Día del Niño (Day of the Child) is celebrated in many Hispanic countries.

Singular or Plural - Let's . . .

Let's _____ - *VAMOS A* _____
play - *jugar*
draw - *dibujar*
color - *colorear*
paint - *pintar / color*
listen - *escuchar*
sing - *cantar*
pray - *orar*
read - *leer*

Did you know? In Mexico, there are approximately three million children that work selling candy and cigarettes in the streets.

CORITOS FOR CHILDREN

Songs can be heard at www.spanishwithamission.com

1. GLORIA A DIOS (PRAISE YE THE LORD)

A. Alelu, alelu, alelu, aleluya.

B. gloria a Dios   (divide into 2 groups

A. gloria a Dios   each group stands

B. aleluya   as they sing their part)

A & B. GLORIA A DIOS   (everyone stands)

Anonymous translation.

2. GRANDE ES (DEEP AND WIDE)

Grande es, grande es,

el amor de Cristo mi Señor.   (motion "big" with hands)

Grande es, grande es,   *Big is the love of Christ my Lord*

El amor de Cristo mi Señor.

Anonymous translation.

3. MI DIOS ES TAN GRANDE (MY GOD IS SO GREAT)

Mi Dios es tan grande,

tan fuerte y potente

no hay nada que Él no puede hacer.   *There is nothing He can't do*

Los montes son de Él   (put hands like a mountain)

los ríos son de Él   (put hands together and wave like a river)

las estrellas son de Él también   (do stars in air)

Mi Dios es tan grande   (motion BIG with hands)

tan fuerte y potente   (flex muscles)

no hay nada que Él no puede hacer.   (shake finger and shake head, NO)

Anonymous translation.

4. DIOS BUENO ES (GOD IS SO GOOD)

Dios bueno es, Dios bueno es,

Dios bueno es, bueno es mi Dios.   *God is so good*

Dios me ama a mí, Dios me ama a mí,   *God loves me so*

Dios me ama a mí, Él me ama a mí.

Anonymous translation.

5. ADENTRO, AFUERA, ARRIBA, ABAJO
(I'M INRIGHT, OUTRIGHT, UPRIGHT, DOWNRIGHT, HAPPY ALL THE TIME)

Adentro, afuera, arriba, abajo,	(Point to yourself, then out, then up then down.)
Qué feliz estoy. (2x)	(clap 3 times to beat) *I am so happy.*
Pues Cristo me salvó,	(point to yourself) *Christ saved me*
Y mi corazón limpió	(circular motion over your heart) *And cleaned my heart*
Adentro, afuera, arriba, abajo,	(repeat song—sing it a little faster every time)
¡Qué feliz estoy!	

Anonymous translation.

6. TENGO GOZO, GOZO EN MI CORAZÓN
(JOY, JOY, JOY, DOWN IN MY HEART)

Yo tengo gozo, gozo en mi corazón,	*Joy, joy, joy, down in my heart*
¿Dónde?	
En mi corazón.	
¿Dónde?	*Where?*
En mi corazón.	*Down in my heart*
Yo tengo gozo, gozo en mi corazón,	*I have joy in my heart*
¿Por qué? Porque Cristo me salvó.	*Because Christ saved me.*
Y estoy alegre, sí muy alegre.	*And I'm happy, yes, so happy*
Yo tengo el amor de Cristo en mi corazón	*I have Christ's love in my heart*
Y estoy alegre, sí muy alegre,	*And I'm so happy*
Porque Cristo me salvó	*Because Christ saved me.*

Anonymous translation.

7. HAY VIDA EN JESÚS (THERE IS LIFE IN JESUS)

Hay <u>vida</u>, hay <u>vida</u>, hay <u>vida</u> en Jesús.	*There is life in Jesus*
Hay <u>vida</u>, hay <u>vida</u>, hay <u>vida</u> en Jesús.	
Yo voy a morar en la Patria Celestial,	*I'm going to live in heaven*
Porque hay <u>vida</u>, hay <u>vida</u> en Jesús.	*because there is life in Jesus.*
- <u>Gozo</u>	*There is JOY in Jesus*
- <u>Canto</u>	*There is SONG in Jesus*

Traditional song from *Cancionero Latinoamericano.*

8. TENGO UN AMIGO QUE ME AMA (I HAVE A FRIEND THAT LOVES ME)

Yo tengo un amigo que me ama,   (point to yourself)
me ama, me ama.
Yo tengo un amigo que me ama,   *I have a friend that loves me*
Su nombre es Jesús.   *His name is Jesus.*
Que me ama, que me ama,
Me ama, sí, con tierno amor.   *He loves me with tender love*
Que me ama, que me ama,
Su nombre es Jesús.   *His name is Jesus.*
- Tú tienes un amigo que te ama.   (point to a child) *a friend who loves YOU*
- Tenemos un amigo que nos ama.   (motion "all of us") *a friend who loves US*

Traditional song from Cancionero Latinoamericano.

9. CRISTO EN LA MAÑANA (JESUS IN THE MORNING)

Cristo, Cristo,
te alabo en la mañana,   *I praise you in the morning*
te alabo a mediodía,   *I praise you at noon*
Cristo, Cristo,
Te alabo al ponerse el sol.   *I praise you when the sun goes down.*

Anonymous translation.

10. JEHOVÁ ES MI PASTOR (THE LORD IS MY SHEPHERD)

Jehová es mi pastor,   *The Lord is my shepherd (3 X)*
Y nada me faltará.   *Nothing will I lack.*
Ungiste mi cabeza con aceite,   *You anointed my head with oil.*
Y nada me faltará.
Mi copa está rebozando,   *My cup runneth over.*
Y nada me faltará

Traditional song from *Cancionero Latinoamericano*.

11. CRISTO ME AMA BIEN LO SÉ (JESUS LOVES ME THIS I KNOW)

Cristo me ama, bien lo sé.   *Jesus loves me, I know it well*
Su palabra me hace ver,   *His word makes me see*
que los niños son de aquél,   *That the children belong to Him*
quien es nuestro amigo fiel.   *Who is our friend.*

(Sí), Cristo me ama.   *Christ loves me*
(Sí), Cristo me ama.   (Same motions as in English, except
(Sí), Cristo me ama.   point to yourself before doing arms crossed for LOVE)
La Biblia dice así.

Words, Anna B. Wagner, translation. Music, William B. Bradbury. Himnario Bautista.

12. ESTE ES EL DÍA (THIS IS THE DAY)

Éste es el día, éste es el día	*This is the day*
Que el Señor nos dio, que el Señor nos dio.	*That the Lord gave us*
Me gozaré, me gozaré,	*I will rejoice*
Y me alegraré, y me alegraré.	*And be glad*
Éste es el día que el Señor nos dio,	
Me gozaré y me alegraré.	
Éste es el día, éste es el día,	
Que el Señor nos dio.	Anonymous translation.

13. JESÚS ES EL CAMINO (JESUS IS THE WAY)

Jesús es el camino,	(can be sung in a round)
yo voy al cielo con Él.	
Jesús es el camino,	*Jesus is the way*
yo voy al cielo con Él.	*I'm going to heaven with Him.*
Con Él, yo voy,	*With Him, I'm going*
Yo voy al cielo con Él.	*I'm going to heaven with Him.*
Con Él, yo voy,	
Yo voy al cielo con Él.	Traditional song from *Cancionero Latinoamericano.*

14. PADRE ABRAHAM (FATHER ABRAHAM)

Padre Abraham, tenía muchos hijos,	(march to the beat)
Muchos hijos, tenía Padre Abraham	*Many sons had father Abraham.*
Tú eres uno,	*You are one* (Stop marching- Point to them)
Y yo también	*I am too.* (Point to yourself)
Por eso todos alabamos a Jehová.	*That's why we all praise Jehova.* (wave hands in air)
• Mano derecha	(right hand)
• Mano izquierda	(left hand)
• Pie derecho	(right foot)
• Pie izquierdo	(left foot)
• La cabeza	(nod your head)
• Den la vuelta	(turn around)
• ¡Siéntense!	(sit down)
	Anonymous translation.

15. SI EN VERDAD ERES SALVO (IF YOU'RE HAPPY AND YOU KNOW IT)

1) Si en verdad eres salvo <u>di, "amén", AMÉN,</u>   *If you truly are saved say amen.*
Si en verdad eres salvo <u>di "amen", AMEN</u>
Si en verdad eres salvo, testifica con tu vida   *If you truly are saved, testify with your life.*
Si en verdad eres salvo <u>di "amen", AMEN.</u>   (Yell out the 2nd AMEN)

2) Si en verdad eres salvo, <u>con las manos,</u>   *...with your hands* (clap your hands)
3) Si en verdad eres salvo, <u>con los pies,</u>   *...with your feet* (stomp your feet)

Anonymous translation.

16. YO TE ALABO DE CORAZÓN, YO TE ALABO CON MI VOZ (I WILL PRAISE YOU WITH MY HEART, I WILL PRAISE YOU WITH MY VOICE)

Yo te alabo de corazón,   (point to heart) *I will praise you with my heart*
Yo te alabo con mi voz   (point to mouth) *I will praise you with my voice*
Y si me falta la voz,   *And if I lack my voice.*
Yo te alabo con las manos.   (clap to beat) *I will praise you with my hands*
Y si me faltan las manos,   *And if I lack my hands.*
Yo te alabo con los pies.   (stomp feet to beat) *I will praise you with my feet*
Y si me faltan los pies,   *And if I lack my feet*
Yo te alabo con el alma.   (point to yourself) *I will praise you with my soul*
Y si me falta el alma,   *And if I lack my soul*
Es que ya me fui con Él.   (point to the sky) *It's because I left with Him.*
Es que ya me fui con Él.

Traditional song from *Cancionero Latinoamericano.*

17. YO ESTOY ALEGRE (I AM SO HAPPY)

Separate into 2 groups.

(A) Yo estoy alegre   *I'm happy*
(B) ¿Por qué estás alegre?   *Why are you happy?*

(A) Yo estoy alegre   *I'm happy*
(B) Cuéntame por qué.   *tell me why*

(A) Yo estoy alegre   *I'm happy*
(B) ¿Por qué estás alegre? Eso quiero yo saber.   *Why? I want to know*

(A) Voy a contarte   *I'm going to tell you*
(B) Puedes contarme, la razón de estar alegre así.   *You can tell me the reason*

(A & B) Pa, di, am , pam, pam, pam

(A) Cristo un día me salvó,   *Christ one day saved me*
Y mi vida transformó,   *And transformed my life*
Por eso yo alegre estoy.   *That's why I'm so happy*

Traditional song from *Cancionero Latinoamericano.*

Praise & Worship Songs

1. HOSANNA (HOSANNA) - HILLSONG©

Veo al rey de Gloria, viene con fuego y poder.
Todos verán, todos verán.

Veo su amor y gracia, mi pecado perdonó,
Le alabaré, le alabaré.

//Hosanna, Hosanna, Hosanna en las Alturas.//

Veo cómo se levanta, una gran generación,
Con compasión, con compasión.

Veo avivamiento, al buscarte y al orar,
Me postraré, me postraré.

Sáname y límpiame,
Con mis ojos tus obras quiero ver.
Quiero amarte como Tú me amas.

Muéstrame tu corazón
Todo lo que soy por tu reino Dios,
Contigo quiero estar por la eternidad.

---

2. NO HAY NADIE COMO TÚ (LORD, THERE IS NONE LIKE YOU) - MARCO BARRIENTOS

Señor, aquí estamos,
Dispuestos ante ti para adorarte.
Señor, hoy te entregamos nuestro corazón,
Como una ofrenda de amor.
Señor, hemos venido a ministrarte, a adorarte.
Señor, reconocemos que no hay nadie como Tú y hoy te cantamos.

//No hay nadie como Tú,//
Precioso y glorioso
Tan bello y tan hermoso.
No hay nadie como Tú,
Precioso y glorioso,
Tan bello y tan hermoso.
Jesús, Jesús, precioso Jesús.

Quiero decirte que mi vida te pertenece
Porque tú Señor, tu vida diste por mí
Y en este canto yo te entrego mi amor
Para exaltarte y que todo el mundo sepa.

3. PODEROSO (STRONGER) - HILLSONG©

Su amor me alcanzó, en la cruz por mi murió
Mi pecado Él llevó, con poder resucitó.

Sigues siendo siempre fiel, mi refugio mi sostén.
Jesucristo es la verdad, que me dio la libertad.

Poderoso, poderoso,
Me libraste, me salvaste.
Está escrito, haz vencido
Cristo, Tú eres Señor.

Sin principio sin final, esperanza sin igual.
El perdido encontró, en Jesús la salvación.

Que tu nombre sea exaltado, sea exaltado, sea exaltado.

---

4. SÓLO DIOS PUEDE SALVAR (MIGHTY TO SAVE) - HILLSONG©

Todos necesitan amor que nunca falla,
Tu gracia y compasión.
Todos necesitan perdón y esperanza,
Y un Dios que salva.

Cristo puede mover montes.
¡Sólo Dios puede salvar, mi Dios puede salvar!
Por siempre, Autor de Salvación,
Jesús la muerte venció, Él la muerte venció.

Aun con mis temores, sé que me aceptas,
Lléname otra vez.
Mi vida te ofrezco, para seguir tus pasos.
A Ti me rindo (a Ti me rindo).

En la tierra, Tu luz brillará,
Cantamos por la gloria de Tu majestad, Jesús.
En la tierra, Tu luz brillará,
Cantamos por la gloria de Tu majestad

5. TU FIDELIDAD (YOUR FAITHFULNESS) - MARCOS WITT

Tu fidelidad es grande,
Tu fidelidad incomparable es.
Nadie como Tú, bendito Dios.
Grande es tu fidelidad.

---

6. LA NIÑA DE TUS OJOS (THE APPLE OF YOUR EYE) - DANIEL CALVETI

Me viste a mí, cuando nadie me vio
Me amaste a mí, cuando nadie me amó

Y me diste nombre.
Yo soy tu niña,
La niña de tus ojos,
Porque me amaste a mí.
///Me amaste a mí///

//Te amo más que a mi vida, //
Te amo más que a mi vida, más.

---

7. VENGO A ADORARTE (HERE I AM TO WORSHIP) - HILLSONG©

Oh luz del mundo bajaste a la oscuridad,
Mis ojos abriste, pude ver.
Belleza que causa que mi ser te adore,
Esperanza de vida en ti.

Vengo adorarte, vengo a postrarme,
Vengo a decir que eres mi Dios.
Eres simplemente bello, simplemente digno,
Tan maravilloso para mí.

Oh Rey eterno, tan alto y exaltado,
Glorioso en el cielo eres Tú.
Al mundo que hiciste, humilde viniste,
Pobre te hiciste por amor.

////Nunca sabré cuanto costó, Ver mi pecado en la cruz.////

8. ALABARÉ (I WILL PRAY) - TRADITIONAL SONG FROM CANCIONERO LATINOAMERICANO

// Alabaré, alabaré, alabaré, alabaré,
Alabaré a mi Señor. //

Juan vio el número de los redimidos
Y todos alababan al Señor
Unos oraban, otros cantaban,
Pero todos alababan al Señor.

Alabaré, alabaré, alabaré, alabaré,
Alabaré a mi Señor.

---

9. TODOPODEROSO (ALL POWERFUL) - DANILO MONTERO

La única razón de mi adoración
Eres tú mi Jesús
Mi único motivo para vivir
Eres tú mi Señor

Mi única verdad
Está en ti, eres mi luz
Y mi salvación
Mi único amor
Eres tú, Señor
Y por siempre te alabaré

//Tú eres todopoderoso
Eres grande y majestuoso,
Eres fuerte, invencible
y no hay nadie como Tú//

---

10. SI EL ESPÍRITU DE DIOS SE MUEVE EN MÍ (IF THE SPIRIT OF GOD MOVES IN ME) – TRADITIONAL SONG FROM CANCIONERO LATINOAMERICANO

//Si el Espíritu de Dios se mueve en mí, yo canto como David.//
//Yo canto, yo canto, yo canto como David.//
- Alabo
- Oro

11. ÉL ES EL REY (HE IS THE KING) - DANILO MONTERO

Él es el Rey infinito en Poder,
Él es el rey de los cielos
seré para Él siervo fiel,
pues mi vida compró con su amor.

Él es el Rey lo confiesa mi ser,
Él es el rey de los siglos
mi vida la rindo a sus pies,
Él es Rey sobre mi corazón.

Él es el Rey, Él es el Rey,
Él es el Rey de mi vida.
Él es el Rey, Él es el Rey
reina con autoridad.

Su reino eterno es, su trono el cielo es.
Él es el Rey que viene a su pueblo a llevar.

---

12. TÚ ESTÁS AQUÍ (YOU ARE HERE) – JESÚS ADRIAN ROMERO

Aunque mis ojos no te puedan ver,
Te puedo sentir, sé que estás aquí.
Aunque mis manos no puedan tocar,
Tu rostro señor, sé que estás aquí.

Mi corazón puede sentir tu presencia,
Tú estás aquí, Tú estás aquí.
Puedo sentir tu majestad,
Tú estás aquí, Tú estás aquí.

Mi corazón puede mirar tu hermosura,
Tú estás aquí, Tú estás aquí.
Puedo sentir tu gran amor,
Tú estás aquí, Tú estás aquí.

13. DAME TUS OJOS (GIVE ME YOUR EYES) – MARCELA GÁNDARA

Dame tus ojos, quiero ver,
Dame tus palabras, quiero hablar,
Dame tu parecer.
Dame tus pies, yo quiero ir,
Dame tus deseos para sentir,
Dame tu parecer.

Dame lo que necesito para ser como tú.
Dame tu voz, dame tu aliento.
Todo mi tiempo es para ti.
Dame el camino que debo seguir.
Dame tus sueños, tus anhelos,
Tus pensamientos, tu sentir.
Dame tu vida para vivir.

Déjame ver lo que tú ves,
Dame de tu gracia, tu poder
Dame tu corazón.
Déjame ver en tu interior.
Para ser cambiado por tu amor,
Dame tu corazón.

Spanish with a Mission

Appendices

APPENDIX I: QUICK LISTS of VOCABULARY, Verbs and Phrases: English to Spanish

accept - aceptar	**finish** - terminar	**respond** - responder
ache - doler	**follow, continue** - seguir	**rest** - descansar
adore - adorar	**forget** - olvidar	**return** - volver
answer - contestar	**forgive** - perdonar	**run** - correr
arrive - llegar	**form** - formar	**say** - decir
ask - preguntar	**fulfill, complete** - cumplir	**see** - ver
ask for - pedir	**garden** - jardinear	**sell** - vender
baptize - bautizar	**get up** - levantarse	**serve** - servir
bathe - bañarse	**give** - dar	**share** - compartir
be - ser	**go** - ir	**shed, spill** - derramar
be able to - poder	**go out** - salir	**shop** - ir de compras
begin - comezar	**go to bed** - acostarse	**shower** - ducharse
be worth - valer	**have** - tener	**sing** - cantar
believe - creer	**hear** - oír	**sleep** - dormir
bless - bendecir	**help** - ayudar	**speak** - hablar
break - romper, quebrar	**invite** - invitar	**start** - comenzar
bring - traer	**jump** - saltar	**study** - estudiar
buy - comprar	**know** (knowledge) - saber	**suffer** - sufrir
camp out - acampar	**know** (a person) - conocer	**swim** - nadar
call - llamar	**learn** - aprender	**take** - llevar
chat - charlar	**leave** - irse, salir	**take, drink** - tomar
change - cambiar	**leave** (behind) - dejar	**take off** (clothes) - quitarse
clean - limpiar	**listen** - escuchar	**teach** - enseñar
close - cerrar	**live** - vivir	**think** - pensar
come - venir	**look for** - buscar	**touch,** (play instrument) -
comprehend - comprender	**lose** - perder	tocar (un instrumento)
confess - confesar	**love** - amar	**translate** - traducir
converse - conversar, platicar	**need** - necesitar	**travel** - viajar
cook - cocinar	**open** - abrir	**try** - intentar, tratar
cover - cubrir	**organizer** - organize	**turn , bend , fold** - doblar
crucify - crucificar	**pass** (time) - pasar(tiempo)	**turn on, light** - encender
curse - maldecir	**pay** - pagar	**understand** - entender
dance - bailar	**permit** - permitir	**unite, join** - unir
decide - decidir	**play** - jugar	**use** - usar
defeat, conquer - vencer	**please, like** - gustar	**visit** - visitar
desire, wish - desear	**praise** - alabar	**wake up** - despertarse
dig - cavar	**pray** - orar	**wait for, hope** - esperar,
do or make - hacer	**preach** - predicar	expect
dream - soñar	**prepare** - preparar	**walk** - caminar
drive - manejar, conducir	**present** - presentar	**want** - querer
drink - beber	**put** - poner	**wash** - lavar
eat - comer	**put on** - ponerse	**watch, look** - mirar
enter - entrar	**read** - leer	**wear, take** - llevar
exist - existir	**receive** - recibir	**win** - ganar
explain - explicar	**redeem** - redimir	**write** - escribir
fall asleep - dormirse	**remember** - recordar	**witness** - testificar
feel - sentir	**repent** - arrepentir	**work** - trabajar

PHRASES TO USE WITH INFINITIVES

1. **I want to** _____. = Yo quiero + infinitive.
2. **I need to** _____. = Yo necesito + infinitive
3. **I can** _____. = Yo puedo + infinitive
4. **I like to** _____. = Me gusta + infinitive
5. **I love to** _____. = Me encanta + infinitive
6. **I have to** _____. = Yo tengo que + infinitive
7. **I'm going to** _____. = Yo voy + a + infinitive
8. **I'm thinking (planning) to** _____. = Pienso + infinitive
9. **It is important to** _____. = Es importante + infinitive
10. **It is impossible to** _____. = Es imposible + infinitve

* #9 and #10 are impersonal expressions and are not conjugated like the others.

CLASSROOM | *EL SALÓN DE CLASE*

book - el libro	**homework, task** - la tarea
pencil - el lápiz	**computer** - la computadora
pen - la pluma	**(cell) phone** - el teléfono (celular)
paper - el papel	**student** - el/la estudiante
desk - el escritorio	**student** - el alumno/a
chair - la silla	**teacher** - el/la maestro/a
light - la luz	**professor** - el/la profesor/a
lights - las luces	**little boy** - el niño
window - la ventana	**little girl** - la niña
door - la puerta	**guy (boy)** - el chico
map - el mapa, plano	**young lady (girl)** - la chica
notebook - el cuaderno	**man** - el hombre
backpack - la mochila	**woman** - la mujer
blackboard - la pizarra, el pizarrón	**question** - la pregunta
clock - el reloj	**answer** - la respuesta
table - la mesa	**school** - la escuela, el colegio
page - la página	**church** - la iglesia
bathroom - el baño	**university** - la universidad
Sunday School - la escuela dominical	**library** - la biblioteca
Bible class - la clase bíblica	

TO GATHER INFORMATION

How do you spell it? - ¿Cómo se escribe?	**name** - nombre
	last name - apellido
How many children do you have? - ¿Cuántos hijos tiene?	**telephone #** - número de teléfono
	address - la dirección / el domicilio
Slower, please. - Más despacio, por favor.	**the street** - la calle

LOS SALUDOS | *GREETINGS*

Hello, good morning / good afternoon.	- Hola, buenos días / Buenas tardes.
Good evening / How's it going?	- Buenas noches /¿Qué tal?
How are you?	- ¿Cómo está usted?
Fine, thank you?	- Bien, gracias.
Very well, and you?	- Muy bien, ¿y usted?
What is your name?	- ¿Cómo se llama usted?
My name is ___ (I call myself _)	- Me llamo _____.
His/her name is __ (He/she calls him/herself __)	- Se llama _____.
Where are you from?	- ¿De dónde es usted?
And you?	- ¿Y usted?
I'm from ___.	- (Yo) soy de...
Nice to meet you.	- Mucho gusto.
The pleasure is mine.	- El gusto es mío.
Please / thank you / you're welcome	- Por favor / Gracias / de nada
I'm (very) sorry.	- lo siento (mucho)

PROFESIONES | *PROFESSIONS* (ALPHABETICAL)

accountant - contador/a	**missionary** - misionero/a
actor - actor/actriz	**manager** - gerente
architect - arquitecto/a	**musician** - músico/a
artist - artista	**nurse** - enfermero/a
author - autor/a	**painter** - pintor/a
boss - jefe/a	**pastor** - pastor
business man - hombre de negocios	**priest** - cura, padre
business woman - mujer de negocios	**pharmacist** - farmacéutico/a
cook - cocinero/a	**photographer** - fotógrafo/a
counselor - consejero/a	**plumber** - plomero
dentist - el/la dentista	**police** - policía
director - director/a	**politician** - político
doctor - médico/a	**professional** - profesional
doctor - doctor/a	**professor** - profesor/a
driver - conductor/a, chofer	**retired** - jubilado/a, retirado/a
employee - empleado/a	**salesperson** - vendedor/a
engineer - ingeniero/a	**secretary** - secretario/a
gardener - jardinero/a	**singer** - cantante
housewife - ama de casa	**soldier** - soldado
journalist - periodista	**student** - estudiante
judge - juez/a	**teacher** - maestro/a
lawyer - abogado/a	**waiter/waitress** - mesero/a
librarian - bibliotecario/a	**worker/laborer** - trabajador/a

LOS NÚMEROS | *NUMBERS*

0 **cero**	9 **nueve**	18 **dieciocho**	90 **noventa**	900 **novecientos**
1 **uno**	10 **diez**	19 **diecinueve**	100 **cien**	1.000 **mil**
2 **dos**	11 **once**	20 **veinte**	200 **doscientos**	2.000 **dos mil**
3 **tres**	12 **doce**	30 **treinta**	300 **trescientos**	10.000 **diez mil**
4 **cuatro**	13 **trece**	40 **cuarenta**	400 **cuatrocientos**	100.000 **cien mil**
5 **cinco**	14 **catorce**	50 **cincuenta**	500 **quinientos**	1.000.000 **un millón**
6 **seis**	15 **quince**	60 **sesenta**	600 **seiscientos**	
7 **siete**	16 **dieciséis**	70 **setenta**	700 **setecientos**	
8 **ocho**	17 **diecisiete**	80 **ochenta**	800 **ochocientos**	

LOS DÍAS | DAYS

Sunday - domingo	**weekdays** - los días de la semana
Monday - lunes	**weekend** - el fin de semana
Tuesday - martes	**all the days, every day** - todos los días
Wednesday - miércoles	**each** - cada
Thursday - jueves	**each (and every) Sunday** - cada domingo
Friday - viernes	**this** - este, esta
Saturday - sábado	**this Monday/this week** - este lunes / esta semana

MONTHS | *LOS MESES*

January - enero	**May** - mayo	**September** - septiembre
February - febrero	**June** - junio	**October** - octubre
March - marzo	**July** - julio	**November** - noviembre
April - abril	**August** - agosto	**December** - diciembre

SEASONS / HOLIDAYS | *LAS ESTACIONES / LOS DÍAS FERIADOS*

spring - la primavera	**Christmas** - Navidad	**New Year** - Año nuevo
summer - el verano	**Christmas Eve** - Noche Buena	**Holy Week** - Semana Santa
autumn - el otoño	**Day of the Wise Men** - Día de los Reyes	**Easter** - Pascua
winter - el invierno		**Mother's Day/Father's Day** - Día de la Madre / Día del Padre

WEATHER | *EL TIEMPO / EL CLIMA*

What's the weather? - ¿Qué tiempo hace?	**it's hot** - hace calor
it's nice weather - hace buen tiempo	**it's cool** - hace fresco
it's bad weather - hace mal tiempo	**it's cold** - hace frío
it's raining / it rains - llueve	**it's windy** - hace viento
it's snowing / it snows - nieva	**it's sunny** - hace sol

PREPOSITIONS

to, at - a **of, from, about** - de	**in, at** - en **with / without** - con / sin	**during, through, for** - por **for, in order to** - para

FAMILY | *LA FAMILIA*

el padre, papá - father	**son** - el hijo
mother - la madre, mamá	**daughter** - la hija
parents - los padres	**children** - los hijos
brother - el hermano	**grandson** - el nieto
sister - la hermana	**grandaughter** - la nieta
siblings - los hermanos	**granchildren** - los nietos
grandfather - el abuelo	**male cousin** - el primo
grandmother - la abuela	**female cousin** - la prima
grandparents - los abuelos	**cousins** - los primos
	niece / nephew - el sobrino / la sobrina
uncle - el tío	
aunt - la tía	**brother-in-law** - el cuñado
aunts and uncles - los tíos	**sister-in-law** - la cuñada
father-in-law - el suegro	**son-in-law** - el yerno
mother-in-law - la suegra	**daughter-in-law** - la nuera
parents-in-law - los suegros	
	boyfriend (groom) - el novio
husband - el esposo	**girlfriend (bride)** - la novia
wife - la esposa	

ADJECTIVES FOR PEOPLE (USE WITH THE VERB *SER*)

very - muy	**dark skinned** - moreno/a	**shy** - tímido/a
tall - alto/a	**skinny** - flaco/a	**patient** - paciente
short - bajo/a	**young** - joven	**believer** - creyente
pretty - bonito/a	**old** - viejo/a	**married** - casado/a
ugly - feo/a	**nice, pleasant** - simpático/a	**single** - soltero/a
beautiful - hermoso/a	**intelligent** - inteligente	**Christian** - cristiano/a
handsome - guapo/a	**generous** - generoso/a	**Baptist** - bautista
cute - lindo/a	**hard working** - trabajador/a	**Evangelical** - evangélico/a
blond(e) - rubio/a	**organized** - organizado/a	**Methodist** - metodista
fat - gordo/a	**funny** - chistoso/a	**Catholic** - católico
thin - delgado/a	**fun** - divertido/a	**Presbyterian** - presbiteriano
punctual - puntual	**friendly** - amable	**Pentecostal** - pentecostal

FEELINGS (USE WITH THE VERB *ESTAR*)

well, fine - bien	**bad off** - mal	**nervous** - nervioso/a
happy - feliz, alegre	**tired** - cansado/a	**sick** - enfermo/a
content - contento/a	**bored** - aburrido/a	**busy** - ocupado/a
sad - triste	**mad, angry** - enojado/a	**worried** - preocupado/a

THINGS YOU CAN HAVE

house - la casa	**dog** - el perro
apartment - el apartamento	**cat** - el gato
car - el auto, carro, coche	**bird** - el pájaro
truck - la camioneta	**cell phone** - el teléfono celular, móvil
bicycle - la bicicleta	**television** - la televisión
motorcycle - la moto	**radio** - el/la radio
computer - la computadora	**purse** - la cartera
watch, clock - el reloj	**wallet** - la billetera
problem - un problema	**job** - el trabajo
money - el dinero	**liberty, freedom** - la libertad
food - la comida	**love of Christ** - el amor de Cristo
health - salud	**peace of Christ** - la paz de Cristo
happiness - la felicidad	**salvation** - salvación
sadness - la tristeza	**the meeting** - la reunión

FEELINGS AND CONDITIONS YOU CAN HAVE

hunger - el hambre	**cold** - el frío	**haste, hurriedness** - la prisa
thirst - la sed	**fear** - el miedo	**stress** - el estrés
heat - el calor	**sleepiness** - el sueño	**good health** - la buena salud

DESCRIPTIVE ADJECTIVES FOR THINGS

new - nuevo/a	**good** - bueno/a	**long in length** - largo
old - viejo/a	**bad** - malo/a	**short in length** - corto
big - grande	**fast** - rápido/a	**expensive** - caro
small - pequeño/a	**slow** - lento/a	**inexpensive, cheap** - barato
small - chico/a	**comfortable** - cómodo	**free** - gratis
little - chiquito/a		

COLORS | *COLORES*

orange - anaranjado	**yellow** - amarillo	**brown** - café, marrón
white - blanco	**black** - negro	**green** - verde
blue - azul	**red** - rojo	**purple** - morado/violeta
light blue - celeste	**pink** - rosado	**gray** - gris

CLOTHING | *ROPA*

dress - el vestido	**bathing suit** - el traje de baño	**glasses** - los lentes
pants - los pantalones	**shorts** - los pantalones cortos	**glasses** - los anteojos
shirt - la camisa	**jeans** - los bluyines, jeans	**scarf** - bufanda
suit - el traje	**belt** - el cinturón	**watch** - el reloj
blouse - la blusa	**tie** - la corbata	**necklace** - el collar
skirt - la falda	**hat** - el sombrero	**ring** - el anillo
jacket - la chaqueta	**shoes** - los zapatos	**closet** - el armario, el ropero
sweater - el suéter	**tennis shoes** - los zapatos tenis	
coat - el abrigo	**boots** - las botas	
t-shirt - la camiseta	**sandals** - las sandalias	

MEAT - *CARNE*
beef - la carne de res
chicken - el pollo
pork chops - las (chuletas de) cerdo
hotdog, sausage - la salchicha
sausage - el chorizo
fish - el pescado
shrimp - los camarones
tuna - el atún
ham - el jamón
bacon - el tocino

VEGETABLES - *VERDURAS/VEGETALES*
lettuce - la lechuga
tomato - el tomate
carrot - la zanahoria
onion - la cebolla
spinach - la espinaca
corn - el maíz
potato - la papa
cucumber, pickle - el pepino
broccoli - el brócoli
peas - los guisantes, las arvejas, los chícharos

FRUIT - *FRUTA*
apple - la manzana
orange - la naranja
banana - la banana
grapes - las uvas
melon - el melón
strawberries - las fresas
peach - el melocotón, durazno
pineapple - la piña
pear - la pera
lemon - el limón
cherries - las cerezas
kiwi - el kiwi
grapefruit - la toronja
watermelon - la sandía

DESSERT - *POSTRE*
sweet - dulce
cake - la torta, el queque
pie, cake - el pastel
cookies - las galletas

MORE FOOD - *MÁS COMIDA*
rice - el arroz
beans - los frijoles
pasta - la pasta
eggs - los huevos
yogurt - el yogur
cheese - el queso
peanut butter - la mantequilla de maní
jelly - la jalea, la mermelada
(toasted) bread - pan (tostado)
crackers - las galletas saladas
olives - las aceitunas
popcorn - las palomitas
cereal - el cereal

CONDIMENTS - *CONDIMENTOS*
salt - la sal
pepper - la pimienta
sugar - el azúcar
sweetener - el edulcorante
mayonaise - la mayonesa
mustard - la mostaza
butter - la mantequilla
oil - el aceite
vinegar - el vinagre
cream - la crema
garlic - el ajo
dressing - el aderezo

DRINKS - *BEBIDAS*
water - el agua
tea - el té
coffee - el café
milk - la leche
(orange) juice - el jugo (de naranja)
ice - el hielo
soda pop - una soda, gaseosa
soda water - el agua con gas
shake, smoothie - el licuado
wine - el vino
beer - la cerveza
candy - los dulces, caramelos
chocolate - el chocolate
vanilla - la vainilla
ice cream - el helado

*AGRICULTURE VOCABULARY FOUND AT 6.2

THE BODY | *EL CUERPO*

body - el cuerpo	**shoulders** - los hombros	**heart** - el corazón
hair - el pelo	**arm** - el brazo	**stomach** - el estómago
head - la cabeza	**elbow** - el codo	**lungs** - los pulmones
forehead - la frente	**wrist** - la muñeca	**blood** - la sangre
face - la cara	**hand** - la mano	**bone** - el hueso
eyes - los ojos	**finger** - el dedo	**skin** - la piel
ears - las orejas	**nails** - las uñas	**bones** - los huesos
inner ears - los oídos	**waist** - la cintura	**skull** - el cráneo
nose - la nariz	**hip** - la cadera	**brain** - el cerebro
cheek - la mejilla	**thigh** - el muslo	**liver** - el hígado
mouth - la boca	**leg** - la pierna	**gall bladder** - la vesícula
lips - los labios	**knee** - la rodilla	**kidneys** - los riñones
teeth - los dientes	**ankle** - el tobillo	**bladder** - la vejiga
gums - las encías	**foot** - el pie	**spleen** - el bazo
neck - el cuello	**toe** - el dedo del pie	**muscles** - los músculos
back - la espalda	**throat** - la garganta	**veins** - las venas
chest - el pecho		

*MEDICAL MISSION VOCABULARY FOUND AT 8.3

SPORTS AND ACTIVITIES | *LOS DEPORTES Y LAS ACTIVIDADES*

to exercise - hacer ejercicio	**to swim** - nadar
soccer - el fútbol	**ride a horse** - montar a caballo
football - el fútbol americano	**to go to the beach** - ir a la playa
baseball - el béisbol	**to go camping** - acampar
baketball - el básquetbol, baloncesto	**video games** - video juegos
golf - el golf	**outside** - afuera
volleyball - el voleibol	**inside** - adentro
tennis - el tenis	**outside** - al aire libre

NATURE | *LA NATURALEZA*

mountains - las montañas	**sky** - el cielo
river - e l río	**sun** - el sol
lake - el lago	**moon** - la luna
earth, dirt - la tierra	**the stars** - las estrellas
above, on top of - arriba de	**below, underneath** - debajo de

POSITIVE AND NEGATIVE WORDS

something - algo	**nada** - nothing
someone - alguien	**no one** - nadie
also - también	**either, neither** - tampoco
always - siempre	**never/ never ever** - nunca / jamás
some - algún	**none, not any** - ningún
any, some - alguno/a/os/as	**not one, not any** - nunguno/a
and / or - y/o	**neither...nor** - ni...ni

HOUSE/HOME – *LA CASA*
door – la puerta
window – la ventana
chimney - la chimenea
floor/ground – el suelo
floor – el piso
two floors – dos pisos

LIVINGROOM – *LA SALA*
sofa – el sofá
rug – la alfombra
wall picture – el cuadro
curtains – las cortinas
lamp – la lámpara
shelves – los estantes
arm chair – el sillón
television – la televisión/el televisor

DINING ROOM – *EL COMEDOR*
table – la mesa
chairs – las sillas
flower vase – el florero
dishes – los platos
glasses – los vasos
dinnerware – las vajillas
tablecloth - el mantel

KITCHEN – *LA COCINA*
stove – la estufa
oven – el horno
microwave - el microonda
sink – el fregadero, la pileta
dish washer – el lavaplatos
refrigerator – el refrigerador
refrigerator - la refrigeradora
cabinets - los gabinetes
washing machine – la lavadora

ROOM - *LA HABITACIÓN*
room – el cuarto
bedroom – el dormitorio, la recámara, alcoba
bed – la cama
pillow – la almohada
blanket – la manta, cobija
night stand – la mesita de noche
lamp - la lámpara
closet – el ropero, el armario

BATHROOM - *EL BAÑO*
bathtub – la bañera, la tina
toilet – el inodoro
bathroom sink – el lavamanos
mirror - el espejo
shower - la ducha
towel – la toalla
soap – el jabón
shampoo – el champú
conditioner – el acondicionador
toothbrush – el cepillo de dientes
toothpaste – la pasta de dientes

BACK YARD – *EL PATIO*
outside – afuera
garden - el jardín
trees – los árboles
bushes - los arbustos
garage - el garaje
lawn – el césped
flowers – las flores
pool – la piscina, la alberca

DESCRIPTIONS
roomy – amplio/a
bright/clear – claro/a
comfortable – cómodo/a
it's clean – está limpio/a
it's dirty – está sucio/a
it's organized – está organizado/a

HOME ACTIVITIES | *LAS ACTIVIDADES DE LA CASA*

to clean - limpiar
to clean the floor - limpiar el piso
to wash dishes - lavar platos
to wash clothes - lavar ropa

to cook - cocinar
to organize - organizar
to make the bed - hacer la cama
to garden - trabajar en el jardín

THINGS IN A CITY/TOWN

CITY AND TOWN - *LA CIUDAD Y EL PUEBLO*
church/cathedral - la iglesia/la catedral
school - la escuela
school (incl. high school) - el colegio
university - la universidad
orphanage - el orfanato
children's home - el hogar de niños
hotel - el hotel
town square, plaza - la plaza
park - el parque
store - la tienda
market - el mercado
supermarket - el supermercado
mall or group of stores - el centro comercial
bread store, bakery - la panadería
fruit store - la frutería
vegetable store - la verdulería
meat store - la carnicería
neighborhood - la vecindad
small neighborhood store -la pulpería (C. America)
small neighborhood store - el quiosko (S. America)

TRANSPORTATION - *TRANSPORTE*
car - el carro, coche, auto
truck - la camioneta
(big) truck - el camión
bus - el bus, autobús, camión (mex.),
        la guagua (P.R., Dom. Rep.)
taxi - el taxi
train - el tren
subway - el subterráneo, metro
ship - el barco
boat - la lancha, el bote
cruise (ship) - el crucero
horse - el caballo
street - la calle
highway - la carretera, autopista
map - el mapa, plano

THE AIRPORT - *EL AEROPUERTO*
airplane - el avión
airline - la aerolínea
luggage - el equipaje
suitcase - la maleta
carry on baggage - la maleta de mano
ticket - el boleto
round trip - ida y vuelta
no smoking section - la sección de no fumar
seat - el asiento
window - la ventana
aisle - el pasillo
exit - la salida

HOTEL - *EL HOTEL*
reservation - la reservación
lobby - el vestíbulo
room - el cuarto, habitación
bed - la cama
sheets - las sábanas
towels - las toallas
soap - jabón
toilet paper - el papel higiénico
the chamber maid - el camarero/a
the employee (clerk) - el empleado
the employee (maid) - la empleada
room service - servicio de cuarto

BANK - *EL BANCO*
currency change - cambio de moneda
ATM - el cajero automático
change (in money) - el cambio
cash - el efectivo
account - la cuenta
(travelers') checks - los cheques (de viajeros)
credit card - la tarjeta de crédito
debit card - la tarjeta de débito

LOCATIONS

close to - cerca de
far from - lejos de
in front of - enfrente de
next to, beside - al lado de
next to - junto a
in between - entre

behind - detrás de
on top of, on - encima de
underneath of - debajo de
here/there - aquí/allí
around here/around there - acá/allá

testimony - el testimonio	**God's people** - el pueblo de Dios
Bible - la Biblia	**the way** - el camino
God's Word -la Palabra de Dios	**the truth** - la verdad
Bible verse - el versículo	**spiritual gift** - el don espiritual
church - la iglesia	**to repent** - arrepentirse
service - servicio, culto	**redeemed** - redimido(s)
pulpit - el púlpito	**redeemer** - redentor
last supper - la santa cena	**death** - la muerte
Jesus Christ - Jesucristo	**blood** - la sangre
to baptize - bautizar	**to shed, spill** - derramar
to forgive - perdonar	**cross** - la cruz
forgiveness - el perdón	**to crucify** - crucificar
God's will - la voluntad de Dios	**crucified** - crucificado
to give your heart -entregar tu corazón	**Virgin Mary** - la Virgen María
sin/sinner - el pecado / el pecador	**John the baptist** - Juan el bautista
heaven(s) - el cielo, los cielos	**prophet** - el profeta
angel - el ángel	**satan** - satanás
decision - la decisión	**devil** - el diablo
to make a decision - tomar una decisión	**enemy** - el enemigo
invitation - la invitación	**demons** - los demonios
to invite - invitar	**hell** - el infierno
victory - la victoria	**to know as personal Savior** - conocer como Salvador personal
to be saved - ser salvo	
plan of salvation - El plan de salvación	**power/powerful** - poder/poderoso
faith - la fe	**to conquer/conqueror** - vencer/vencedor
Father, Son and Holy Spirit - el Padre, el Hijo y el Espíritu Santo	**worthy** - digno
	mercy - la misericordia

the creation - la creación	**Birth of Jesus** - El nacimiento de Jesús
heavens and earth - los cielos y la tierra	**manger** - el pesebre
Adam and Eve - Adán y Eva	**star** - la estrella
la serpiente - serpente	**Jesus calms the storm** - Jesús calma la tormenta
el pecado - sin	**boat** - el barco
Noah's Ark - El arca de Noé	**Jesus calms storm** - Jesús calma la tormenta
the rain - la lluvia	**Parable of the Prodigal Son** - La parábola del hijo perdido
the animals - los animales	
David and Goliath - David y Goliat	**inheritance** - la herencia
sling and rocks - una honda y piedras	**Parable of the Good Samaritan** - La parábola del buen samaritano.
Daniel in the Den of Lions - Daniel en el foso de los leones	**herido** - wounded
Josephs coat of many colors - José y la túnica de muchos colores	

Appendix II: Present Tense Verb Conjugations

PRESENT INDICATIVE TENSE

REGULAR VERBS

	-ar	-er	-ir
yo	-o	-o	-o
tú	-as	-es	-es
él / ella / Ud.	-a	-e	-e
nosotros	-amos	-emos	-imos
ellos / ellas / Uds.	-an	-en	-en

With this chart, you can conjugate any REGULAR Spanish verb.

STEM + ending = conjugation

	LLEVAR	*BEBER*	*VIVIR*
yo	llevo	bebo	vivo
tú	llevas	bebes	vives
él / ella / Ud.	lleva	bebe	vive
nosotros	llevamos	bebemos	vivimos
ellos / ellas / Uds.	llevan	beben	viven

IRREGULAR VERBS

ALPHABETICAL

CONOCER - to know / to be familiar with

yo	conozco	nosotros/as	conocemos
tú	conoces		
él, ella, Ud.	conoce	ellos, ellas, Uds.	conocen

DAR - to give

yo	doy	nosotros/as	damos
tú	das		
él, ella, Ud.	da	ellos, ellas, Uds.	dan

DECIR - to say/to tell

yo	digo	nosotros/as	decimos
tú	dices		
él, ella, Ud.	dice	ellos, ellas, Uds.	dicen

ENTENDER - to understand

yo	**entiendo**	nosotros/as	**entendemos**
tú	**entiendes**		
él, ella, Ud.	**entiende**	ellos, ellas, Uds.	**entienden**

ESTAR - to be

yo	**estoy**	nosotros/as	**estamos**
tú	**estás**		
él, ella, Ud.	**está**	ellos, ellas, Uds.	**están**

HACER - to do / to make

yo	**hago**	nosotros/as	**hacemos**
tú	**haces**		
él, ella, Ud.	**hace**	ellos, ellas, Uds.	**hacen**

IR - to go

yo	**voy**	nosotros/as	**vamos**
tú	**vas**		
él, ella, Ud.	**va**	ellos, ellas, Uds.	**van**

IRSE - to leave (to take oneself away)

yo	**me voy**	nosotros/as	**nos vamos**
tú	**te vas**		
él, ella, Ud.	**te va**	ellos, ellas, Uds.	**se van**

JUGAR - to play

yo	**juego**	nosotros/as	**jugamos**
tú	**juegas**		
él, ella, Ud.	**juega**	ellos, ellas, Uds.	**juegan**

LEVANTARSE - to get up (reflexive)

yo	**me levanto**	nosotros/as	**nos levantamos**
tú	**te levantas**		
él, ella, Ud.	**se levanta**	ellos, ellas, Uds.	**se levantan**

OÍR - to hear (this verb changes the -i to a -y between 2 vowels)

yo	**oigo**	nosotros/as	**oímos**
tú	**oyes**		
él, ella, Ud.	**oye**	ellos, ellas, Uds.	**oyen**

PEDIR - to ask for

yo	**pido**	nosotros/as	**pedimos**
tú	**pides**		
él, ella, Ud.	**pide**	ellos, ellas, Uds.	**piden**

PENSAR - to think

yo	pienso	nosotros/as	pensamos
tú	piensas		
él, ella, Ud.	piensa	ellos, ellas, Uds.	piensan

PODER - to be able to (can)

yo	puedo	nosotros/as	podemos
tú	puedes		
él, ella, Ud.	puede	ellos, ellas, Uds.	pueden

PONER - to put

yo	pongo	nosotros/as	ponemos
tú	pones		
él, ella, Ud.	pone	ellos, ellas, Uds.	ponen

QUERER - to want

yo	quiero	nosotros/as	queremos
tú	quieres		
él, ella, Ud.	quiere	ellos, ellas, Uds.	quieren

SABER - to know (knowledge)

yo	sé	nosotros/as	sabemos
tú	sabes		
él, ella, Ud.	sabe	ellos, ellas, Uds.	saben

SALIR - to go out

yo	salgo	nosotros/as	salimos
tú	sales		
él, ella, Ud.	sale	ellos, ellas, Uds.	salen

SEGUIR - to continue, to follow

yo	sigo	nosotros/as	seguimos
tú	sigues		
él, ella, Ud.	sigue	ellos, ellas, Uds.	siguen

SER - to be

yo	soy	nosotros/as	somos
tú	eres		
él, ella, Ud.	es	ellos, ellas, Uds.	son

SENTIR - to feel

yo	siento	nosotros/as	sentimos
tú	sientes		
él, ella, Ud.	siente	ellos, ellas, Uds.	sienten

TENER - to have

yo	tengo	nosotros/as	tenemos
tú	tienes		
él, ella, Ud.	tiene	ellos, ellas, Uds.	tienen

TRADUCIR - to translate

yo	traduzco	nosotros/as	traducimos
tú	traduces		
él, ella, Ud.	traduce	ellos, ellas, Uds.	traducen

TRAER - to bring

yo	traigo	nosotros/as	traemos
tú	traes		
él, ella, Ud.	trae	ellos, ellas, Uds.	traen

VALER - to be worth

yo	valgo	nosotros/as	valemos
tú	vales		
él, ella, Ud.	vale	ellos, ellas, Uds.	valen

VER - to see

yo	veo	nosotros/as	vemos
tú	ves		
él, ella, Ud.	ve	ellos, ellas, Uds.	ven

VENIR - to come

yo	vengo	nosotros/as	venimos
tú	vienes		
él, ella, Ud.	viene	ellos, ellas, Uds.	vienen

Spanish with a Mission | For Ministry, Witnessing and Mission Trips

Appendix III: Quick List of Other Verb Tenses

PRESENT PROGRESSIVE
estar + present participle (-ndo)
To form the present participle (gerund) of a verb, take the stem and add the ending.
-ar verbs end in -ando.
-er and -ir verbs en in -iendo.

HABLAR: I am speaking, you are speaking, he is speaking, etc...

yo	estoy hablando	nosotros/as	estamos hablando
tú	estás hablando		
él, ella, Ud.	está hablando	ellos, ellas, Uds.	están hablando

COMER: I am eating, you are eating, he is eating, etc...

yo	estoy comiendo	nosotros/as	estamos comiendo
tú	estás comiendo		
él, ella, Ud.	está comiendo	ellos, ellas, Uds.	están comiendo

ESCRIBIR: I am writing, you are writing, he is writing, etc...

yo	estoy escribiendo	nosotros/as	estamos escribiendo
tú	estás escribiendo		
él, ella, Ud.	está escribiendo	ellos, ellas, Uds.	están escribiendo

Irregulars: *leyendo* (reading) , *trayendo* (bringing) , *oyendo* (hearing).

INFORMAL FUTURE
IR + A + Infinitive. Equivalent to the phrase "Going to..." that is used in English.

ESTUDIAR - to study (I am going to study, you are going to study...)

yo	voy a estudiar	nosotros/as	vamos a estudiar
tú	vas a estudiar		
él, ella, Ud.	Va a estudiar	ellos, ellas, Uds.	van a estudiar

PAST PERFECT
The present perfect the present tense of the auxiliary verb **HABER + past participle.**
The auxiliary verb *HABER* is like our auxiliary HAVE. This is the present tense:

yo	he	nosotros/as	hemos
tú	has		
él, ella, Ud.	ha	ellos, ellas, Uds.	han

The present perfect of the verb *hablar* is as follows:

yo **he hablado I have spoken**	nosotros/as **hemos hablado we have spoken**
tú **has hablado you have spoken**	
él **ha hablado he has spoken**	ellos, ellas, Uds. **han hablado they have spoken**

PAST TENSE (PRETERITE) - SIMPLE PAST TENSE

The preterite (simple past) tense is one of the tenses with the most irregular forms. Here are the regular endings, followed by some irregular common verbs.

HABLAR - to speak (I spoke…)

yo	**hablé**	nosotros/as	**hablamos**
tú	**hablaste**		
él, ella, Ud.	**habló**	ellos, ellas, Uds.	**hablaron**

Regular -*ar*: amar: me amó - he loved me./ salvar: me salvó - (he) saved me./ orar, yo oré - I prayed.

COMER - to EAT (I ate…)

yo	**comí**	nosotros/as	**comimos**
tú	**comiste**		
él, ella, Ud.	**comió**	ellos, ellas, Uds.	**comieron**

VIVIR - to live (I lived…)

yo	**viví**	nosotros/as	**vivimos**
tú	**viviste**		
él, ella, Ud.	**vivió**	ellos, ellas, Uds.	**vivieron**

IR and *SER* have the same conjugations, meaning will be understood by context.
In the sentence, *IR* will be followed by "*a*."

VERB	YO	TÚ	ÉL, ELLA, UD.	NOSOTROS	ELLOS/UDS.
Ir - ser	fui	fuiste	fue	fuimos	fueron

DAR and *VER* are conjugated similarly.

dar	di	diste	dio	dimos	dieron
ver	vi	viste	vio	vimos	vieron

The following verbs have the indicated endings (no accents). The stem changes.
Sometimes with a -*u* othertimes with an -*i*. Notice the endings: **-e, -iste, -o, -imos, -ieron.**

tener	tuve	tuviste	tuvo	tuvimos	tuvieron
estar	estuve	estuviste	estuvo	estuvimos	estuvieron
poder	pude	pudiste	pudo	pudimos	pudieron
hacer	hice	hiciste	hizo	hicimos	hicieron
querer	quise	quisiste	quiso	quisimos	quisieron
venir	vine	viniste	vino	vinimos	vinieron

The following verbs have a -*j* in the stem and drop the -*i* in the *ellos/Uds.* form.

decir	dije	dijiste	dijo	dijimos	dijeron
traer	traje	trajiste	trajo	trajimos	trajeron

El sábado pasado **fui** a la tienda.	*Last Saturday I **went** to the store.*
Dios nos **dio** el Espíritu Santo.	*God **gave** us the Holy Spirit.*
¿**Viste** el programa anoche?	***Did you see** the program last night?*
Yo **tuve** que trabajar la semana pasada.	***I had** to work last week.*
Nosotros **pudimos** correr 10 millas^miles el fin de semana pasado.	***We were able** to run 10 miles last week end.*

Appendix IV: Written Accent Rules

RULES FOR ACCENTS PART I - SYLLABLES & DIPTHONGS

These rules and the pronunciation of the words can be heard at www.spanishwithamission.com.

Dipthongs are important to understand to know how many syllables are in a word. And this is important to know so you can understand about accents.

In Spanish, every vowel sound is a syllable nucleus.

Example:		
libro	li-bro	<u>2 syllables</u>
pluma	plu-ma	<u>2 syllables</u>
profesor	pro-fe-sor	<u>3 syllables</u>
universidad	u-ni-ver-si-dad	<u>5 syllables</u>

Listen to these words, can you write how many syllables are in each?

mesa _____   silla _____   mochila _____   pregunta _____

Sometimes you have 2 or 3 vowels together. If they are strong vowels, (-a, -e, -o), they will separate into different syllables.

Example:		
sea	se-a	2 syllables
toalla	to-a-lla	3 syllables
cereal	ce-re-al	3 syllables

In lesson A.9, you learned that the weak vowels, -u and -i can be joined with a strong vowel, -a, -e, -o and will make a **diphthong** which means it will not separate into 2 syllables, but will remain as one.

Listen to your teacher and repeat these words with **diphthongs.**

Mario, puerta, escuela, cuaderno, seis, veinte, nueve, escritorio

Repeat the words again, and figure out how many syllables each word has.

Example:	Mario	<u>Ma-rio</u>	<u>2 syllables because the second one is a dipthong</u>

If the weak vowel needs to be separated from the strong vowel in order to make 2 separate syllables, an accent mark will be added to the weak vowel and it will be stressed. This means it will **NOT** be a dipthong and the weak vowel will now become a strong vowel with its own syllable.

Now say these words. Remember, the -i and -u no longer are weak vowels.

María, púa, día, baúl, biología, fotografía, alegría

Look at the contrast of these words:
Mario (2 syllables, 1 dipthong)   María (3 syllables, no dipthong)
diario (2 syllables, 2 dipthongs)   día (2 syllables, no dipthong)

How many syllables? Gracias _____   diecinueve _____   iglesia _____

RULES FOR ACCENTS PART II

These rules and the pronunciation of the words can be heard at www.spanishwithamission.com.

The rules in Spanish for syllable stress are very clear and easy to understand.
Once you know how to separate syllables, you can know which syllable is the one that is stressed when you say the word. These are rules for which syllable to stress.

**Rule #1** - words that end with a vowel, -n or -s will be stressed on the NEXT TO THE LAST syllable.

_____ _____
here

Examples (listen and repeat) :   a-**mi**-go, com-pu-ta-**do**-ra, **Bi**-blia , **a**-gua, **can**-tan, **pal**mas, **ri**co, Guate**ma**la, **si**lla, **ca**rro, co**ri**to.

****

**Rule #2** - words that end with anything esle other than a vowel, -n or -s will be stressed on the LAST syllable.

_____ _____
here

Examples (listen and repeat) : Rule #2 - hos-pi-**tal**, can-**tar**, es-pa-**ñol**, ca-ri-**dad**, ha-**blar,** a**zul**.

****

**Rule #3** - If a word does not follow rule #1 or #2, then it will carry a WRITTEN ACCENT MARK over the syllable that is to be stressed.

Notice that these words do not follow the rules, and for this reason they have a written accent. The stress is on the vowel with the accent mark: Listen and repeat: cárcel, esdrújula, sofá, huérfano, fácil, ñandú, jóvenes, siéntense, versículo, teléfono. **Be sure you practice stressing the correct syllable!**

The following words have the stressed syllable in bold print with underline. When the word is said, that is the syllable that must be stressed more than the others.
By reviewing the rules, figure out if the word will need an written accent mark or not. If there is more than one vowel (dipthong), make sure you place it over the correct one. (the strong vowel)

1. Mar**le**na
2. pa**pe**les
3. te**le**fonos
4. **ar**bol
5. profe**so**ra

6. Pana**ma**
7. fotogra**fia**
8. **cli**nica
9. sep**tiem**bre
10. litera**tu**ra

11. japo**nes**
12. traba**jar**
13. a**zul**
14. **sa**bado
15. **me**dico

16. jala**pe**ño
17. universi**dad**
18. **la**piz
19. choco**la**te
20. **mu**sica

Answers: The only ones that need accent marks:
teléfonos, árbol, Panamá, fotografía, clínica, japonés, sábado, médico, lápiz, música.

Appendix V: Vos and Vosotros Conjugations

Vos and *vosotros* are two subject pronouns not usually covered in Spanish classes because of their limited use. *Vos* is used in Central America and some parts of South America, especially Argentina. *Vos,* in Central America, is used with children and peers, and not usually used to address someone older than yourself. In Argentina, however, it is used by all generations. Almost one-third of Hispanics use *vos*. It is equivalent to the use of *tú*. Usually, where *vos* is used, they will not use *tú*.

Vosotros is only used in Spain, though you will find it in many versions of the Bible. It is equivalent to the Latin American use of *ustedes*, however, *vosotros* is never used in Latin America.

If you go to a region that uses either *vos* or *vosotros*, these conjugations can be easily learned and used.

VOS

The present tense conjugation for the *vos* subject pronoun is as follows. It is very simple to conjugate—drop the final "*-r*" and add an "*-s*" keeping the stress on the last vowel sound.

Note: Stem-changing verbs do not exist in the *vos* conjugation.

PRESENT TENSE *VOS*

-ar verbs	-er verbs	-ir verbs
-ás	-és	-ís
hablás	comés	vivís
orás	querés	pedís

> **IRREGULARS**
>
> *ser = sos*
>
> Monosyllable verbs don't change: *vas, das, ves*

Vos hablás con tu mamá todos los días.   *You talk to your mom every day.*
Vos comés mucho.   *You eat a lot.*
¿Vivís en Buenos Aires?   *Do you live in Buenos Aires?*
¿Orás antes de comer?   *Do you pray before eating?*
¿Querés ver la película?   *Do you want to watch the movie?*
Vos sos un buen estudiante.   *You are a good student.*

The *vos* commands are very easy to form. Simply drop the "*r*" and stress the last vowel sound.

Note: Stem-changing verbs do not exist in the *vos* commands.

VOS COMMANDS

-ar verbs	-er verbs	-ir verbs
-á	-é	-í
hablá	comé	viví
mirá	hacé	vení

> **IRREGULARS**
>
> *Ir* is not used in the command. Instead, the verb *andar* is used.
>
> Andá al mercado. *Go to the market.*

Hablame.   *Talk to me.*
Negative: No me hablés.   *Don't talk to me.*
Mirá lo que tengo.   *Look at what I have.*
Vení aquí.   *Come here.*

Note: The direct and indirect object pronoun and reflexive pronoun is **te**. The past and future tenses are the same as the *tú* conjugation.

VOSOTROS/VOSOTRAS

Vosotros/as is the informal second person plural used in Spain. It is equivalent to the use of *ustedes* in Latin America. The present tense conjugation for the *vosotros/as* subject pronoun is as follows. It is simple to conjugate—with *-ar* and *-er* verbs, drop the "*-r*" and add an "*-is*" keeping the stress on the last strong vowel. The *-i* will make a dipthong with the *-a* and the *-e*. With *-ir* verbs, the ending is *-ís*.

Note: Stem-changing verbs do not exist in the *vosotros/as* present tense conjugation.

PRESENT TENSE *VOSOTROS/AS*

-ar verbs	-er verbs	-ir verbs
-áis	-éis	-ís
habláis	coméis	vivís
oráis	queréis	pedís

IRREGULARS

ser = sois

One syllable verbs do not take an accent mark:
ir = vais
dar = dais   ver = veis

IRREGULARS

ser = sois

One syllable verbs do not take an accent mark:
ir = vais
dar = dais   ver = veis

Vosotros habláis en la clase.	*You (plural) speak in class.*
¿Vosotros vivís en Buenos Aires?	*Do you (plural) live in Buenos Aires?*
¿Queréis ver la película?	*Do you (plural) want to watch the movie?*
Vosotros sois buenos estudiantes.	*You (plural) are good students.*

PRESENT PERFECT *VOSOTROS/AS*

Vosotros habéis + past participle

Vosotros habéis hablado.	*You (plural) have spoken.*
Vosotros habéis terminado el proyecto.	*You (plural) have finished the project.*

VOSOTROS/AS COMMANDS

The commands are very easy to form. Simply exchange the "*-r*" for a "*-d*" and stress the last vowel sound.
Note: Stem-changing verbs do not exist in the *vosotros/as* commands.

-ar verbs	-er verbs	-ir verbs
-á	-é	-í
hablad	comed	vivid
mirad	haced	venid

Habladme. *Talk to me.*	**Negative:** No me habléis. *Don't talk to me.*
Id y haced discípulos.	*Go and make disciples.*

Note: The direct and indirect object and reflexive pronoun is **os,** the possessive adjective and pronouns is **vuestro/a(s).**   Abrid vuestros libros. *Open your books.*   Os digo la verdad. *I tell you the truth.*

PRETERITE *VOSOTROS/AS*

To form the preterite tense (past tense), take the stem used in the preterite "*tú*" form, and add "*-is*".

-ar	-er	-ir
-asteis	-isteis	-isteis
hablasteis	comisteis	vivisteis
soñasteis	escribisteis	fuisteis

Ayer vosotros comisteis en el restaurante elegante.   *Yesterday you (plural) ate in the elegant restaurant.*
Vosotros has conjugations in all the tenses. You will see the pattern of the conjugation ending in *-is*.

Appendix VI: DOUBLE OBJECT PRONOUNS
(DIRECT AND INDIRECT OBJECT PRONOUNS USED TOGETHER)

In lessons *5* and *6*, direct and indirect object pronouns were introduced.
If there is a sentence which contains a direct object and an indirect object, you may have a sentence where two pronouns are used together.

I give you the book: *Yo te doy el libro.* (**Te** is the indirect object pronoun **to you.**) If we replace *LIBRO* with a direct object pronoun. The sentence will have 2 object pronouns.
The indirect object pronoun will go first, then be followed by the direct object pronoun. Both pronouns must be placed before the conjugated verb.
*Remember the indirect object is what answers the questions: **To whom?** or **For whom?**

Yo **te** doy el libro.	*I give **you** the book.*
Yo **te lo** doy.	*I give **it to you**.* (literally: To you, it, I give)
Ella **me** compra los libros.	*She buys **me** the books.*
Ella **me los** compra.	*She buys **them for me.***
Yo **te** digo la verdad.	*I tell **you** the truth.*
Yo **te la** digo.	*I tell **it to you.***

Note: There is a change that happens when the third person of both the indirect and the direct object are together. For example: (*le/les* + *lo/la/los/las*)
The **LE** or **LES** will change to **SE.**
The combinations possible are: ***se lo, se la, se los, se las.***
Since **le** and **les** change to **se**, it can have various meanings and will have to be clarified if not understood in the context.

SE →	a él	*to him*
	a ella	*to her*
	a usted	*to you (formal)*
	a ellos	*to them*
	a ellas	*to them (females only)*
	a ustedes	*to you (plural)*

Yo **le** doy el libro a mi papá.   *I give the book to my father.* (Here "a mi papá" clarifies **le**.)
If we take out *"el libro"* and replace it with the direct object pronoun, **lo**, it would read like this.

Yo **se lo** doy a mi papá.   *I give it to him, to my father.*

Rewrite the following sentences. (Remember **le/les** change to **se**)

1. Yo **te** leo <u>la Biblia</u>. _____Yo te la leo._____

2. Tú **nos** compras <u>el almuerzo</u>. _____

3. Ella **le** escribe <u>la carta</u> a su esposo. _____

4. Nosotros **les** decimos <u>la verdad</u>. _____

5. Dios **nos** da <u>la paz</u>. _____

2. Tú nos lo compras.   3. Ella se la escribe.   4. Nosotros se la decimos.   5. Dios nos la da.

Appendix VII:
Spanish-English Glossary of Spanish with a Mission

A

a - to, at
abecedario - alphabet
abogado/a - lawyer
abrigo - coat
abril - April
abrir - open
abuela - grandmother
abuelo - grandfather
abuelos - grandparents
aburrido/a - bored
acá - around here
acampar - to go camping
aceptar - accept
aceite - oil
aceitunas - olives
acondicionador - conditioner
acostarse - go to bed
actor - actor
actriz - actress
Adán - Adam
adentro - inside
aderezo - dressing
adiós - bye
adonde - where to
adoración - adoration
adorar - to adore
aerolínea - airline
aeropuerto - airport
afuera - outside
agosto - August
agricultura - agriculture
agua - water
agua con gas - soda water
aire libre - outside
ajo - garlic
al lado de - next to, beside
alabanza - praise
alabar - to praise
alambre - wire
alcoba - bedroom
alegre - happy

alfombra - rug
algo - something
alguien - someone
algún - some
alguno/a/os/as - any, some
allá - over there
allí - there
alma - soul
almohada - pillow
almuerzo - lunch
alto/a - tall
alumno/a - student
ama de casa - housewife
amable - friendly
amar - love
amarillo - yellow
amor - love
amplio/a - roomy
anaranjado - orange
andamio - scaffold
andar - walk , ride
ángel - angel
anillo - ring
animales - animals
año - year
anteojos - glasses
apartamento - apartment
apellido - last name
aprender - learn
aquel - over there
aquí - here
árboles - trees
arbustos - bushes
arca - ark
arena - sand
armario - closet
arquitecto - architect
arreglar - to fix
arrepentirse - to repent
arriba de - above, on top of
arroz - rice
artista - artist

arvejas - peas
así - like this, like so
asiento - seat
atún - tuna
auto - car
autobús - bus
autopista - highway
autor/a - autor
avión - plane
avivamiento - revival
ayudar - help
azadón - hoe
azúcar - sugar
azul - blue

B

bailar - dance
balón - ball
bajar - to go down
bajo/a - short
baloncesto - basketball
banana - banana
bañarse - bathe
banco - bank
bañera - bathtub
baño - bathroom
barato - inexpensive, cheap
barco - boat, ship
barrer - to sweep
básquetbol - basketball
basura - trash
bautista - Baptist
bautizar - baptize
bautizo - baptism
bazo - spleen
beber - drink
bebidas - drinks
béisbol - baseball
bello/a - beautiful
bendecir - bless
bendito - blessed
biberón - baby bottle

Biblia - Bible
biblioteca - library
bicicleta - bicycle
bien - well, fine
billetera - wallet
bistec - beef steak
blanco - white
blusa - blouse
bluyines - jeans
boca - mouth
boleto - ticket
bonito/a - pretty
botas - boots
bote - boat
botella - bottle
brazo - arm
brillar - to shine
brocha - (paint) brush
brócoli - broccoli
bueno/a - good
bufanda - scarf
burro - donkey
bus - bus
buscar - look for

C

caballo - horse
cabeza - head
cabra - goat
cadera - hip
café - coffee
café - brown
cajero automático - ATM
calle - street
calmar - to calm
calor - heat
calor - hot
cama - bed
camarera - maid, waitress
camarones - shrimp
cambiar - change
cambio - change
caminar - walk
camino - the way, walkway
camión - (big) truck
camioneta - truck
camisa - shirt
camiseta - t-shirt
campo - field

cancha – sport field
cansado/a - tired
cantante - singer
cantar - sing
canto - song
capilla - chapel
cara - face
carne - meat
carnicería - meat store
caro - expensive
carretera - highway
carro - car
cartera - purse
casa - house
casado/a - married
catedral - cathedral
católico - Catholic
catorce - fourteen
cavar - to dig
cebolla - onion
celeste - light blue
cemento - cement
cena - dinner
centro comercial - mall
cepillo - brush
cerca de - close to
cerdo - pig
cereal - cereal
cerebro - brain
cerezas - cherries
cero - zero
cerrar - close
cerveza - beer
césped - lawn
champú - shampoo
chancho - pig
chaqueta - jacket
charlar - chat
cheques - checks
chica - young lady (girl)
chícharos - peas
chico - guy (boy)
chico/a - small
chivo/a - goat
chimenea - chimney
chiquito/a - little
chistoso/a - funny
chocolate - chocolate
chofer - driver
chorizo - sausage

chuletas de cerdo - pork chops
cielo - sky, heaven
cien - one hundred
cinco - five
cincuenta - fifty
cintura - waist
cinturón - belt
ciudad - city
claro/a - bright, clear
clavar - to nail
clavo - a nail (to build)
cobija - blanket
coca (cola) - a coke
coche - car
cochino/a - pig
cocina - kitchen
cocinar - cook
cocinero/a - cook
coco - coconut
codo - elbow
colegio - school
colegio - school (high school)
collar - necklace
colorear – to color
comedor - dining room
comenzar - start, begin
comer - eat
comida - food
como - how, like
cómodo/a - comfortable
compartir - share
compasión – compassion
comprar - buy
compras - shopping
comprender - comprehend
computadora - computer
con - with
condimentos - condiments
conducir - drive
conductor - driver
conejo - rabbit
confesar – confess
conmigo - with me
conocer - know, be familiar
consejero/a - counselor
consuelo - comfort
construir - to construct, build
contador/a - accountant
contento/a - happy
contestar - to answer

contigo - with you
conversar - converse
corazón - heart
corbata - tie
correr - run
cortinas - curtains
corto - short in length
cosechar - to harvest
cráneo - skull
creación - creation
creer - believe
crema - cream
creyente - a believer
cristiano/a - Christian
Cristo – Christ
crucero - cruise (ship)
crucificado - crucified
crucificar - to crucify
cruz - cross
cuaderno - notebook
cuadro - wall picture
cuál - which
cuándo - when
cuánto - how much
cuántos - how many
cuarenta - forty
cuarto - quarter, room
cuatro - four
cuatrocientos - four hundred
cubrir - cover
cuchara - spoon
cuchillo - knife
cuello - neck
cuenta - account
cuenta - bill
cuento - story
cuidado - careful
culto - service
cumplir - fulfill, complete
cuñada - sister-in-law
cuñado - brother-in-law
cura - priest

D

dar - to give
de - of, from, about
debajo de - below, underneath
débito - debit
decidir - decide
decir - say

decisión - decision
dedo - finger
dedo del pie - toe
dejar - leave (behind)
delgado/a - thin
delicioso - delicious
demonios - demons
dentista - dentist
derecha - to the right
derecho - straight
derramar - to shed, spill
desayuno - breakfast
descansar - rest
desde - from
desear - desire, wish
desmayar - to faint
despertarse - wake up
destornillador - screw driver
detrás de - behind
diablo - devil
dibujar – to draw
diciembre - December
diecinueve - nineteen
dieciocho - eighteen
dieciséis - sixteen
diecisiete - seventeen
dientes - teeth
diez - ten
digno - worthy
dinero - money
Dios - God
dirección - address, direction
director/a - director
dispuesto – willing
divertido/a - fun
doblar - turn, bend, fold
doce - twelve
doctor/a - doctor
doler - to ache
dolor - pain, ache
domicilio - address, home
domingo - Sunday
dominical - Sunday (adj.)
Don - title of respect (m)
Doña - title of respect (f)
donde - where
dones - gifts (spiritual)
dormir - sleep
dormirse - fall asleep
dormitorio - bedroom

dos - two
dos piso - two floors
doscientos - two hundred
ducha - shower (ducharse - to shower)
dulce - sweet
dulces, caramelos - candy
durazno - peach

E

each - cada
edulcorante - sweetener
efectivo - cash
ejercicio - exercise
embarazada – pregnant
empezar – to start, begin
empleado/a - employee
en - in, at
encantar - to love, be enchanted
encender - turn on, light
encías - gums
encima - on top of
encima de - on top of, on
enemigo - enemy
enero - January
enfermero/a - nurse
enfermo/a - sick
enfrente de - in front of
enojado/a - mad, angry
enseñar - teach
entender - understand
entrar - enter
entre - in between
entregar - to give
equipaje - luggage
escoba - broom
escribir - write
escritorio - desk
escuchar - listen
escuela - school
ese - that
espalda - back
espejo - mirror
esperanza - hope
esperar - wait for, hope
espinaca - spinach
espíritu - spirit
esposa - wife
esposo - husband
esquina - corner

esta - this
estación - station, season
estantes - shelves
este - this
estómago - stomach
estrella - star
estrés - stress
estudiante - student
estudiar - study
estufa - stove
eterno/a - eternal
eternidad – eternity
Eva - Eve
evangélico – evangelical
existir - exist
explicar - explain

F

falda - skirt
fallar – to fail
farmacéutico/a - pharmacist
febrero - February
feliz - happy
feo/a - ugly
fidelidad – faithfulness
fiebre - fever
fiel - faithful
fierro - iron
fin de semana - weekend
finca - farm
flan - egg custard
florero - flower vase
flores - flowers
formar - form
foso - den (of animals)
fotógrafo - photographer
fotos - photos
fregadero - sink
frente - forehead
fresas - strawberries
fresco - cool
frijoles - beans
frío - cold
fruta - fruit
frutería - fruit store
fuego – fire
fumar - to smoke
fútbol - soccer
fútbol americano - football

G

gabinetes - cabinets
galletas - cookies
gallina - hen
gallo - rooster
ganar - win
garaje - garage
garganta - throat
gaseosa - soda pop
gasolinera - gas station
gato - cat
generoso/a - generous
gerente - manager
gloria - glory
Goliat - Goliath
gordo/a - fat
gozo - joy
gracia – grace
gracias- thank you
grande - big
granja - farm
gratis - free
gris - grey
guapo/a - handsome
guisantes - peas
gustar - pleasing to, like

H

habitación- room
hablar - speak
hacer - do or make
hambre - hunger
hasta - until
helado - ice cream
herida - wound
hermana - sister
hermano - brother
hermanos - siblings
hermoso/a - beautiful
herramientas - tools
hielo - ice
hierro - iron
hígado - liver
hija - daughter
hijo - son
hijos - children
hogar de niños - childrens' home
hola - hello
hombre - man

hombros - shoulders
honda - sling
hora - hour
horno - oven
hotel - hotel
hueso - bone
huevos - eggs
humilde – humble

I

ida y vuelta - round trip
iglesia - church
infierno – hell
infinito/a – infinite
ingeniero/a - engineer
inodoro - toilet
inteligente - intelligent
intentar - try
invierno - winter
invitación - invitation
invitar - invite
inyección - injection
ir - go
irse - leave
izquierda - left

J

jabón - soap
jalea - jelly
jamás - never ever
jamón - ham
jardín - garden
jardinear - to garden
jardinero/a - gardener
jefe/a - boss
Jesús - Jesus
joven - young
jubilado/a - retired
juegos - games
jueves - Thursday
juez - judge
jugar - play
jugo- juice
julio - July
junio - June
junto a - next to
junto/a - together

K

kiwi - kiwi

L

la - it, her
labios - lips
lado - side
lago - lake
lámpara - lamp
lancha - boat
lápiz - pencil
largo - long in length
las - them, you (pl. fem.)
lavamano - bathroom sink
lavar - wash
le - to/for him, her, you (formal)
leche - milk
lechuga - lettuce
leer - read
lejos de - far from
lentes - glasses
lento/a - slow
león - lion
les - to/for them, you (pl.)
levantar - to raise
levantarse - get up
libertad - liberty, freedom
libro - book
licuado - shake, smoothie
limón - lemon
limpiar - to clean
limpio/a - clean
lindo/a - cute
llamar - call
llamarse - to be called
llegar - arrive
llenar - to fill
llevar - take, wear
llover - to rain
lluvia - rain
lo - it, him
lo siento - I'm sorry
los - them, you (pl. masc.)
luces - lights
luna - moon
lunes - Monday
luz - light

M

madera - wood
madre - mother
maestro/a - teacher
maíz - corn
majestad - majesty
mal - bad off
maldecir - curse
maleta - suitcase
malo/a - bad
mamá - mom
mamadera - baby bottle
mañana - tomorrow, morning
manejar - drive
mano - hand
manta - blanket
mantequilla - butter
manzana - apple
mapa - map
mariscos - seafood
marrón - brown
martes - Tuesday
martillo - hammer
marzo - March
más - more
mayo - May
mayonesa - mayonaise
mayor - older
me - me, to me
media - half
medianoche - midnight
médico/a - doctor
mediodía - noon
mejilla - cheek
mejor - better
melocotón - peach
melón - melon
menor - younger
menos - minus
mercado - market
merienda - snack
mermelada - marmalade, jelly
mesa - table
mesero/a - waiter, waitress
mesita de noche - night stand
metodista - Methodist
metro - subway (mex.)
mezclar - mix
mi - my

mí - me
microondas - microwave
miedo - fear
miércoles - Wednesday
minuto - minute
mío - mine
mirar - watch, look
misionero/a - missionary
misericordia - mercy
mochila - backpack
moneda - coin, currency
montañas - mountains
montar - to ride (a horse)
montes - mountains
morado - purple
moreno/a - dark skinned
mostaza - mustard
moto - motorcycle
muerte - death
mujer - woman
muletas - crutches
muñeca - wrist
músculos - muscles
músico/a - musician
muslo - thigh
muy - very

N

nacimiento - birth
nada - nothing
nadar - swim
nadie - no one
naranja - orange
nariz - nose
Navidad - Christmas
necesitar - need
negocios - business
negro - black
nervioso/a - nervous
nevar - to snow
ni - neither…nor
nieta - grandaughter
nieto - grandson
nietos - granchildren
niña - little girl
ningún - none, not any
ninguno/a - not one, not any
niño - little boy
noche - night

noche buena - Christmas eve
Noé - Noah
nombre - name
nos - us, to us
nosotros - we
novecientos - nine hundred
noventa - ninety
novia - girlfriend (bride)
noviembre - November
novio - boyfriend (groom)
nuera - daughter-in-law
nuestro - our, ours
nueve - nine
nuevo/a - new
número - number
nunca - never

O

o - or
obedecer - to obey
obra - (great) work
océano - ocean
ochenta - eighty
ocho - eight
ochocientos - eight hundred
octubre - October
ocupado/a - busy
ofrecer - to offer
oídos - inner ears
oír - hear
ojos - eyes
olvidar - forget
once - eleven
optimista - optimist
oración - prayer
orar - pray
orejas - ears
orfanato - orphanage
orfanatorio - orphanage
organizado/a - organized
organizar - to organize
oscuridad - darkness
oscuro - dark
otoño - autumn

P

paciente - patient
padre - father
padre - priest
padres - parents

pagar - pay
página - page
pájaro - bird
pala - shovel
palabra - word
palomitas - popcorn
pan (tostado) - (toasted) bread
panadería - bread store
pantalones - pants
pantalones cortos - shorts
panqueque – pancake
pañal - diaper
papá - dad
papa - potato
papel - paper
papel higiénico - toilet paper
para - for, in order to
parábola - parable
parque - park
pasar (tiempo) - pass (time)
pascua - easter
pasillo - aisle
pasta - pasta
pasta de dientes - toothpaste
pasta de maní - peanut butter
pastel - pie, cake
pastillas - pills
pastor - pastor
patio - backyard
pato - duck
pavo - turkey
paz- peace
pecado - sin
pecador - sinner
pecho - chest
pedir - ask for
pegamento - glue
pelo - hair
pensar - think
peor - worse
pepino - cucumber, pickle
pequeño/a - small
pera - pear
perder - lose
perdido - lost, prodigal
perdón - forgiveness
perdonar - to forgive
periódico - newspaper
periodista - journalist
permitir - permit

perro - dog
pescado - fish
pesebre - manger
pertenecer - to belong
pie - foot
piedras - rocks
piel - skin
pierna - leg
pileta - sink
pimienta - pepper
piña - pineapple
pintar – to paint
pintor/a - painter
pintura - paint
piscina - pool
piso - floor
pizarra - blackboard
plano - map
plantar - to plant
platos - dishes
playa -beach
plaza - town square
plomero - plumber
pluma - pen
poco - little, few
poder - be able to
poder - power
poderoso - powerful
policía - police
político - politician
pollo - chicken
poner - put
ponerse - put on
por - during, through, for
por favor - please
por qué - why
porque - because
postrarse - bow before
postre - dessert
precioso - precious
predicar - preach
pregunta - question
preguntar - ask
preocupado/a - worried
preparar - prepare
presbiteriano - Presbyterian
presentar - present
presión sanguínea - blood
pressure

prima - female cousin
primavera - spring
primo - male cousin
primos - cousins
prisa - haste, hurriedness
problema - problem
profesional - professional
profesor/a - professor
profeta - prophet
propina - tip
pueblo - town, people
puerco - pig
puerta - door
pulmones - lungs
pulpería - small store
púlpito - pulpit
pulso - pulse
puntual - punctual

Q

que - what
quebrar - to break
queque - cake
querer - want
queso - cheese
quien - who
quince - fifteen
quinientos - five hundred
quiosko - small store
quitarse - take off(clothes)

R

radio - radio
rancho - ranch
rápido/a - fast
razón - reason
rebozar - overflow
recamara - bedroom
receta - prescription, recipe
recibir - receive
recordar - remember
redención - redemption
redentor - redeemer
redimido(s) - redeemed
redimir - to redeem
refrigerador/a - refrigerator
refugio - refuge
regalo - gift
reino - kingdom

reloj - watch, clock
res - cow, beef
reservación - reservation
responder - respond
respuesta - answer
retirado - retired
reunión - meeting
rey - king
reyes - kings, wise men
riñones - kidneys
río - river
rodilla - knee
rojo - red
romper - break
ropa - clothes
ropero - closet
rosado - pink
rubio/a - blond(e)

S

sábado - Saturday
sábanas - sheets
saber - know (knowledge)
sal - salt
sala - livingroom
salada - salty
salchicha - sausage, hotdog
salida - exit
salir - to go out
saltar - jump
salud - health
saludable - healthy
salvación - salvation
salvador - savior
salvar - to save
samaritano - samaritan
sanar - to heal
sandalias - sandals
sandía - watermelon
sangre - blood
sano - healthy
santo/a - holy
satanás - satan
se - him, her, them, you
sé - I know
secretario/a - secretary
sed - thirst
seguir - follow, continue
segundos - seconds

seis - six
seiscientos - six hundred
semana - week
sembrar - to plant
semilla - seed
sentir - feel
señor - mister
Señor - Lord
señora - Mrs.
señorita - miss
septiembre - September
ser - to be, being
serpiente - serpent
serrucho - saw
servicio de cuarto - room
                    service
servilleta - napkin
servir - serve
sesenta - sixty
setecientos - seven hundred
setenta - seventy
siempre - always
sierra - saw
siervo - servant
siete - seven
siglo - century
silla - chair
sillón - arm chair
simpático/a - nice, pleasant
sin - without
Sion - Zion
sobrino/a - niece, nephew
soda - carbonated drink
sofá - sofá
sol - sun
soldado - soldier
soltero/a - single
sombrero - hat
soñar - to dream
sostén - support
su - his, her, your, their
subir - to go up
subterráneo - subway
sucio/a - dirty
suegra - mother-in-law
suegro - father-in-law
suegros - parents-in-law
suelo - floor
sueño - sleepiness

suéter - sweater
sufrir - suffer
supermercado - supermarket
suyo - his, hers, yours, theirs

T

también - also
tampoco - either, neither
tarde - afternoon
tarea - homework, task
tarjeta - card
taxi - taxi
té - tea
te - you, to you
teléfono (celular) - cell phone
televisor - television
temor - fear
tenazas - pliers
tenedor - fork
tener - have
tenis - tennis
terminar - finish
testificar - witness
testigo - witness
testimonio - testimony
ti - you
tía - aunt
tiempo - time, weather
tienda - store
tierra - earth, dirt
tímido/a - shy
tina - bathtub
tío - uncle
tíos - aunts and uncles
toallas - towels
tobillo - ankle
tocar - touch, (play instrument)
tocino - bacon
todo(s) - all, everything
todopoderoso - almighty
tomar - take, drink
tomate - tomato
tormenta - storm
tornillos - screws
toro - bull
toronja - grapefruit
torta - cake, sandwich (Mex.)
tos - cough
trabajador/a - hard working

trabajador/a - worker, laborer
trabajar - work
trabajo - job
traducir - translate
traer - bring
traje - suit
traje de baño - bathing suit
transporte - transportation
tratar - try, treat
trece - thirteen
treinta - thirty
tren - train
tres - three
trescientos - three hundred
triste - sad
trono - throne
tu - your
tú - you (sing. fam.)
túnica - coat
tuyo - yours

U

uñas - nails
único - only
unir - unite, join
universidad - university
uno - one
usar - use
usted - you (sing. form.)
ustedes - you (pl.)
uvas - grapes

V

vaca - cow
vainilla - vanilla
vajillas - dinnerware
valer - be worth
vasos - glasses
vecindad - neighborhood
vegetales - vegetables
veinte - twenty
vejiga - bladder
venas - veins
vencer - defeat, conquer
vencedor - conqueror
vendedor/a - salesperson
vender - sell
venir - come
ventana - window

ver - see
verano - summer
verdad - truth
verde - green
verdulería - vegetable store
verduras - vegetables
vergüenza - embarrassment, shame
versículo - verse
vesícula - gall bladder
vestíbulo - lobby
vestido - dress
vez - time (in a series)
viajar - travel
victoria - victory
vida - life
viejo/a - old
viento - wind
viernes - Friday
vinagre - vinegar
vino - wine
violeta - purple
virgen - virgin
visitar - visit
vivir - live
voleibol - volleyball
voluntad - will
volver - to return
vos - you (sing.)
vosotros - you (pl.) (Spain)
vuestro/a(s) – your (poss. adj. for vosotros)

Y

y - and
yerno - son-in-law
yeso - cast
yo - I
yogur - yogurt

Z

zanahoria - carrot
zapatillas - tennis shoes
zapatos - shoes
zapatos tenis - tennis shoes
zumo - juice (Spain)

Appendix VIII:
Answers to Written Work At the End of Lessons

Lección A:

B) 0- cero
1 - uno
2- dos
3- tres
4- cuatro
5- cinco
6- seis

7- siete
8- ocho
9- nueve
10- diez
11- once
12- doce
13- trece

14- catorce
15- quince
16- dieciséis
20- veinte
21- veintiuno
30- treinta
35- treinta y cinco

C) 1. la   2. las   3. los   4. el   5. los   6. las   7. la   8. la   9. la

D) 1. Los hospitales   2. Los profesores   3. Las chicas   4. Las cruces   5. Las calles
6. Los nombres   7. Las estudiantes   8. Las universidades   9. Los apellidos   10. Las luces

Lección B:

A) 1. Buenos, Cómo   2. bien, y   3. Me   (tu nombre)   4. Yo   (where you are from)   5. gusto   6. es

B) Yo ---Soy   Tú---eres   Él---es   Ella--- es   Usted---es   Nosotros---somos
Ellos---son   Ellas---son   Ustedes---son

C) 1. Sí, yo soy estudiante. /   No, yo no soy estudiante.
2. Sí, yo soy mexicano. /   No, yo no soy mexicano.
3. Sí, nosotros somos de los Estados Unidos. /   No, nosotros no somos de los Estados Unidos.

D) 1. Hay treinta y cuatro plumas.   2. Hay veinticinco estudiantes.   3. Hay siete escritorios.
4. Hay dieciocho mochilas. 5. Hay cincuenta y nueve libros.

E)

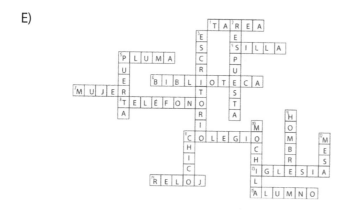

F)   1. un / a paper 2. un / a pencil   3. una / a light   4. unos / some notebooks   5. unas / some doors
6. un / a map 7. unos / some children   8. una / a question   9. unas / some schools   10. un / a man

G)   1. están 2. está 3. están 4. está 5. está

H)   1. La profesora no es de California. / The professor is not from California. 2. Los niños no son
estudiantes. / The children are not students. 3. Yo no soy profesora. / I am not a professor.
4. Los libros no están allí. /The books are not there. 5. Ellos no son argentinos. /They are not Argentine.

J)   Father, Son, Holy Spirit, King, Love, Peace, Comfort, Eternal Life, Good, Faithful

Lección 1
A) 1. Un médico, una enfermera… 2. Un mesero…   3. Un juez…   4. Una profesora…   5. Un actor…

B)   1. yo   2. tú   3. ella / el   4. nosotros   5. ellos / ellas

C)   1. yo   2. tú   3. él / ella   4. nosotros   5. ellas / ellos

D)   1. alto / guapo 2. vieja / fea 3. amables   4. bonita / simpática   5. muy generoso
6. bajos / gordos 7. organizadas   8. rubias / delgadas.

E) 1. cansado / enfermo 2. preocupada   3. nerviosos 4. feliz / contenta   5. muy ocupado
6. aburridos / tristes   7. enojadas

F) 1. está   2. es   3. está   4. están   5. es   6. es   7. está

G) Answers vary

H) 1. El/La misionero/a es muy generoso/a.   2. El/La cocinero/a es puntual.   3. El soldado es inteligente.
4. El/La vendedor/a está ocupado/a.   5.El/La juez/a es creyente.

Lección 2
A) 1. tiene   2. tienen   3. tienes   4. tiene   5. tenemos   6. tiene

B) Answers vary

C) 1. nieto 2. abuelos 3. tía 4. prima 5. hermano

D)   1. las casas de él.   2. las casas de ustedes.   3. las casas de ellas.   4. las casas de ella.
5. las casas de ellos.   6. las casas de usted.

E)   1. ¿Qué? 2. ¿Quién? 3. ¿Cuándo? 4. ¿Por qué?   5. ¿Cuál? 6. ¿Dónde?

F)   1. Hay alguien en la iglesia.   2. I don't have anything in my car. Tengo algo en mi carro.
3. I never have any money. Siempre tengo dinero.

G) , H) Answers vary

I) 1. La clase tiene veintidós estudiantes.   2. Mi cuñado tiene cuarenta y siete años.
3. Nosotros tenemos la mochila de él.   4. ¿Tienen nuestras Biblias?
5. Los libros son míos.   6. Yo no tengo tus sillas.
7. ¿Dónde está su iglesia?   8. Yo tengo muchos amigos en mi clase bíblica.

Lección 3

A) 1. qué 2. son 3. la 4. a 5. hora

B)   lunes, martes, miércoles, jueves, viernes, sábado , domingo

C) and D) answers vary

E) enero   febrero   marzo
abril   mayo   junio
julio   agosto   septiembre
octubre   noviembre   diciembre

F) 1. otoño, hace fresco   2. verano, hace calor.   3. otoño, hace viento
4. primavera, hace buen tiempo, llueve   5. invierno, nieva, hace frío 6. primavera, hace sol
7. invierno, hace frío, nieva

G) 2. El primero de enero   3. El cuatro de julio

H)   1. veinticinco   2. setenta y seis   3. cien   4. ciento cuarenta y ocho
5. quinientos setenta.   6. mil ochocientos cincuenta y dos

I)   1. El cuatro de julio de mil setecientos setenta y seis.
2. El doce de octubre de mil cuatrocientos noventa y dos.
3. El siete de diciembre de mil novecientos cuarenta y uno.
4. El primero de enero de mil novecientos noventa y nueve.

J) In the name of the Father, of the Son and of the Holy Spirit. Amen.

Lección 4

A)   Answers vary.

B) 1. My brother-in-law likes to travel to Central America.   2. I like to live in the mountains.
3. I don't like to go to the hospital.   4. Do you like Chinese food?
5. My cousins like to witness.   6. We like to study Spanish in our class.

C) Answers vary

D)   1. le   2. les   3. le   4. me   5. te

E)   1. Yo tengo su pluma nueva.   2. Ellos tienen my computadora vieja.
3. Me gusta salir con mis amigos. 4. Me gusta leer libros, pero a ella le gusta ver televisión.

F)   1. por   2. para   3. por 4. por   5. para   6. en, de, por   7. a, para
8. con,   conmigo

G)   1. tengo, calor   2. tiene, frío   3. tengo, hambre   4. tengo, sed   5. tiene, sueño
6. tiene estrés, miedo.

H)   Tengo frio, tengo miedo , tengo calor, tengo sed y hambre, tengo prisa, tengo sueño

I), J). Answers vary.

Lección 5
A)   1. una chaqueta, un abrigo, un suéter   2. unas botas.   3. unos pantalones cortos, una camisa.
4. un traje, un vestido, unos pantalones.   5. un vestido, unos pantalones cortos…

B) canto	cantas	--	cantamos	cantan
escucho	escuchas	escucha	escuchamos	--
viajo	--	viaja	viajamos	viajan
compro	compras	compra	--	compran
---	esperas	espera	esperamos	esperan
ayudo	ayudas	ayuda	ayudamos	ayudan
estudio	estudiasestudia	estudiamos	estudian	
necesito	--	necesita	--	necesitan
oro	oras	ora	oramos	oran
---	predicas	predica	predicamos	predican
trabajo	trabajas trabaja	trabajamos	--	
toco	tocas	--	tocamos	tocan

C)   1. viaja   2. cocino   3. cantamos   4. camina   5. trabajan   6. terminas
7. habla   8. enseña   9. escucho   10. miran

D)   1. X   2. a   3. X   4. a   5. X   6. a

E)   1. me   2. te   3. nos

F) 1. da   2. va   3. van   4. doy   5. da   6. vas

G)   1. How much are the black pants?   2. How much is the green shirt?
3. I don't like that for you.   4. That church has someone that plays the guitar very well.

H)   1. Confió en ti.   2. Tú eres mi Dios.   3. Mi vida está en tus manos.
4. Que brille tu faz sobre tu siervo.   5. Sálvame.

Lección 6
A) Yo como el desayuno a las ocho de la mañana.   Yo como el almuerzo a la una de la tarde.
Yo como la cena a las seis de la tarde.   Yo como la merienda a las 3 de la tarde.

B) 1. el plato, el tenedor, el cuchillo, la cuchara, la servilleta   2. los mariscos, el pollo, el pescado, el atún,
el pavo.   3. la lechuga, la espinaca, el apio, el pepino, el bróculi, los guisantes, las arvejas, las uvas,
el melón, el kiwi, la pera.   4. el tomate, la manzana, la naranja, el melocotón, las fresas, la sandía,
la cereza. 5. el agua, el té, el café, la leche, el vino, el jugo.

C) ---	lees	lee	leemos	leen
corro	corres	corre	corremos	---
escribo	escribes	---	escribimos	escriben
olvido	---	olvida	olvidamos	olvidan
decido	decides	decide	---	deciden
---	enseñas	enseña	enseñamos	enseñan
creo	crees	cree	creemos	---
sufro	sufres	sufre	---	sufren
veo	---	ve	vemos	ven
abro	abres	---	abrimos	abren

1. creemos   2. escribe   3. pongo

D) ---	pones	pone	---	ponen
salgo	sales	---	salimos	salen
conozco	---	conoce	---	conocen
hago	---	hace	hacemos	---
se	sabes	---	sabemos	saben
---	oyes	oye	oímos	---
traduzco	traduces	traduce	---	traducen
quiero	---	quiere	---	quieren

1. traduzco   2. hago   3. sé   4. valgo, vales   5. oye   6. hacen   7. veo 8. sabe

E), F), G). Answers vary.

H)   1. quiero   2. quieren   3. quiere   4. quieres   5. quiere   6. queremos

I)   1. lo   2. los   3. la   4. me   5. te   6. las   7. las   8. los

J) 1. conocen   2. sé   3. sabemos   4. conoce   5. sabes   6. conoces

Lección 7
A) 1. sala   2. habitación, dormitorio, recámara, alcoba   3. comedor   4. cocina   5. baño

C)   Yo estoy escuchando. / Tú estas escuchando. / El está escuchando.
       Nosotros estamos escuchando. / Ellos están escuchando.

E)				
quiero	quieres	---	queremos	quieren
cierro	---	cierra	cerramos	---
---	sientes	---	sentimos	sienten
pienso	piensas	piensa	---	piensan
---	pierdes	---	perdimos	---
entiendo	entiendes	entiende	---	entienden
---	vienes	viene	venimos	---

F)

pido	---	pide	pedimos	piden
---	sirves	sirve	servimos	---
sigo	sigues	sigue	---	siguen
---	dices	---	decimos	dicen
bendigo	---	bendice	bendecimos	---

G)

---	duermes	---	dormimos	---
puedo	puedes	puede	---	pueden
juego	---	juega	jugamos	juegan
---	recuerdas	recuerda	---	recuerdan
vuelvo	vuelves	---	volvemos	---

H)   1. siento   2. va   3. entiendes   4. siguen   5. recuerdo   6. duermen 7. jugamos   8. Vuelven

I) Answers vary

J) 1. va   2. voy / I'm not going to visit Honduras.   3. vas / When are you going to work?   4. vamos / We are going to sing in the choir.   5. van / Are you (plural) going to bring your friends to church?

K)   1. Los voy a estudiar.   2. La vamos a visitar.   3. La vas a hacer.   4. Mariana lo va a limpiar.
5. Los católicoas lo van a ver.   6. Ustedes lo van a preparar.

L)   1. worship   2. Justice   3. I want to sing praises   4. rectitude.

Lección 8
A) 1. le   2. te   3. le   4. me   5. les   6. nos

B)   1. se despierta   2. me pongo   3. nos vamos   4. te levantas   5. se baña
6. se duermen   7. se acuestan   8. se lava   9. me voy   10. se quita

C)   1. preparada   2. dormidos   3. terminado   4. contestadas.

D)   1. has - Have you traveled to Spain?   2. ha - David has prepared a good Bible lesson.
3. ha - Cristina has accepted the Lord as her Savior.   4. ha - The professor has taught the class.
5. han - The children already have gone to bed.   6. has - Have you seen an angel?
7. he -   I have returned from the missionary trip.

E)   1. Sí, la he leído.   2. Sí, la he estudiado.   3. Sí, lo he bebido.
4. Sí, los hemos visto.   5. Sí, la hemos comprado   6. Sí, los ha preparado.

F) I have decided to follow Jesus. I won't go back.

Lección 9
A) 1. Yo compro ropa.   2. Compro el pan.   3. Compro las frutas.   4. Compro las verduras.
5. Compro los jugos.   6. Compro la comida.   7. Compro carne.   8. Compro libros.
9. Compro zapatos.

C)   1. near my house   2. under the table   3. far from my church   4. next to the supermarket
5. between the cinema and the school

D)   1. Go to the doctor.   2. Come to the meeting.   3. Turn to the right.   4. Turn to the left.
5. Go straight .   6. Have a good day.   7. Everyone come to church.

F)   1. Levántese   2. Cante   3. Lea   4. Hable   5. Diga   6. Tenga
7. Trabaje y juegue   8. Salga   9. Viva   10. Ame

G) Estudien mucho.   Limpien su cuarto. No hablen mucho, etc.

H) Lea la Biblia. Ore a Dios. Acepte a Jesús como Salvador, etc.

I) 1. No doble a la derecha. 2. No vaya a la esquina.   3. No me diga. 4. No lo haga.

Lección 10
A) San Mateo, San Marcos, San Lucas, San Juan.

B) Answers will vary.

C) pregunté	preguntaste	preguntó	------	preguntaron
-----	tomaste	tomó	tomamos	tomaron
amé	amaste	amó	amamos	------
escribí	escribiste	-----	escribimos	escribieron
olvidé	------	olvidó	olvidamos	olvidaron
decidí	decidiste	------	decidimos	decidieron
-----	fuiste	fue	fuimos	fueron
leí	leíste	leyó	leímos	-----
sufrí	sufriste	sufrió	-----	sufrieron
vencí	-----	venció	vencimos	vencieron
di	diste	-----	dimos	dieron
------	creíste	------	creímos	creyeron
vi	------	vio	------	vieron
hice	hiciste	------	hicimos	hicieron
------	dijiste	dijo	dijimos	------

D) 1. limpié 2. preguntaron 3. cocinó 4. viven 5. bebió 6. hicieron 7. esperaron 8. fuimos
9. dijo 10. cantaste 11. leí 12. venció

E) 1. Conozco a Jesucristo hace cinco años. 2. No bebo gaseosas hace ocho semanas. 3. Voy a la
Iglesia Nueva Vida hace doce años. 4. Mario habla por teléfono hace cuarenta minutos. 5. Yo miro/veo
televisión hace una hora. 6. Fui al supermercado hace una semana. 7. Mi hijo hizo la tarea hace quince
minutos. 8. Carlos comió hace dos horas.

G) Jesus said, "The kingdom of Heaven is like this: a merchant searched for fine pearls. When he found
one of great value, he went and sold everything then bought it."

ACKNOWLEDGEMENTS AND COPYRIGHTS

Pictures:
All pictures taken and copyrights owned by Cristina Balyeat or Alicia Morcillo.
Permission granted to use in *SPANISH WITH A MISSION*.
Unless otherwise noted, copyright will be stated by the picture.

All drawings made and copyrights owned by Alicia Morcillo.
Permission granted to use in *SPANISH WITH A MISSION*.
Unless otherwise noted.

Lupita Cortés, pg. 73
Jack Matlick, pg. 145
ThinkStock.com, pg. 111 (4 & 6), 87 (4& 6), 73

Scripture taken from the HOLY Bible, NEW INTERNATIONAL VERSION®.
Copyright © 1973, 1978, 1984 by International Bible Society.

Texto Bíblico tomado de la SANTA Biblia, NUEVA VERSIÓN INTERNACIONAL. © 1999 POR LA Sociedad Bíblica Internacional.

Songs:
Tu fidelidad, Eres Todopoderoso, Él es el Rey, La niña de tus ojos.
Permission granted by CANZION GROUP, LP. License no. 2002

Mighty to Save, Hosanna, Here I am to Worship and Stronger.
Permission given by HILLSONG©. through EMI MUSIC, CMG Publishing. License no. 540012

Tú estás aquí, Dame tus ojos.
Permission given by VASTAGO PRODUCTIONS.

No hay nadie como tú.
Permission granted by Marco Barrientos.

Pictures and biographies of Christian artists:

Marco Barrientos - permission given by Marco Barrientos.

Marcos Witt, Danilo Montero, Daniel Calveti - permission given by CANZION GROUP, LP.

Jesús Adrián Romero, Marcela Gándara - permission given by VASTAGO PRODUCTIONS.

Printed in the USA
CPSIA information can be obtained
at www.ICGtesting.com
LVHW081238110823
754955LV00015B/1190